THE PROSECUTION OF JOHN WYCLYF

THE PROSECUTION OF John Wyclyf

BY JOSEPH H. DAHMUS

ARCHON BOOKS, 1970

ISBN: 0-208-00953-1
Library of Congress Catalog Card Number: 76-120371
Printed in the United States of America

INTRODUCTION

One of the problems in the religious-political field of the later Middle Ages which has remained largely unsolved is that concerning the controversy between John Wyclyf and the church. To what extent were the ecclesiastical authorities successful in silencing Wyclyf? Or were they at all successful? If they were not, how can one account for the escape from punishment of the leading religious revolutionary of the period? The topic has invited considerable attention, but the conclusions offered have usually lacked conviction if not objectivity. Now that time has dulled the feeling which was permitted to color almost every discussion of Wyclyf in the past, it is possible that this particular problem may lend itself today to something approaching definitive treatment.

This study presumes to correct several major misconceptions about Wyclyf's career in general, about his struggle with the church in particular. It seeks to establish in the process a number of new interpretations which should modify the traditional treatment of the religious and political history of England in the late 14th century. Among the significant contributions which are claimed for the study as providing it with substance and justifying its appearance are the following:

It recasts the political role of John of Gaunt, the duke of Lancaster, and his relationship with Wyclyf: the duke emerges not as an unscrupulous, anticlerical aristocrat who exploited Wyclyf for his own selfish ends but rather as a politician of considerable merit who had learned of Wyclyf's intellectual attainments and felt the crown could use the bright clerk.

It re-creates the scene at St. Paul's in 1377 to show the aristocracy supporting Wyclyf, the citizenry indifferent if not hostile.

It attributes Pope Gregory's intervention in the English church's quarrel with Wyclyf to his concern about doctrinal orthodoxy, not to his fear lest Wyclyf's propositions lead to the impairment of the church's political position.

It pictures Wyclyf at Lambeth as qualifying his position on several propositions under cross-examination by the prelates.

It sharply reduces Wyclyf's political stature: it is extremely improbable that Wyclyf at any time had the honor of addressing Parliament or that the great council ever asked his opinion as to the legality of withholding money from Rome.

46632

It insists that the government in 1378 ordered Wyclyf, for practical purposes, to terminate his attacks on the church—not simply to cease discussing the question of withholding money from Rome.

It correlates the silencing of the Benedictine John de Acley in 1378 with the injunction the crown placed upon Wyclyf: in the interest of national tranquillity, the former was enjoined not to attack Wyclyf, while Wyclyf was ordered to cease his attacks on the church.

It establishes a direct sequence between Pope Gregory's representations to the king and the crown's prohibition on Wyclyf.

It emphasizes, on the other hand, the necessity that the state cooperate if the medieval church was to succeed in suppressing heresy: indicative of the secular spirit motivating governmental policy was the punishment meted out to the vice-chancellor of Oxford for having dared to imprison Wyclyf upon the pope's authority.

It weighs the consequences of Pope Urban's election upon Wyclyf's fortunes and finds them to have been serious.

It appraises the government's attitude toward Lollardy as consistently hostile from king to Commons inclusive: the anti-Catholic sentiments of Parliament in the 17th century may not be traced back to the late 14th.

It provides a thorough analysis of all the circumstances which played a part in saving Wyclyf from physical punishment, noting at the same time the extent to which he was disciplined.

It establishes the genuineness of the disputed letter of 1384 which Wyclyf addressed to Pope Urban; it authenticates, furthermore, the manuscript date of 1384, both points being of decisive significance in the solution of the problem at hand.

It furnishes numerous translations of documents, many of which have hitherto been closed to students who were unable to read them in the original Latin.

It provides an indispensable corrective to Workman's standard biography of Wyclyf.

In the preparation of this study I wish to acknowledge the gracious cooperation of the libraries of the Pennsylvania State College and the University of Illinois, the Bodleian Library, and the Lambeth Palace Library. I am indebted to the Council on Research of the Pennsylvania State College for financial assistance in the preparation and publication of the manuscript. To two individuals am I especially grateful for advice and encouragement, Frederick C. Dietz, chairman of the Department of History at the University of Illinois, and Robert E. Dengler, chairman of the Department of Classics at the Pennsylvania State College.

Note on the Spelling "Wyclyf"

John Wyclyf's name has appeared in as great a variety of spellings as that of any figure in history.[1] The medieval scribe who depended upon the sound of the word for his spelling not only doubled the *c*, *l*, and *f* or added an *e* to the ending as he chose but substituted a *k* for the *c* and used either *i* or *y* or both with little or no concern for consistency. The spelling "Wycleph" is frequently found in Continental manuscripts. S. H. Thomson has concluded from an examination of five documents which he assigns to Wyclyf's life that the spelling "Wyclyf" has the greatest validity.[2] This point of view finds support in the manner in which Archbishop Courteney's clerks spelled Wyclyf's name.[3] The registers of Archbishop Sudbury and Bishop Buckingham, on the other hand, which are as old as the documents which Thomson used, at no time give his name that particular spelling, although the variance is not marked. Yet one cannot escape the conclusion that there is no overwhelming evidence which will eventually compel the adoption of any one spelling, especially since the dissolution of the Wyclif Society in 1924.[4] The distress such a statement might occasion the exacting scholar will be more than offset by the confidence with which the constitutional misspeller will attack the word. One must make a choice, however, and it is only for reasons of consistency that I use the spelling "Wyclyf."

1. "By medieval writers Wyclif's name was spelt in over thirty ways, Walsingham alone giving eight forms." Workman, *John Wyclif*, *1*, 22 n. 3.

2. Thomson, "Wyclif or Wyclyf?" *EHR*, 53, 678.

3. See my article, "Further Evidence for the Spelling 'Wyclyf,'" *Speculum, 16*, 225.

4. There is some objection to employing the simplest spelling, which is "Wiclif." Workman (*1, 22*) has this to say: "The first syllable is Wy 'water,' not wick or wic. The German form 'Wiclif' should therefore be avoided."

Since the appearance of *The Prosecution of John Wyclyf* in 1952, all but universal preference for the spelling "Wyclif" has rendered pedantic any further discussion of that problem. I have used "Wyclif" in several articles published since 1952 which touched upon the Reformer and in *William Courtenay, Archbishop of Canterbury* (Pennsylvania State University Press, 1966). The cost of changing "Wyclyf" to read "Wyclif" in this Archon edition is, unfortunately, prohibitive. My biography of William Courtenay incorporated what new analyses have appeared relative to those phases of Wyclif's career with which the *Prosecution* was concerned. Their impact upon the Wyclif of the *Prosecution* has been negligible.

J. H. D.—March 1970

ABBREVIATIONS

Apos.	*De Apostasia*
Blas.	*De Blasphemia*
Chron. Angl.	*Chronicon Angliae*
Civ. Dom.	*De Civili Dominio*
Eccles.	*De Ecclesia*
EHR	*English Historical Review*
Euch.	*De Eucharistia*
Eulog.	*Eulogium Historiarum sive Temporis*
Fas. Ziz.	*Fasciculi Zizaniorum*
Hist. Angl.	*Historia Anglicana*
HZ	*Historische Zeitschrift*
Knighton	*Chronicon Henrici Knighton*
Op. Min.	*Opera Minora*
Op. Evang.	*Opus Evangelicum*
Pol. Works	*Polemical Works in Latin*
"Reg. Buck."	"Register of John Buckingham"
"Reg. Court."	"Register of William Courteney"
"Reg. Sud."	"Register of Simon Sudbury"
Rot. Parl.	*Rotuli Parliamentorum*
Serm.	*Sermones*
SKAW	*Sitzungsberichte der philosophisch-historischen Classe der Kaiserlichen Akademie der Wissenschaften*
Transcript	*Transcript of a Chronicle*
Trial.	*Joannis Wiclif Trialogus*
Ver. Script.	*De Veritate Sacrae Scripturae*

Unless otherwise indicated, footnote references are to the following books of the authors listed:

Lechler	*Johann von Wiclif und die Vorgeschichte der Reformation*
Lewis	*The History of the Life and Sufferings of the Reverend and Learned John Wiclif*
Salter	*Snappe's Formulary*
Vaughan	*The Life and Opinions of John de Wycliffe*
Wilkins	*Concilia Magnae Britanniae et Hiberniae*

TABLE OF CONTENTS

1. WYCLYF'S EARLY YEARS AT OXFORD

While almost every aspect of the life of John Wyclyf is the occasion of controversy, "over his earlier years there hangs a more than medieval obscurity . . ."[5] Fortunately, there is no need here for more than a sketch of these years. Wyclyf was born about 1330 in Yorkshire of middle-class parentage and about 1360 became lord of the manor of Wycliffe. It may be worth noting that for some 30 years John of Gaunt was his overlord. He probably entered Oxford about the year 1345, and three colleges, Queen's, Merton, and Balliol, claim the honor of his residence. Balliol can establish as a fact that he was its master in 1360.

There is no record of his ordination to the priesthood, but it must have been shortly before May 14, 1361, when he was instituted to the college living of Fillingham in Lincolnshire. As was required, he resigned his fellowship at the university and in all probability served his parish in person until August, 1363, when his bishop, John Buckingham, granted him license for nonresidence for a period of one year.[6] The year before, upon the request of the university, the pope had provided him with the prebend of Aust in the collegiate church of Westbury-on-Trym near Bristol. His name was listed among those presented in the annual roll of masters, and the pope was petitioned to make the grant "notwithstanding that he has the church of Filingham . . ."[7] The income from these benefices enabled Wyclyf to continue and complete his studies, and except for the few years at Lutterworth after 1378,[8] Wyclyf's name is almost continuously associated with Oxford.

What little is known of Wyclyf's early years at Oxford suggests that they did not differ appreciably from those of the usual clerk. Actually in view of his subsequent fame and the confidence with which some

5. Workman, *1*, 3. To this obscurity a number of Wyclyf's admirers have added a great deal of confusion through their ingeniousness in filling in the extensive gaps in his career.

6. "Reg. Buck.," Memoranda, fol. 7. This license for nonresidence was granted for one year, not for five as Workman implies, *1*, 153, 194.

7. *Calendar of Entries in the Papal Registers, Petitions to the Pope, 1*, 390. See below, p. 3.

8. See below, p. 129.

1

of his biographers describe his activities during that time, one is astonished at the well-nigh complete blank these years present in his career. One of the first of the manifold controversies which continue to plague Wyclyf scholars—whether it was he or another Wyclyf who served as warden of Canterbury Hall from December, 1365, to March, 1367—emphasizes the obscurity of these years. Because of Wyclyf's possible reaction to his experiences at Canterbury Hall—assuming, as is probable,[9] that the subject of this study and not some other Wyclyf was involved—it may be pertinent to review the history of his relationship with that college.

Archbishop Islip established Canterbury Hall early in 1361 in order to encourage more of the clergy, secular as well as regular, to attend the university. Since he was obliged to alienate the lucrative living of Pagham which belonged to Canterbury in order to provide the necessary income for the new college, the monks of the Canterbury chapter were able to secure his promise that the warden would always be a monk. In December, 1365, Islip expelled the regulars and appointed a "John de Wyclyve" as warden.[1] Upon the death of Islip, Simon Langham, the new archbishop, reversed this action, demoted Wyclyf, and reinstated the monks. When Wyclyf and the seculars refused to accept the new situation, they were forthwith expelled. Wyclyf appealed the matter to Pope Urban V,[2] but his case was weak and his suit unsuccessful. According to the testimony of Wyclyf's contemporary and colleague, the Franciscan William Woodford, the incident rankled,[3] but Wyclyf's subsequent attacks on the possessioners can just as easily be laid to coincidence as to malice. His experiences at Canterbury

9. Cronin ("John Wycliffe, the Reformer, and Canterbury Hall, Oxford," *Transactions of the Royal Historical Society,* Third Series, 8, 55–76) presents a fairly conclusive case in support of this view. But see *Fas. Ziz.,* App., "Note On The Two John Wyclifs," pp. 513–28.

1. Vaughan, *The Life and Opinions of John De Wycliffe, 1,* App., 417.

2. See Foxe, *The Acts and Monuments, 2,* App., 927–8, for Wyclyf's appeal.

3. William Woodford, who had earlier been a friend of Wyclyf—the two apparently collaborated in the preparation of their lectures (Little, *The Grey Friars in Oxford,* p. 81)—only to attack him with vehemence in the eighties, declared that "before he had been expelled by the monks and the prelates from the hall of the monks of Canterbury, he had attempted nothing of any moment against the monks . . ." *Fas. Ziz.,* App., pp. 517–18. Similarly damaging are Walsingham's words, namely, that Wyclyf took up his attack on the church "for the reason that he had been justly deprived by the archbishop of Canterbury of a certain benefice which he unjustly held within the city of Oxford." *Chron. Angl.,* p. 115. Yet Manning ("Wyclif," *Cambridge Medieval History, 7,* 487) insists: "There is no reason to represent him as an aggrieved individual over-ridden by a powerful corporation; the badness of his case explains its failure." Workman inclines to this view, *1,* 192–3.

Hall, however, may have had some influence in helping form his later opinions, such as, for example, the conclusion that the church would be better off if lay directors rather than clergy administered her property.[4]

In 1368 Wyclyf was careful to secure a second license for non-residence from Fillingham, this one for two years.[5] He had been cited in the summer of 1366 upon orders of the bishop of Worcester, William Whittlesey, to show cause why he should not be suspended from office and benefice, together with the other nonresident canons, for failure to provide a chaplain for his prebend of Aust.[6] In the fall of the same year Wyclyf exchanged his parish in Fillingham for that of Ludgershall which was but a short distance from Oxford.[7] It must have been in 1372 or 1373 that he finally obtained his doctorate in theology,[8] and it may have been in recognition of that achievement, as it was upon the request of the university, that Pope Gregory XI reconfirmed to him on December 26, 1373, the provision to a canonry of Lincoln with reservation of a prebend.[9] This last provision should have left Wyclyf well established financially,[1] for just prior to receiving his doctorate he had entered the service of the crown and in the spring of 1374 had received from the king in recognition thereof the rectory of Lutterworth in Lincolnshire.[2]

4. *Op. Min.*, pp. 405, 410, 414.

5. "Reg. Buck.," Mem., fol. 56ᵛ.

6. Wilkins, *Was John Wycliffe a Negligent Pluralist?*, pp. 16–17, 24, 43–6. See Workman, *1*, 159–63, for a discussion of Wyclyf and Aust. Wyclyf retained possession of Aust. Ten years later John of Gaunt saved the prebend for him when the king, upon the advice of the duke, rescinded another appointment he had made to that prebend in the belief it was vacant. *Cal. of Pat. Rolls*, 1374–77, *16*, 393.

7. "Reg. Buck.," Institutions, fol. 419.

8. Workman, *1*, 203. The two papal bulls of January 28, 1371, and December 26, 1373, provide a *terminus a quo* and a *terminus ad quem* for the dating of Wyclyf's doctorate. The first bull refers to Wyclyf as a master of arts (Lloyd, "John Wyclif and the Prebend of Lincoln," *EHR, 61*, 392) while the second bull describes him as a master of theology. *Calendar of Entries in the Papal Registers, Papal Letters, 4*, 193. See also Twemlow, "Wycliffe's Preferments and University Degrees," *EHR, 15*, 530.

9. As doctor in 1373 Wyclyf "was able to obtain permission to hold the two prebends in plurality with his rectory, since doctors were allowed by Chancery Rule to hold benefices amounting to a larger annual sum than were bachelors." Lloyd, *loc. cit.*, p. 389. Miss Lloyd continues: "In view of the historical importance of Wyclif's attitude to the system of papal provisions, it is perhaps worth while emphasizing the fact that not only did he petition in 1370–1 for the prebend of greater value than the one he already held but in 1373 he took the further step of procuring permission to retain his prebend of Aust as well as his rectory of Ludgershall."

1. As it happened, this never materialized. See below, p. 4.

2. *Cal. of Pat. Rolls*, 1370–74, *15*, 424. Wyclyf, soon after receiving Lutter-

After 1373 the sources are more generous with their references to Wyclyf. In 1374 and 1375 two events took place in his life, the importance of which has been exaggerated, that of 1374 by his champions, that of 1375 by his enemies. Both incidents may have had some influence upon Wyclyf's subsequent attitude toward the papacy. On July 26, 1374, he was appointed to a commission which was to treat with a papal delegation at Bruges on the problem of provisions. He was the only theologian of the seven-man commission headed by John Gilbert, bishop of Bangor.[3] While his original appointment demands little explanation,[4] some significance may be attached to his failure to be reappointed to serve on a second commission the following year. The conferences in the late summer of 1374 ended without producing any agreement. We know nothing of Wyclyf's part in the discussions and must be content with the observation that if he there insisted upon putting forward his views on the subject of papal provisions some of the commission's lack of success may be placed upon his shoulders. In any event, Wyclyf was not named to the delegation which resumed negotiations at Bruges the following year and with significantly more success. Yet it is well to remember that if it was his obstinacy which prevented a compromise at Bruges in 1374 he never referred to it, and "Historians, almost without exception, have exaggerated the part that Wyclyf played . . ."[5]

The incident of 1375 which the enemies of Wyclyf have been inclined to magnify was his disappointment at failing to receive the prebend promised him by Gregory XI in 1373.[6] Students are divided on the question of whether the canonry with reservation of a prebend which Gregory had promised remained anything more than a promise

---

worth, surrendered his living at Ludgershall, and another incumbent is noted in possession in May, 1376. "Reg. Buck.," Mem., 143ᵛ.

3. Rymer, *Foedera, Conventiones, Literae, et Cujuscunque Generis Acta Publica*, 7, 41–2.

4. Some writers, as Lechler, *Johann von Wiclif und die Vorgeschichte der Reformation, 1*, 347, are of the opinion that Wyclyf was appointed to the commission because of his antipapal views. He would prevent the crown from being deluded at Bruges. These views he had presumably already set forth in his *Determinatio*. This is improbable. In the first place, it is doubtful if the *Determinatio* appeared before his return from Bruges. See Workman, *1*, 239. In the second place, had Wyclyf by 1374 earned the reputation of being strongly antipapal he would for that reason have been passed over rather than selected. So Loserth, "Studien zur Kirchenpolitik Englands im 14. Jahrhundert," *SKAW, 136*, pt. I, 62. See also Loserth, "The Beginnings of Wyclif's Activity in Ecclesiastical Politics," *EHR, 11*, 328.

5. Workman, *1*, 264.

6. See above, p. 3.

which the pope did not carry out in view of Wyclyf's subsequent attitude at Bruges and the publication of the *Determinatio*.[7] It is doubtful whether the pope would have granted Wyclyf any prebend, an important one at any rate, after what must have transpired at Bruges, and only a saint or a simpleton would have done so after the appearance of the *Determinatio*. Yet as Lloyd reminds us, "It has hardly been appreciated by modern writers, how impersonal was the working of the provision system, and personal animus on the part of the pope has been somewhat too easily assumed." [8]

Wyclyf claims both to have been a canon and to have received a prebend in the church of Lincoln only to have the prebend given to someone else.[9] We are not sure whether he ever received the promised prebend or whether when actually conferred he was then deprived of it.[1] We are sure that he was bitter at his failure to receive the rich prebend of Caistor in 1375, particularly in view of the considerable expense he had undertaken to get it.[2] He had some time before accused his enemies of seeking to denigrate him to the Curia in the hope of having him deprived of his benefices.[3] Sir John Thornbury, the priest who did secure the prebend of Caistor, he vilified as an "idiot." [4] If Wyclyf had been outspoken in his condemnation of papal provisions

7. On this question, see Workman, *1*, 204–5; Cronin, *loc. cit.*, p. 568; Lloyd, *loc. cit.*, 389–92; Salter, "John Wyclif, Canon of Lincoln," *EHR, 35*, 98.

8. Lloyd, *loc. cit.*, p. 389.

9. See *Civ. Dom.*, *1*, 387–8; *3*, 334. Lloyd (*loc. cit.*, p. 389) questions Wyclyf's optimism for "the papal rescript gave Wyclif no immediate right to a benefice, but was merely the first step in a juridical process to be set in motion by the petitioner himself. Having obtained the provision, Wyclif (or his proctor) must watch for a vacancy in a prebend of Lincoln and prove his legal right to it."

1. Lloyd (*loc. cit.*, p. 391) declares: "Whether, as Dr. Rashdall in the *Dictionary of National Biography* states, Wyclif actually received the prebend and was afterwards ousted by Philip de Thornbury [the one who actually received the prebend], or whether the latter made his claim at an earlier stage can hardly be decided."

2. *Civ. Dom.*, *1*, 387–8; *3*, 334. Lloyd (*loc. cit.*, p. 391) and Cronin (*loc. cit.*, p. 568) both agree that this passage in *Civ. Dom.* must refer to his efforts to secure the prebend of Caistor. Workman first contradicts Cronin's view (*1*, 201 n. 2) and then his own (*1*, 206 n. 2).

3. *Op. Min.*, p. 425. See Workman, *1*, 205. On the basis of Wyclyf's fear that his enemies at Oxford would be successful in having him deprived of his reservation, Cronin (*loc. cit.*, p. 567) concludes that Wyclyf's hope of preferment was never very good. Cronin also makes this interesting point, that because of the agreement at Bruges by which the pope gave up all reservations of his predecessors not already used, a provision which Wyclyf would have approved, Wyclyf found himself without the preferment to Lincoln which he had been promised.

4. See Workman, *1*, 206; *Civ. Dom.*, *3*, 334.

at Bruges and if his *Determinatio* had already appeared, both of which contingencies are highly probable,[5] one wonders whether Wyclyf for his optimism might not himself have been more deserving of the appellative "idiot."

While it is not difficult to believe that Wyclyf resented the loss of Caistor,[6] the story which later circulated, that he had turned reformer because of his resentment at being passed over in filling the see of Worcester,[7] appears wholly without foundation. It is customary to dismiss the story as a particularly vicious rumor, but it deserves some examination. John Gilbert, who headed the first delegation to Bruges, was promoted from Bangor to Hereford, while Ralph Erghum, who was a member of the second, received Salisbury.[8] Under normal circumstances Wyclyf's eminence as a theologian should ordinarily have netted him something of a comparable character, and since the see of Worcester was vacant during the whole of 1374 and until September, 1375,[9] he could have had his eye on that diocese. But he did not. We know that in 1375 he was making strenuous efforts to secure the far humbler preferment of Caistor. Both Caistor and Worcester were filled in 1375. In view of this, it is reasonable to conclude that the story had its origin in the mistake of attributing Wyclyf's very real indignation in 1375 not to his actual disappointment at failing to receive Caistor but to his imagined grievance in not securing Worcester. The loss of Worcester would have made, in any event, a much better story than his failure to secure Caistor.

5. For Wyclyf's appointment to Bruges, see above, p. 4; for the publication of the *Determinatio*, see below, p. 22.

6. Even Workman (*1*, 206) admits the matter rankled.

7. According to Netter (*Doctrinale Antiquitatum Fidei Catholicae Ecclesiae, 1*, 560), Robert Hallum, bishop of Salisbury, stated before a great synod of the clergy of Canterbury how Wyclyf turned revolutionary because of his failure to receive Worcester. See Workman, *1*, 252.

8. Workman, *1*, 252.

9. Workman (*1*, 252-3) argues that Wyclyf could not have had his eye on Worcester despite its vacancy because the prior of Worcester, Walter Leigh, had been slated for the appointment as early as December 7, 1373. Yet this may not have been common knowledge, or even had Wyclyf been aware of Leigh's nomination he may have hoped that it would not materialize, as it actually did not.

2. WYCLYF'S ARRAIGNMENT
AT ST. PAUL'S

It was soon after Wyclyf's return from Bruges that he became involved in politics.[1] In doing so he was violating one of his cardinal principles, namely, that the clergy should hold itself aloof from politics and devote its energies to spiritual matters. Wyclyf may have justified this inconsistency on the score that the clergy had grown so self-seeking and at the same time so unresponsive to suggestions of reform that there was no alternative but to use politics to force them out of politics. It may be significant that the only business which Wyclyf undertook for the crown, as far as the records reveal, was concerned with church affairs.[2]

Wyclyf was brought out of the seclusion of Oxford to which he had retired[3] by John of Gaunt who sent him instructions on September 22, 1376, to appear before the king's council.[4] How Gaunt happened upon Wyclyf is a matter of conjecture. The duke had been his overlord for many years,[5] but that would not necessarily have thrown them together. In fact, had they been acquainted, Wyclyf would almost certainly have had his Lincoln prebend. Gaunt had but to say the word. If the duke was instrumental in having Wyclyf appointed to the Bruges commission, this cannot be confirmed, and the fact remains that Wyclyf was left off the second commission in 1375 which was largely under the duke's direction. In the absence of any positive evidence, one may suggest that Gaunt first learned what sort of man Wyclyf was after he took over the negotiations with the papal envoys at Bruges in 1375. In acquainting himself with the ground the earlier commission had been over, he must have learned

1. Loserth (*loc. cit.*, *136*, 62) declares he did not enter politics before 1375: "wenigstens besitzen wir keine Zeugnisse darueber, da jene, die man immer als solche angefuehrt hat, in eine spaetere Zeit gehoeren."

2. We are certain only of his part in the Bruges mission. He may have been approached on the issue of withholding money from Rome (see below, p. 57), and he may also have helped prepare the crown's defense in the case of the Westminster Abbey outrage (see below, p. 77).

3. Wyclyf returned to Oxford from Bruges and is found renting rooms at Queen's in September, 1374. Magrath, *The Queen's College*, *1*, 112 n. 3.

4. *Issues of the Exchequer*, p. 200.

5. For 30 years, from 1342 to 1372, the duke was Wyclyf's overlord. See Workman, *1*, 36–7.

of Wyclyf's part in the proceedings, that is, if his part had been of any consequence.

Why Gaunt sought the support of Wyclyf, if he ever did,[6] is no easier to explain. It is usually assumed that though the motives of the two men were poles apart their goals were essentially the same, namely, the reduction of the power and wealth of the hierarchy. Wyclyf felt that no effective reform of the church could be achieved until this hydra of political power and wealth from which stemmed the manifold evils besetting the church had been cut off. If Gaunt, on the other hand, aimed at reducing the political influence of the hierarchy and despoiling the church of her wealth, the explanation may lie in the muddled political situation of England in the middle seventies.

The unanimity of the Parliament of 1369 had been broken under stress of the reverses in France, and by contrast the closing years of Edward's long reign exhibited a "singular combination or rather confusion of political elements together with a great amount of political activity."[7] In these years may be found "the commencement of those political movements and party combinations which continued throughout the next fifteen years."[8] When the reins of state dropped from the listless hands of the aging king, since the dying Black Prince was incapable of stepping into the breach there came forward individuals and political cliques eager to exploit for their own ends the absence of the once-strong hand.

There was what is sometimes described as the anticlerical party which, "jealous at once of the influence of the church in social life and of the preponderant share of the clergy in the administration of the government, was likely enough for its own ends to ally itself with religious discontent, whilst it steadily resisted moral or spiritual reformation."[9] This group proposed in the Parliament of 1371 that the clergy be deprived of its temporalities which in time of war should be considered the common property of the kingdom. Though the proposal was defeated, the monasteries found little sympathy for their plea that they should be exempted from the proposed war levy. One of the speeches made in this Parliament is of particular interest, for Wyclyf claims to have heard it.[1] It was the fable of the owl which

6. See below, p. 14.
7. Stubbs, *The Constitutional History of England*, 2, 419.
8. Trevelyan, *England in the Age of Wycliffe*, p. 4.
9. Stubbs, 2, 419.
1. *Civ. Dom.*, 2, 7. See Workman, *1*, 210.

had lost its feathers. The other birds listened to its tale of woe and in pity gave it their own feathers. But then a hawk appeared, and when the owl refused to return the feathers to enable the birds the better to meet the hawk's attack they took them back by force.

The moral was not lost upon the English church—that if the church refused to contribute her share to the war effort of the wealth which she had actually received from the English people then that wealth would be forcibly taken from her. The English church was doubly conscious of her wealth in the seventies. The war with France was going badly, and the war was expensive. Inasmuch as the aristocracy wanted the war to continue and yet was unwilling to make the necessary financial sacrifices, what was more natural than to force the church to do so? The richly endowed bishoprics and monasteries looked all the more desirable for their relative vulnerability. At the same time, the antipapal sentiment of the fifties which had produced the statutes of Provisors and Praemunire, far from subsiding, had been aggravated by the pope's demand for John's tribute, by the continued practice of papal reservations and provisions, and by the worsening foreign situation for which many were inclined to hold the "French" pope partly responsible. While nothing so drastic as confiscation was ever widely contemplated, the anticlerical party contrived to force the resignations of Wykeham, bishop of Winchester, and Brantingham, bishop of Exeter, chancellor and treasurer respectively, on the plea that their ecclesiastical character left them unaccountable for their policies.[2]

Attracted to this anticlerical party were elements less worthy in their motivation. Scoundrels like Lord Latimer, the king's chamberlain, and Richard Lyons and John Pecche, London merchants, attached themselves to the new ministers and senile king to the improvement of their own fortunes and the impoverishment of the realm. An associate of similarly dubious character was Alice Perrers, the king's mistress, who by common consent was charged with employing her charms to the ruin of the country. The leader to whom fell the doubtful distinction of coordinating the efforts of this "band of nobles and knaves"[3] into what was known as the court party was John of Gaunt.

Although the treasurer who succeeded Brantingham was Gaunt's faithful adviser Sir Richard le Scrope, the duke's absence from England at the time leaves in doubt the part he played in the late minis-

2. *Rot. Parl.*, 2, 304.
3. Workman, *1*, 217. See Clarke, *Fourteenth Century Studies*, pp. 37–9.

terial changes.[4] The duke appears, in fact, not to have taken an active part in politics prior to 1375. It was chiefly the imminent death of his father and the fatal illness of his brother, the Black Prince, which prompted him to invade the political arena in the conviction that his birth, wealth, and fame made him the logical leader of the court. Though he developed into a skilled politician, it might have been his relative inexperience at the time which led him into the blunders of allying himself with such rascals as Latimer, Lyons, and Perrers and of coming to the assistance of Wyclyf in his difficulties with the English hierarchy.[5]

John of Gaunt continues to puzzle students. Possibly the chief reason why he has been "alternately blackened and whitewashed to a ludicrous extent, first by contemporaries, to whom a man in his position was bound to bulk large, whatever his true character, and (less excusably) by most modern historians," [6] has been the error of crediting him with a program. The duke is invariably represented as having charted a basely ambitious if not sinister course, a charge which neither then nor later required any proof since it was presumably self-evident. Yet once a search is made for evidence to substantiate this view nothing conclusive is forthcoming. And none can be found for the simple reason that the duke had no program, no major political objectives which he sought to achieve. He apparently wanted nothing more extraordinary than to play the dominant role at the court now that his father and brother were incapacitated. The duke's efforts were as a consequence largely negative—to eliminate those who might question his eminence at the court. For this purpose he willingly accepted the coöperation of any group or person, whatever his particular ambitions, whom he felt might serve his own end. Such an analysis explains the strange variety of personalities with whom he found himself allied.

Gaunt is usually classified as an anticlerical, since high among the leaders of the group which was opposing his court party were three bishops, Wykeham of Winchester, Brantingham of Exeter, and Courteney of London. Wykeham and Brantingham, especially the former, had been influential members of the court circle for some time. Courteney's was a new face and needs some introduction; he proved to become not only Gaunt's most persistent antagonist but also the prelate chiefly instrumental in prosecuting John Wyclyf. Courteney's

4. Parliament sat in March, *Rot. Parl.*, 2, 303. Gaunt returned to England in November, Armitage-Smith, *John of Gaunt*, p. 123; *Hist. Angl.*, *1*, 313.

5. See below, p. 14.

6. Steel, *Richard II*, p. 21.

father was the earl of Devon, his mother a granddaughter of Edward I, his parentage so eminent, indeed, as to elicit comment from Gaunt.[7] He attended Oxford, received the degree of doctor of laws,[8] and appears to have done some lecturing.[9] In 1367 he was elected to the chancellorship of Oxford, and for the choice of one "refulgent with the blood of kings" the university returned thanks.[1] Courteney was not wanting in powerful patrons, among whom he counted the Black Prince, and his rise was correspondingly rapid.[2] He was raised to the see of Hereford in 1369, the pope granting him a dispensation to cover his lack of years "inasmuch as by the study of letters and other virtues he had supplied the deficiency of his age . . . and had shown himself as prudent in spiritual matters as he had been circumspect in temporal."[3] Yet if Courteney owed his promotion to the favor of the pope, he soon forgot that kindness. One of the few bits of information which the sources yield relative to this early portion of his career is his threat not to contribute to the tenth voted by convocation in 1373 "until the king should provide a remedy for the grievances the clergy were suffering."[4]

In speaking of "grievances," Courteney had in mind the papal demands on the English church. For if Parliament was justified in complaining about all the money it was sinking into the bottomless war chest, the clergy had double cause for protest. After the bishops in this convocation of 1373 had attacked the burden of royal demands, they drew attention to the all but annual importunities of the pope as the sister cause for their gradual impoverishment. And though convocation did finally vote the king what he had demanded, he was reminded that if this "intolerable yoke [the demands of the Roman Curia] were removed from their necks, they would be able the more easily to aid him in his difficulties."[5]

7. See below, p. 29. Courteney was probably the most important member of the English hierarchy at the time. To quote Lechler (1, 368): "Courtnay . . . Adel und Hierarchie in sich vereignite und in seinem eigenen Person die Coalition der Adelsgeschlechter mit der Praelatur gegen die hochfliegenden Plaene des Herzogs von Lancaster repraesentierte."

8. *Registrum Willelmi de Courtenay*, p. 2; *Fas. Ziz.*, p. 286.

9. *Register of John de Grandisson, 3*, 1260.

1. *Munimenta Academica, 1*, 226.

2. His rise was so rapid that the election of Brantingham by the chapter of Hereford was set aside in order to make possible Courteney's provision. *Register of Thomas de Brantyngham, 2*, vii.

3. *Registrum Willelmi de Courtenay*, pp. 1–2.

4. Wilkins, *Concilia Magnae Britanniae et Hiberniae, 3,* 97.

5. *Ibid.*

In May, 1375, Courteney was translated to the see of London. He must have been gratified by the promotion, for the pre-eminence of that metropolis among the cities of England made it the most important bishopric in the country. This new honor left him one of the most influential men in England, for in contrast to the modest political role of the modern prelate his episcopal predecessor of the Middle Ages was a lord in the full sense of the term. Not only was the bishop the spiritual leader of the laity in an age when the church could vie with the state for prior claim to the loyalty of the people, but he was also expected to be the protector of their civil liberties as well and the champion of their demands against the pretensions of crown and nobility.[6] Incidentally, in return for accepting the recommendations of Wykeham and the Black Prince, who were pressing Courteney's eligibility for promotion to London, it is probable that Gaunt and the court party exacted their *quid pro quo* by requiring the elevation of Sudbury, Courteney's predecessor in London, to Canterbury.

It was in the so-called "Good Parliament" which convened April 28, 1376, that the cleavage among England's political leaders, between Gaunt's or the court party and the opposition, was brought into the open. The initiative was seized by the opposition, a group composed of the powerful bishops mentioned above, many of the Black Prince's friends who were suspicious of the duke, and those nobles who were jealous of Gaunt. They were enabled to do this with the support of a surprisingly assertive Commons which under Peter de la Mare's inspiring leadership almost anticipated something of the parliamentary history of the 17th century.

To the chancellor's request for additional grants, the opposition countered with its own demands, that Latimer, Lyons, and others be prosecuted for fraud, that Alice Perrers be banished from the court, and that an administrative council continuously 'attend and advise the crown upon all important business. In the main the king, with Gaunt acting as intermediary, agreed to these demands. Those who had been charged with fraud he ordered imprisoned, Perrers was sent away from the palace, and a council was appointed, whose authority, however, was not to extend over the king's principal ministers.

But with the adjournment of Parliament in July came the denouement. The opposition, so commanding a few weeks previous, became

6. See below, p. 33, where Courteney promised to secure satisfaction for the grievances of the Londoners against the duke.

negligible overnight. And Gaunt proceeded to ignore it. His leading opponent among the aristocracy, the earl of March, was ordered off to France to inspect English strongholds. When the earl refused to go, he was deprived of his office of lord marshal, which was immediately conferred upon the powerful Percy in order to gain his support. March's steward, Peter de la Mare, who had directed the opposition of Commons in the Good Parliament, was seized and imprisoned. Bishop Wykeham was banished from the court, Latimer and Lyons were recalled, and the exile of Perrers was revoked. To make his victory complete, the duke dismissed the new council and insolently announced that the Good Parliament had been no parliament at all. Since the Black Prince had died in June, Gaunt's position was supreme.

Yet the chronicler's jibe at the hierarchy for conducting themselves "like dume dogs not able to barke" [7] was premature, for though the duke found the new Parliament of early 1377 reasonably cooperative,[8] convocation was in open revolt. The prelates were wroth at the enforced absence of Wykeham who had been forbidden to approach within 20 miles of the court.[9] After Bishop Courteney had harangued the assembled prelates on the injury done the bishop of Winchester, which he pointed out was as much an affront to them all and to the church, they agreed that they would not take up the business of the convocation, chiefly that of a sudsidy, until Wykeham had been recalled. Sudbury was eventually forced to adjourn the meeting and betake himself to the king, who, wanting his subsidy, authorized the archbishop to summon Wykeham.[1]

Now to return to Wyclyf—it was at this time that the association which had sprung up between Gaunt and Wyclyf came into public view. In the early afternoon of February 19, 1377, the same month in which convocation had refused to continue its sessions unless Wykeham's banishment were revoked, Wyclyf appeared before the prelates at St. Paul's in the entourage of the duke to answer to charges of

7. *Transcript, Archaeologia*, 22, 242. See *Chron. Angl.*, p. 104.

8. See Steel, pp. 32–5, and Wedgwood, "John of Gaunt and the Packing of Parliament," *EHR*, 45, 623–5, for a discussion of this Parliament.

9. *Chron. Angl.*, pp. 106–7, 398.

1. *Ibid.*, pp., 113–14; Lowth, *The Life of William of Wykeham*, pp. 131–4. That the king's hand was forced by his desire for a grant is suggested by his express exclusion of Wykeham from a general pardon issued on the occasion of his jubilee. *Rot. Parl.*, 2, 365. The bishop was pardoned and his temporalities restored only three days before Edward's death—against the wishes of Gaunt. Rymer, 7, 148–9.

heresy. We have seen that it was Gaunt who drew Wyclyf from the relative obscurity of Oxford.[2] We must now analyze Gaunt's motives for doing so.

The two motives customarily attributed to Gaunt as impelling him to seek an alliance with Wyclyf were, first, the exclusion of the hierarchy from politics, and second, the secularization of the wealth of the church. The temptation to impute these motives to the duke springs largely from the fact that Wyclyf in these early years was concentrating his attack on the church along those two lines. Wyclyf maintained that the prelate had no place in civil office, that God had given the pope and his ministers supreme spiritual dominion with which they should be content.[3] He proposed further that the civil authorities might justly deprive a corrupt church of its property.[4] Nothing, so it is assumed, would have pleased Gaunt better. He would have been only too happy to bar certain ecclesiastics from public office, specifically such influential adversaries as Wykeham and Courteney. It was believed by many of his contemporaries, as it is still commonly believed today, that he was an unprincipled politician and as such would have grasped at the opportunity of cloaking his own rapacious desire for ever more wealth under the guise of disciplining an unworthy church.

Even though the above analysis is a popular one,[5] it will bear little scrutiny unless there is some cogency in the statement that what is repeated often enough as true in time becomes true. In order to qualify for the charge of seeking to drive the prelatical lords out of politics Gaunt would be obliged to accept the vice of inconsistency along with the many others imputed to him. For how then could one otherwise account for the fact that two of the chief ministers in 1377, the duke's own appointees, were bishops? Adam Houghton, the bishop of St. David's, was made chancellor, while Henry Wakefield, the bishop of Worcester, became treasurer. Gaunt's own chancellor and trusted adviser, Ralph Erghum, was the bishop of Salisbury. The new archbishop, Simon Sudbury, a friend of the duke's though for the moment without high civil office, was murdered as chancellor in 1381. "The duke's treasurers, auditors, receivers, clerks, and higher household officials were all paid in canonries, prebends, bene-

2. See above, p. 7.
3. *Blas.*, p. 261.
4. See below, p. 23.
5. See Workman, *1*, 277–8, Trevelyan, pp. 38–41, Vaughan, *1*, 313, among others.

fices . . ." [6] The claim that Gaunt wanted to humble Wykeham and Courteney is easy to prove. It is a mistake to assert that his attack on them went beyond this immediate if not personal objective.[7]

As little evidence can be marshaled to substantiate the charge that the duke was conspiring to secularize the property of the church, that the "duke made Wyclif's scheme of disendowment . . . his own, untrammelled by Wyclif's social aims or spiritual desires, but with far clearer insight into the consequences. He saw his chance of doubling his estates . . ." [8] In the first place, Gaunt showed himself most generous toward religious establishments during his life and left them handsome bequests in his will.[9] In the second place, Gaunt was already the wealthiest and most powerful man in England. In any general scramble for church property, his more ruthless and less moral rivals—and there were such—would have grown relatively more formidable. Finally, if Gaunt had been aiming at disendowment, we should expect him to have shown more zeal than that of simply coming to Wyclyf's rescue in 1377. The duke shielded him again several years later when Wyclyf had all but forgotten disendowment for more fundamental issues, most of them not at all to Gaunt's liking.[1] There can be no question that the duke would have protected Wyclyf in February, 1377, had the latter not been preaching disendowment.[2]

Equally unhistorical and uncritical is the tendency to read political motivation into Wyclyf's activities of 1376–77 which led to his subsequent summons to St. Paul's in February, 1377. Thus several writers maintain that the duke had been employing Wyclyf as a sort of bulldog during that period in order to frighten into a state of quiescence the prelatical lords who were balking his political ambitions. It is difficult to substantiate the statement that Gaunt had been saving Wyclyf for "just such an occasion" and now gave him directions "to expound his views upon civil and divine dominion, on grace and,

6. Workman *1*, 276. See Armitage-Smith, *op. cit.*, pp. 173–4.

7. The cleavage between Gaunt and Courteney was more than political, see below, p. 29. According to current gossip the duke had good cause for hating Wykeham; see *Chron. Angl.*, Introd., p. 1. Walsingham quotes the duke as threatening to humble the entire English hierarchy (see below, p. 29), but that chronicler was a highly prejudiced reporter; see below, p. 16.

8. Workman, *1*, 278.

9. Armitage-Smith, *op. cit.*, pp. 405–6. Of Gaunt's munificence to the clergy, Armitage-Smith writes: "He is constantly giving gifts, not only the small marks of favour like timber and venison from his forests, but gifts of land, solid endowments, manors, and the advowsons of churches and chapels." *Ibid.*, p. 168.

1. See below, p. 133.

2. See below, p. 18.

above all, on ecclesiastical poverty." [3] Wyclyf had been voicing his views on those subjects for some time, even before he had entered the service of the crown.[4] Furthermore, would not such views distress the duke's numerous friends among the hierarchy as much as his enemies? Finally, if Gaunt were in favor of ecclesiastical poverty, his own munificence had been, and was to continue to be, partly responsible for producing the condition he would now be wishing to correct.

Walsingham is the source of the story that Gaunt was actively encouraging Wyclyf's attacks on the church at this time. The chronicler makes the statement that the duke had long been plotting how he might seize the kingdom and had decided that before this could be accomplished it would be necessary to destroy the liberties of the church and of London. In this infamous scheme he had been able to enlist the services of Wyclyf, for Wyclyf had been attacking the church since being deprived of a benefice.[5]

Walsingham's bold report may be attacked on a number of counts. Its most obvious weakness is the author's lack of objectivity. The chronicler assails the duke "with an animosity that savours of personal hatred," [6] and if he abominated anyone even more than Gaunt it was Wyclyf. In the chronicler's defense, but further weakening the force of his evidence, is the qualification "as it is said" with which he prefaces his account. Possibly Walsingham hoped to be able to ruin Gaunt's and Wyclyf's reputations, yet protect his own as a historian, with the saving "ut fertur." [7]

There is another reason why Walsingham's evidence should be used only with considerable caution to support the view that Gaunt hunted up Wyclyf for political reasons. That is the strong suspicion which the account arouses in the reader that the chronicler was using hindsight in telling of the events which presumably preceded Wyclyf's summons in February, 1377. One wonders whether Walsingham was not read-

3. Steel, p. 35. Steel argues that Gaunt directed Wyclyf to voice such opinions in retaliation for the refusal of convocation to proceed with its business until Wykeham had been recalled. Steel has ignored the pertinent chronology. Convocation met February 2, while Wyclyf was summoned on February 19, hardly an adequate interval to permit effective dissemination of Wyclyf's views. The prelates, in any event, would not have acted with such haste, which would be unusual even today.

4. See below, p. 20.

5. *Chron. Angl.*, p. 115. See above, p. 4, for reference to the deprivation.

6. *Chron. Angl.*, p. xxxviii. For a more recent criticism of Walsingham's objectivity, see Galbraith, "Thomas Walsingham and the Saint Albans Chronicle, 1272–1422," *EHR*, 47, 12–29.

7. *Chron. Angl.*, p. 115.

ing back from the events of February 19 when the duke and Percy appeared as Wyclyf's protectors and simply assumed that since they shielded him on that occasion they must have been promoting him for some time previous. In fact, that they protected him on that occasion the chronicler lays as much to Wyclyf's own design as to Gaunt. To quote Walsingham:

> After he [Wyclyf] had discussed these [theories] and much worse not only openly in the halls of Oxford, but also publicly in the city of London, that he might there certainly gain the favor of the duke and of others, whom he knew were inclined to give thought to his opinions, he found, what he had long been seeking, namely, some nobles . . . who would embrace his absurdities, steel him in blunting the sword of Peter, if they could in any way, and protect him with the secular arm lest he be publicly struck down by it.[8]

Then after telling how Wyclyf had continued his preaching all the more brazenly for this protection, how he gained some followers among the "simple-minded" folk of London,[9] and how he had extolled the mendicants, the chronicler makes this comment: "The duke and Henry Percy commended his opinions, and busied themselves in extolling his knowledge and honesty to the skies." Only after this had been going on for some time did the archbishop finally bestir himself, "although late," and summon Wyclyf.[1]

In evaluating Walsingham's account, scholars have this choice: either to accept his words as evidence that while Gaunt was seeking Wyclyf's support to further his own ambitions Wyclyf was courting the favor of the duke and other nobles to bolster his attack on the church, or to reject the chronicler's statement altogether as that of a violently prejudiced reporter. Yet not only Wyclyf's untutored admirers but students as well have rejected both alternatives. What blackens Gaunt's reputation they approve; what discredits Wyclyf they ignore. They accept without hesitation the chronicler's words as proof that the duke used Wyclyf to advance his own devious designs, while they reject at the same time what the same chronicler has to say in the very same passage about Wyclyf's motives in addressing

8. *Ibid.*, p. 116.
9. "simplices quosdam Londoniensium cives . . ." *Ibid.*
1. *Ibid.*, p. 117. That Percy had gone over to the duke since the adjournment of the Good Parliament was clear from his acceptance of the office of marshal, but the fact of their alliance was hardly so manifest as the chronicler would have us believe—another suggestion of Walsingham's hindsight.

such nobles as Gaunt. This is all the more puzzling in view of the fact that, though little evidence can be marshaled to support Walsingham's statement that the duke protected Wyclyf from political considerations, strong negative confirmation is provided by Wyclyf himself that he was willing to go to inconsistent lengths in order to win the sympathy of the English nobility. Consider, for example, Wyclyf's thesis that one in mortal sin forfeited dominion. He explained at length how this principle should be applied against a corrupt hierarchy, exhorting the nobility to confiscate its wealth without fear of such futile papal gestures at retaliation as excommunication.[2] And what was the reaction of the same nobility to Wyclyf's views on dominion? So carefully did Wyclyf obscure the logical consequences his theories on dominion would have meant for the nobility that the duke, the notoriously immoral son of an equally immoral father, together with the vicious Percy, appeared as his champions at St. Paul's.[3]

If Gaunt's interest in Wyclyf lacked political motivation, so did the summons which Wyclyf received from Archbishop Sudbury to appear at St. Paul's. The charge that the bishops arraigned Wyclyf simply to embarrass Gaunt[4] rests indirectly upon Walsingham's untrustworthy report. Furthermore, if there was an understanding between the duke and Wyclyf, there is nothing other than Walsingham's words to suggest that this was known at the time.[5] Then there is the significant fact that Wyclyf was summoned to appear at St. Paul's by Sudbury, a friend of the duke. Finally, the issues that Wyclyf was raising in his attack on the church were sufficiently odious to the prelates to have warranted his arraignment whatever his political associations.[6] It is true that the prelates, in summoning Wyclyf to St. Paul's when they might have handled the matter quietly at Oxford or some chapter house, may have wished the affair to have some notoriety. But since Gaunt's friend Sudbury did the summoning, if publicity was desired it may more properly have been intended to impress the Londoners rather than the duke.

Too much sinister ambition has been imputed to Gaunt. For instance, he has been accused of seeking to block the accession of

2. See below, p. 24.

3. See below, p. 28.

4. See Workman, 1, 284.

5. "His alliance with the duke was probably secret as yet, or known only to the few." Workman, 1, 282; see also, n. 6.

6. "It was impossible for the bishops and clergy of all England, assembled in the city for Convocation, to allow their authority to be defied with such publicity . . ." Trevelyan, p. 43.

Richard in order to smooth his own path to the throne. "Though naturally anxious to dominate English politics on the failure of his father's and elder brother's health, the contemporary charge that he was aiming at the English throne is groundless." [7] Gaunt's appearance as Wyclyf's champion at St. Paul's requires no more complex an explanation and implies no more reprehensible a motive than that the duke considered it his duty to support Wyclyf since the latter was in the service of the crown.[8] Again it is important to remember that the duke protected Wyclyf some years later not only when Wyclyf was of no value to him but when the association had become actually embarrassing if not injurious.[9]

If Wyclyf's summons to St. Paul's was not politically inspired, what doctrinal grounds did the prelates have for arraigning him? On the basis of what is actually found in the sources about Wyclyf's revolutionary tenets, one might be surprised at the relative suddenness with which he was summoned. According to Netter, Wyclyf's views had not drawn attack for unorthodoxy before he took his degree as doctor, consequently not prior to 1372, although what he might have maintained as a "sententiary" was eventually declared heretical.[1] Workman points out, for example, that Wyclyf's views on the humanity of Christ which he first expressed as a sententiary about 1370 introduced him into formal theological controversy, "at any rate in its published form." [2] This qualification is important, for a sententiary was expected to propose theories which would provoke counterarguments from his fellow sententiaries.[3] How academic such disputations were is revealed by this statement of Woodford, later a bitter critic of Wyclyf: "When I was lecturing at the same time as he was on the *Sentences*

7. Steel, p. 21.

8. And Gaunt, to all intents and purposes, was regent. As Wedgwood writes: "John of Gaunt was practically regent in 1377 . . ." Wedgwood, *loc. cit.*, p. 625.

9. See below, p. 133.

1. Shirley (*Fas. Ziz.*, p. xxvii) says Archbishop Langham condemned Wyclyf's doctrine of the imperishability of matter. Wyclyf must have expressed such views as a sententiary. See below, p. 20.

2. Workman, *1*, 139.

3. "The sin of scholasticism did not lie in any rigid, mechanical uniformity. We might even assert that scholasticism by the very logomachies on which it set such store made it its chief business to prevent uniformity. There was never a time when some angel or demon was not stepping down into the pool and troubling its waters. In consequence the record of scholasticism is the record of all sorts of minor heretics, for differences of thought soon became differences in belief. But as a rule these minor heretics were unreal; their beliefs were mere matters of argument vitiated by the tradition of double truth, or adopted to advertise their Determinations or Quodlibeta." Workman, *1*, 146.

Wyclyf used to write his answers to the arguments which I advanced in a note-book that I sent him with my arguments, and to send me back the note-book." [4]

Netter lists thirteen "heresies which he [Wyclyf] first cast into the air," presumably as a sententiary at Oxford. They are the following:

1. That if anything was or will be, it is.
2. That anything is a thing created, which is any kind of created thing and at the same time all created things.
3. That one animal is every animal and any one of them, and in like fashion with every genus and species.
4. That God can not annihilate a creature.
5. That Christ is his humanity and is his soul and the body itself, which is the second quantitative part of the humanity of Christ; and much more than this, that Christ is the lowest creature, since he is that first matter.
6. That the Son of God can not cease being man.
7. That God of his absolute power can not damn that creature, in order to demonstrate that which is united to Christ.
8. That no one prejudged is a part of the church. [5]
9. That no one in mortal sin is lord, priest, or bishop.
10. That no priest or member of the consecrated can have civil dominion.
11. That no ecclesiastic can live as an owner of property.
12. That temporal lords have the power to take away temporalities from ecclesiastics.
13. That no one is bound to give tithes or offerings to bad-tempered priests. [6]

If Wyclyf expressed these views early in his career, as Netter declares, he must have done so as a sententiary, for several propositions, such as the last five, are not found stated quite so severely in any of his formal writings. These opinions, incidentally, reflect Wyclyf's scholastically trained mind and his pronounced realism. They also indicate that Wyclyf had long pondered over the theses he was in time to set down in his treatises on civil and divine dominion. [7]

This suggests that there is considerable validity in Workman's observation that in the Middle Ages, in contrast to today, "publication

4. Little, *op. cit., p.* 81.

5. The text reads: "Quod nullus praescitus est pars ecclesia"; *ecclesia* should read *ecclesie*. For *praescitus*, see below, p. 94, n. 2.

6. *Fas. Ziz.*, pp. 2–3.

7. See below, p. 24.

marked the culmination of a long tournament in the lecture rooms and schools." [8] But it does not follow necessarily that Wyclyf's repute at this time extended beyond academic and, since Wyclyf was in the service of the crown, court circles. Loserth declares that contemporary writers notice Wyclyf first in 1377.[9] Only Walsingham, who has a penchant for exaggeration, states that Wyclyf had been "barking at the church for many years in single acts in the schools," [1] though the phrase *in scholis* leads one to infer that this "barking" did not extend beyond the halls of Oxford. Yet Walsingham goes on to describe how, before being arraigned by the archbishop, Wyclyf had disseminated his views not only at the university but among the citizenry of London and from church to church. However, since Walsingham notes that Gaunt and Percy had been protecting Wyclyf in these activities, one is inclined to question his chronological accuracy since Gaunt's interest in Wyclyf probably—and Percy's undoubtedly—had not come to view before the incident at St. Paul's in February, 1377.

That Wyclyf was formally summoned to appear at the great church of St. Paul's and that he did so in the company of the duke and Percy have tempted Wyclyf's biographers to exaggerate his fame in 1377 as well as that of his doctrines. This tendency is founded partly on the unwarranted assumption that the duke and Wyclyf had been actively cooperating against the hierarchy, partly on the equally dubious premise that Wyclyf's revolutionary views were common knowledge at this time, and partly on the wild claims of several of Wyclyf's admirers who declare he was a member of Parliament, even a royal chaplain and one to whom the government would soon appeal for an opinion as to the validity of withholding money from Rome.[2] We even find the fantastic statement—this not by a friend—that Wyclyf once lectured to Chaucer.[3]

While modern scholarship is willing to concede the fallacy of these claims,[4] individual scholars have been loath to reduce proportionately these earlier estimates of Wyclyf's eminence, which were largely predi-

8. Workman, *1*, 258.

9. Loserth, *loc. cit.*, *136*, 113. Loserth argues that since Pope Gregory, who was ever on the lookout for heresy, did not notice Wyclyf prior to 1377 the latter must have confined his attack on the church to the university before that date.

1. *Chron. Angl.*, p. 115.

2. See *Fas. Ziz.*, p. xix, and Lechler, *1*, 331–2. For a discussion of the question of whether Wyclyf's opinion was sought on the matter of holding back money from Rome, see below, pp. 57–9.

3. Wood, *History and Antiquities of the University of Oxford*, *1*, 485.

4. See especially Workman, and Manning, "Wyclif," *Cambridge Medieval History*.

cated upon such gratuitous assertions. It might be added that part of this reluctance may be traced to the faulty translation of the editor of the *Chronicon Angliae* who abstracted on the margin, "He [Wyclyf] gains many followers among the nobles," when the text actually reads "some." [5]

We do not know the specific charges on which Wyclyf was arraigned at St. Paul's on February 19. Walsingham leads us to believe that it was the following theses which prompted the summons: that the pope could excommunicate no one but that if someone granted the pope that power then any priest would have as much authority to remove the sentence as the pope himself; that neither king nor lay lord might make a grant to any person or to the church in perpetuity, since the lay lords might meritoriously deprive such persons of what had been given them in the event they were habitual sinners; that temporal lords in need might lawfully appropriate the goods of the possessioners in order to relieve their poverty. "These and opinions far more serious" had Wyclyf been preaching about London. The chronicler notes finally that Wyclyf had extolled the perfection of the friars and their poverty, which he must have contrasted with the wealth of the church in general and with that of the possessioners in particular.[6]

The controversial views which Walsingham ascribes to Wyclyf are found expressed in Wyclyf's *Determinatio* and in his treatises on civil and divine dominion. The *Determinatio* introduced the theme upon which he elaborated in his subsequent works on the subject of dominion. Various dates have been assigned to its appearance. Because of Wyclyf's discussion of the papal demand for payment of the tribute, some scholars have dated it unnecessarily early on the mistaken assumption that the pope made only one such request, that made in July, 1365.[7] The *Eulogium* declares a second request was made in 1374.[8] Though the accuracy of this statement has been challenged, it is supported by the fact that Wyclyf in the *Determinatio* replies to the arguments of John Uhtred of Durham, one of the canonists who the *Eulogium* states was selected to advise the council on the question of the tribute. In the *Determinatio* Wyclyf also accuses William Binham of attacking him for his position on the tribute in the hope that the Curia might deprive him of his ecclesiastical benefices.[9] This last must

5. *quosdam* (*Chron. Angl.*, p. 116).

6. *Ibid.*

7. *Cal. of Papal Letters*, 4, 16. See Loserth, *loc. cit.*, *136*, 30–1, 118–19.

8. *Eulog.*, 3, 337.

9. *Op. Min.*, p. 425. Uhtred's name appears as Outredus in the *Opera Minora* (p. 403), Binham's as Vrinham and Wiham (p. 415).

have been in reference to his discouragement in 1374–75 when he saw his prospects for a prebend at Lincoln fading.[1] Finally, the *Determinatio* could scarcely have appeared before 1374, "for that would have stamped him as a partisan rather than a commissioner" and he would never have been appointed to the Bruges commission.[2]

The *Determinatio* is a short work divided into two parts. The first answers the arguments of Uhtred, a doctor and lecturer at Oxford who had assailed Wyclyf's thesis that the state might discipline a negligent church and deprive her of her secular power and wealth. At this early point in his career Wyclyf was willing to recommend such interference only as a last resort, namely, when the ecclesiastical authorities refused to correct the situation. Yet he insisted that the less the church concerned herself with wealth and secular affairs, the more properly would she fulfill her mission.

The second part of the *Determinatio*, largely a rebuttal of Binham's arguments, examines the legality of the pope's claim to tribute. Wyclyf here justifies the confiscation of the church's goods under certain conditions, although he grants that a priest may resist a lay lord whom greed alone inspires to such action. He charges benefactors with serious sin when their gifts contribute to luxurious living, and he justifies the civil prosecution of criminal priests. Next he introduces the speeches of seven lords whom he claims to have heard attacking the papal demand.[3] The first lord disallowed the claim which he declared had been acquired through force and could therefore be repudiated since the pope was not sufficiently strong to enforce it. The second lord opposed tribute because the pope had no right to exercise civil dominion which such payment would imply since Christ had not done so. The third lord denied the papal claim to tribute since the pope was benefiting England "nec spiritualiter nec corporaliter" but was taking English money to favor England's enemies. The fourth lord declared the pope had forfeited what rights he may have enjoyed, even to church property, for by collecting first fruits he had denied the king his feudal superiority. The fifth lord denounced the tribute as a simoniacal concession which the pope had demanded in return for absolving John and which "smacked more of avarice than of penance." The sixth lord

---

1. See above, p. 5.

2. Workman, *1*, 239. See above, p. 4, n. 4. Loserth (*loc. cit., 136*, 35) dates it 1377, as does Cronin (*loc. cit.*, p. 67 n. 1).

3. Wyclyf's account has been described as "the earliest instance . . . of a report of a parliamentary debate." *Fas. Ziz.*, p. xix. See also Lechler, *1*, 333. Workman attacks this interpretation (*1*, 236) and ridicules the suggestion that Wyclyf was a member of Parliament (pp. 340–1).

took the position that if England belonged to the pope he had no right to sell it so cheaply, and that, furthermore, since the pope was peccable he could not establish his claim to England, for his dominion lapsed when he fell into sin. The seventh lord opposed the payment of the tribute inasmuch as John never had the right to surrender his kingdom to the pope without the consent of the people.[4]

The *Determinatio* served to introduce Wyclyf's more exhaustive treatises on the subject of dominion which he developed in the *De Dominio Divino* and *De Civili Dominio*. According to Wyclyf dominion is held directly and only from God Himself, never mediately through human lords. God is the lord, man is His vassal. God grants dominion to those in His grace, but mortal sin, being tantamount to treason, results in the loss or forfeiture of dominion. Conversely the good Christian has dominion whatever his status in society, for all share alike as sons of God in the duty and privilege of reciprocal service. In fact, one might logically attack all distinctions of rank and estate as established upon injustice.

While Wyclyf did not press the implications of his theories on dominion against king or nobility, he wanted to implement them immediately against the church.[5] A sinful priest might be deprived of his benefice, and since the church might be directed by sinful men no grants should be made in perpetuity to the church. Since lay action to enforce such principles would elicit excommunication, Wyclyf declares any such excommunication futile unless for strictly spiritual offenses. He even suggests that the power of excommunication be exercised by secular authorities when laymen are involved. Tithes may be paid since they are alms, yet if the clergy neglects its duties these alms should be paid directly to the poor. Since popes are but human and may err, they are not essential to the government of the church.

In keeping with his premise that the church should eschew wealth, Wyclyf leveled a bitter attack on the possessioners while he commended the friars for their desire to "more strictly follow Christ in His poverty." Just as Christ and His apostles lived lives of complete poverty, so the church should hold no property except insofar as it was necessary

---

4. For the arguments of the seven lords, see *Op. Min.*, pp. 425–30.

5. Wyclyf taught that obedience was due to lay authorities whether in the state of grace or not but was to be denied to clergymen whose state was doubtful. Manning, p. 498, does not consider this inconsistent since "the Church should be judged by a different standard from the world." Actually given Wyclyf's premise that all dominion is based upon grace, no such sweeping qualification is logically possible.

to aid the poor. Under no circumstances whatsoever might the church exercise civil jurisdiction.

The first volume of Wyclyf's treatises on civil dominion must have appeared in book or pamphlet form by the close of 1376, in time for them to serve as a basis for the summons he received from the prelates. Wyclyf was arraigned in February, 1377. In May of that year Pope Gregory prepared a list of 19 propositions, for which he drew heavily upon the views Wyclyf set forth in the *De Civili Dominio*. In fact, eight of Gregory's propositions agree word for word with identical passages in the *De Civili Dominio* while another seven vary but slightly. Furthermore, the sequence in which they are listed in Gregory's schedule follows roughly the manner in which Wyclyf discussed them in the *De Civili Dominio*. That the Curia in Rome was able to use these treatises as a basis for its charges in May, 1377, proves that they must have been current in England sometime before that date.[6]

Before the events are described which attended Wyclyf's appearance at St. Paul's to answer to charges of heresy, a word should be said about some of the earlier occasions when his views were called into question. Wyclyf declares that the "year previous"[7] to the production of the *Determinatio* he had become involved in a controversy with the Franciscan William Woodford on the question of civil dominion and the right of the clergy to possess property.[8] Their controversy remained in the main on an amicable plane. It was only later that Woodford accused Wyclyf of attacking the monks out of simple malice.[9] Similarly friendly were the early exchanges between Wyclyf and the Carmelite John Cunningham. Their dispute dates from the early seventies when Cunningham attacked Wyclyf for his unquestioning reliance on the authority of the Bible and his extreme realism, which he warned would lead to pantheism and a denial of transubstantiation.[1] There were others who questioned or attacked Wyclyf, some simply in the role of scholastic disputants, others to answer such direct assaults as those he had made upon the possessioners.[2]

Had Wyclyf restricted his activities to oral controversy at Oxford,

6. Loserth (*loc. cit.*, *156*, Pt. VI, 7) is not sure whether the theses appeared before Wyclyf's first book of the *De Civili Dominio*.

7. *Op. Min.*, p. 415.

8. *Ibid.*, pp. 415–16; *Civ. Dom.*, 2, 1; 3, 351, 358.

9. See above, pp. 19–20. Cronin (*loc. cit.*, p. 564 n. 5) dates this controversy as the very end of 1376.

1. *Fas. Ziz.*, pp. 4–103.

2. See Workman, 2, 122–9.

the hierarchy would probably not have molested him. Such distasteful theories as the necessity of apostolic poverty or that secular authorities should deprive sinful priests of their offices would have occasioned but negligible injury and scandal under those circumstances. In fact, several years later Wyclyf would even have been permitted to theorize upon such a fundamental doctrine as transubstantiation, despite the dubiousness of his views, had he limited his discussions to the halls of Oxford.[3] Quite a different matter was the publication of revolutionary views. These opinions would immediately become, at least potentially, public knowledge. Furthermore, until a controversialist's theses had been published, he might maintain under question that he was simply speculating upon, not maintaining, them. And if, as Walsingham states, Wyclyf had been going about London airing his views to the citizenry, he might have been able to escape censure by insisting that his accusers had misunderstood his sermons or had been misinformed.[4]

It is probable that Wyclyf informed the duke that he had been summoned to appear before the bishops at St. Paul's, for Walsingham describes how Gaunt sought to reassure Wyclyf in his anxiety as to what to answer to his questioners by appointing four friars to assist him. The four were theologians, and each represented a different mendicant order.[5] The chronicler states that the duke played upon the "natural and ancient antagonism" between the friars and the monks, wherefore "nether was yt difficult to compell the willynge freires to aide hym in this poynt."[6]

The appearance of these friars as advisers to Wyclyf at a date as late as 1377 has caused historians some concern. Thus Thompson writes: "It is indeed almost hopeless to account for such a glaring perversion of facts otherwise than by an assumption of the writer's ignorance, and yet one hardly dares to allow such ignorance in a contemporary writer."[7] Actually the problem is not so mystifying today as it was 75 years ago. Through the work of more recent Wyclyf scholars the chronological pattern of Wyclyf's publications has been completely revised. In the De Civili Dominio, for instance, of which some treatises appeared shortly before 1377, others shortly after, Wyclyf has nothing

3. See below, p. 133.

4. Courteney's apologist used this same argument. See below, p. 87. See below, p. 128, when Stokes, accused of heresy, defended himself on the ground that he had been merely speculating.

5. "quatuor theologiae magistros, unum ex singulis ordinibus Mendicantium . . ." Chron. Angl., p. 118.

6. Transcript, p. 256. See Chron. Angl., p. 118.

7. Chron. Angl., p. liii.

but praise for the friars.[8] And it should be borne in mind that Wyclyf did not consider any of his opinions "heretical."[9] He bitterly denounced Pope Gregory the following year for presuming to condemn 19 of his theses. Indeed there were many theologians at Oxford who were inclined to agree with him.[1] Among the friars who accompanied him to St. Paul's, the Franciscan, were he a member of the "Spirituals," might not have considered his views particularly novel or revolutionary or even debatable.

A few other comments might be made concerning the cooperation of these friars. In view of Wyclyf's denunciation of the wealth of the church and of the growing establishments of the possessioners, it is easy to understand how in contrast he could still in 1377 describe the friars as "most pleasing to God."[2] Being human, the friars might have been glad to reciprocate such sentiment, all the more so since it was so rare for them to receive commendation from any secular. Workman suggests that Wyclyf's association with the friars at Oxford may have favorably impressed him.[3] Surely his clash with the monks of Canterbury Hall would have left him somewhat skeptical of the quality of their poverty and self-abnegation. Furthermore, the friars might have been all the more willing to assist Wyclyf because the man who directed his prosecution was Courteney, now bishop of London. Courteney had become so involved in the dispute raging at Oxford in the sixties on the side of the university against the mendicants that when he was elected chancellor in 1367 the king had to interpose to block the attempt of the friars to cite him to Rome.[4] Finally, the duke was a good friend of the friars, and it was he who must have suggested their accompanying Wyclyf to St. Paul's.[5]

Just as it had been necessary to prod Archbishop Sudbury into appealing to the king to permit Wykeham to attend convocation,[6] so now it required Courteney's vigorous insistence and that of other bishops before he issued the summons to Wyclyf. "Wherefor (although somewhat late) the bishoppes beynge moved, wakened the archbishopp,

8. *Civ. Dom.*, *3*, 4, 6, 57. Loserth (*loc. cit.*, *136*, 107) writes: "In dem Buch von der buergerlichen Herrschaft spricht er von den Bettelmoenchen nur Gutes. Sie sind es ja, die seinem Ideal von der christlichen Geistlichkeit am naechsten stehen."

9. See below, p. 73.

1. See Workman, *2*, 130–40, and below, p. 66.

2. *Eulog.*, *3*, 345.

3. Workman, *1*, 77, 281.

4. Wood, *1*, 480.

5. Loserth, *loc. cit.*, *136*, 93.

6. See above, p. 13.

there father, as out of a greate sleep, and as a myghtye man drunken with wyne . . ." [7] A summons was accordingly sent to Wyclyf, requiring him to present himself at St. Paul's for questioning.

In the early afternoon of Thursday, February 19, 1377, Wyclyf duly presented himself in company of the duke, Henry Percy, the four mendicants, and "some others who by their prestige might be able to awe the timid." [8] On the way Wyclyf was again reassured that he had nothing to fear from the bishops, who "compared with him were almost illiterate," and that he need not be uneasy about any possible assault by some of the people "since his body was protected on every side by so many lords." It was, consequently, with supreme confidence that he entered the church.

The street in front of the cathedral was so congested with people eager to see what might happen that the duke's party had to push and elbow its way inside. The situation inside was no better, and Henry Percy, presuming on his authority as marshal, proceeded to order the people about in an arrogant fashion, whereupon Bishop Courteney, who had noted his imperiousness as he came down the aisle to meet the party, interposed and warned him not to exercise any magisterial rights in the church. The bishop declared that had he suspected that Percy would act with such insolence he would never have permitted him to enter the church, to which Gaunt retorted that they would do as they pleased, whether the bishop liked it or not.

The duke's party and Courteney made their way to the Chapel of Our Lady where the archbishop and the rest of the conclave awaited them. When the prelates and lords had been seated, Percy bade Wyclyf to sit also, pointing out that as "he haythe much to answeare he haith neede of a better seate." [9] Percy's proposal sprang not from concern about Wyclyf's comfort but from a desire to humiliate the assembled bishops. In the first place he had no authority to make the suggestion. In the second place, as Courteney was quick to remonstrate, it was contrary to "reason and law" that one should sit who had been cited to answer before his ordinary to charges which had been brought against him. "He would therefore stand during the period of his examination, however long his case might be deliberated." This rejoinder led to

7. *Transcript*, p. 255. Sudbury was by nature irresolute and he was a friend of Gaunt. Workman (*1*, 284–5) suggests he may have had some sympathy for Wyclyf's views.

8. "et nonnullis aliis, qui pro sui magnitudine valerent turbare pusillanimes . . ." *Chron. Angl.*, p. 118.

9. *Transcript*, p. 258. See *Chron. Angl.*, p. 119.

heated words between Percy and the bishop, and the "entire assembly became alarmed."

Then the duke joined in the altercation. He assailed the bishop with abusive words and was similarly attacked in return. When Gaunt saw that his mere interposition did not silence the spirited prelate, he began to threaten and swore that he would humble Courteney and the entire English hierarchy as well. "You put your trust in your parents, but they will not be able to help you, for they will have enough to do in defending themselves." To this Courteney made the apt rejoinder: "I do not trust in my parents, nor in you, nor in any man, but in my God, who is not one who 'trusts in Himself.' " [1]

The jibe at the duke's grandiloquence was not lost on Lancaster, and he muttered something about dragging the bishop out of the church by his hair rather than endure any further contumely. This proved to be the spark which ignited the smoldering wrath of the crowd, already aroused because of the events of the morning, when a bill had been proposed in parliament which would have taken the government of the city out of the hands of the mayor and turned it over to any captain the court might select. In addition to other opprobrious proposals which "manifestly would have infringed upon the liberties of the city" was one to extend the jurisdiction of the marshal over the city so that "in that city as elsewhere he might make arrests." The marshal who would exercise these powers was Percy, the man who had so rudely jostled the spectators a few moments before. And joining Percy in insulting their bishop was Gaunt who had presided over parliament when these infamous measures were broached and who, as the most powerful man in the government, would appoint their "captain."

The people, accordingly, gave free rein to their indignation when they heard the duke threaten Bishop Courteney and began to riot. They shouted that they would not permit their bishop to be browbeaten, "that they would rather lose their lives than that their bishop should be insulted in his church or dragged violently therefrom . . ." The meeting broke up in an uproar, and "thus had the devil taken care lest so great a champion of his perish." [2]

We would prefer a less partisan and more informative account. Walsingham leads us to suppose that Wyclyf made an abrupt departure with the somewhat discomfited Gaunt and Percy and that this first

1. *Chron. Angl.*, p. 120. In this passage Walsingham outdoes himself in blackening Gaunt. The duke is accused of planning to humble not only the hierarchy but also those barons who might dare to interfere.
2. *Chron. Angl.*, p. 121.

attempt to silence Wyclyf had misfired. In keeping with the remarkably impersonal tone of his own writing, Wyclyf does not help us out with even a reference to the incident. Was it that he would have been just as well pleased if his readers never knew or were not reminded that he had at one time had such a dubious champion as Henry Percy?

There is a short reference in Walsingham's *Historia Anglicana* to this appearance of Wyclyf at St. Paul's. The chronicler here describes how, after the opinions of Wyclyf had been examined, the archbishop, "in the presence of the duke of Lancaster and Lord Henry Percy, enjoined silence upon him [Wyclyf] and upon all others concerning that matter [his opinions]." [3] Walsingham, however, seriously compromises the force of his testimony by stating that prior to the imposition of this sentence the pope had condemned 23 of Wyclyf's theses and had sent bulls to the archbishop and bishop of London directing them to proceed against Wyclyf. There is no record of any bulls being received in England concerning Wyclyf before those issued in May, 1377,[4] which led to Wyclyf's second appearance before an ecclesiastical tribunal. The discrepancy between Walsingham's two accounts has been clarified by Galbraith. It seems that in time, with the continued boiling and ferment of English politics, Gaunt became a *persona grata* to St. Albans. Walsingham was accordingly called upon to gloss over the duke's part in the proceedings at St. Paul's. This he did in such valiant fashion that in censoring his earlier account he muddled it as well.[5]

The meeting at St. Paul's broke up in confusion before the prelates were able to censure Wyclyf. This is clear from Walsingham who prefaces his detailed description of the quarrel between Percy, Gaunt, and Courteney with a hint as to what the sequel will be—how the resourceful devil will sow dissension between the prelates and the lords and thereby will Wyclyf escape punishment.[6]

It is worth the time to examine the factors which might have aroused the crowd to tumult. According to the chronicler, the proximate cause—

3. *Hist. Angl.*, *1*, 325. This reference to a "silencing" is not found in the other two accounts which correspond so closely to that of the *Historia Anglicana*, namely, the *Continuatio Adami Murimuthensis* (p. 223) and the *Chronicon Angliae* (App., p. 397).

4. See below, p. 35.

5. Galbraith, *loc. cit.*, pp. 21–3.

6. "Jam jamque tali occasione alumnum suum, multorum mortibus evasurum e praelatorum manibus, astute subtrahere diabolus viam invenerat; ut, primum facta dissensione inter magnatos et episcopos, ejus responsio dilationem acciperet." *Chron. Angl.*, 119.

and as it happened, the most impelling, for without it there would have been no tumult—was the insults and threats the duke cast at Courteney. For, in contrast to the unpopular Sudbury, Courteney was well liked by the Londoners. They graphically demonstrated their attachment to him the following year when a letter bearing the common seal of the city was sent to Pope Urban "deprecating the raising of William Courtenay, Bishop of London, to the dignity of Cardinal, and thereby depriving the citizens of his personal influence." [7] And as if to convince Urban that this appeal reflected no passing fancy, two similar requests were sent him the following spring.[8] That he was popular with the masses of the citizenry as well as with the upper classes was made evident when in the aftermath of the events at St. Paul's he was able to dissuade the mob from destroying Savoy, the duke's palatial residence.[9]

The jostling the people had suffered at the hands of Percy would have inflamed tempers already excited by the proposals made that forenoon in Parliament. While the Londoners would have suffered most should these bills have been adopted, the two archvillains who had most to gain were Gaunt and Percy. Gaunt, as director of the court, would have appointed the captain, while Percy as marshal would have been free to arrest at will in the city. Since the people were already in a dangerous mood because of these attempts upon their liberties, it is easy to understand how the indignities these two detested lords heaped upon "their bishop" [1] should have precipitated the tumult.

Workman believes the crowd began to riot not because of the bitter words that passed between the duke and Courteney but upon learning about the odious proposals which had been presented that morning in Parliament. To quote Workman: "On hearing of the outrage [the presenting of the bills] the crowd in the cathedral with cries of vengeance

7. Sharpe, *Cal. of Letter-Books, Letter-Book H*, p. 116. See *Hist. Angl., 1*, 382. The letter is dated December 4, 1378. In stating this was "nine months later" rather than 21 and a half, Workman (*1*, 286 n. 2) ironically slips into making the same mistake he had corrected in others.

8. *Cal. of Letter-Books*, p. 117. These are dated April 25 and May 16, 1379. Urban was contemplating raising Courteney to the dignity of cardinal along with many others to replace those whom he had deprived of hats for supporting Clement VII. Either Courteney refused the proffered honor or Urban respected the wishes of the Londoners, for he bestowed the dignity on the bishop of Norwich, Adam Easton.

9. See below, p. 33.

1. "Londonienses vero . . . jurantes non passuros se talem injuriam suo inferri episcopo . . ." *Chron. Angl.*, p. 120.

broke in upon Lancaster's guard and rescued their bishop . . ." [2]
Staid scholar though he is, Workman's words prove that when called
upon his mind can create imagery as rich as any medieval chronicler's.
There is nothing in Walsingham's account which would support that
sequence of events, although the editor of the *Chronicon Angliae* gives
that impression through his incorrect marginal comment.[3] In any event,
why should the news of what transpired that morning in Parliament
take longer to reach St. Paul's than the duke himself, who probably
had some refreshments between the adjournment of that assembly and
his appearance at St. Paul's? It makes a good story, but only a story,
to tell how, in the few minutes between the duke's arrival at St. Paul's
and the wrangling in the Lady chapel, the ominous news of what had
transpired that morning reached the crowd, and immediately hell broke
loose.

There is no reason to suppose that the hostility of the crowd toward
Wyclyf hastened in any way the rioting. Though the chronicler is outspoken in his detestation of the man, the only suggestion he drops of any
popular hostility toward Wyclyf is in noting that the duke reassured
Wyclyf before entering St. Paul's not to be uneasy about a possible attack by any of the people.[4] That his appearance in the company of
Gaunt, Percy, and other lords did his cause considerable damage is,
on the other hand, highly probable.[5] And it is especially significant that
those who shielded Wyclyf at St. Paul's in 1377 were not the citizenry
but the interested nobility.

While Walsingham is silent about what happened to Wyclyf after
the trial at St. Paul's, he takes delight in describing at length the misfortunes which dogged the duke's footsteps after his undignified departure from the Lady chapel. The next morning the leading citizens
of the city gathered to take counsel as to how they might safeguard
their threatened liberties. While they were deliberating, two lords
walked in, Sir Guy de Bryan and Walter Fitzwalter. Only by swearing
to the friendliness of their mission did they escape immediate manhand-
ling. Fitzwalter took the stand and assured the assembled citizens that
inasmuch as they too were citizens of the city and at the same time
owners of extensive property any menace to the burghers' liberties was
as much a threat to theirs. He warned them to be vigilant, for their liber-

2. Workman, *1,* 287.
3. "Their anger is increased by an attempt, by the duke, on their liberties."
Chron. Angl., p. 120.
4. "admonitus est . . . ne . . . alicujus populi vereretur incursum." *Ibid.,*
p. 119.
5. As Workman states, *1, 279.*

ties were in greater danger than they suspected. In fact, he said that they had come to report that Percy had already had the audacity to seize a man and was even then holding him in his residence. Unless Percy's presumptions were checked forthwith, worse would follow and there would be no stopping it.[6]

Fitzwalter's warning had the desired effect. With what arms they could muster, the people rushed to the marshal's house. They broke down the doors, released the prisoner, and celebrated their triumph around the burning stocks with which he had been secured. Fortunately for Percy, a thorough search of the house found him missing. The marshal happened to be dining with Lancaster at the home of John Ypres. They had not yet finished their oysters when several of the duke's attendants came rushing in with the disquieting news that the mob was seeking them. With a pair of bruised shins which he had barked in his haste to leave the table, Gaunt followed Percy to the river, whence they eventually made their way to Kensington Manor, the home of the widow of the Black Prince.[7]

The Londoners meanwhile grew more tumultuous in their license and in their disappointment at not finding Percy. They continued their search, moving out of the city toward Savoy, the duke's home. On the way they met a priest who asked them the reason for all the excitement. When they explained that they hoped to capture the duke and Percy and force them to release Peter de la Mare,[8] the priest—"the fool, not knowing how to give way to such mobs"—remarked that the Peter of whom they were speaking was a traitor to the king and had for many years richly deserved hanging. They beat the priest to death.

By this time Courteney had learned of the tumult. Leaving his dinner, he hurried to Savoy and managed to arrive in time to save the place from the mob's vengeance. He reminded the citizens that this was the holy season of Lent, hardly the time in which to be plotting sedition. Upon the bishop's promise to secure full satisfaction for its grievances, the crowd gave up its more destructive intentions [9] and contented itself

6. *Chron. Angl.*, pp. 121–3. Percy evidently had anticipated the adoption of the bill which would have given him that power. See above, p. 29.

7. *Ibid.*, pp. 123–4.

8. Peter de la Mare had been in prison since the dissolution of the Good Parliament. See above, p. 13.

9. "And had similar words of the bishop not been able to soothe their frenzied passions, without doubt both duke and Henry Percy would that day have lost either life or limbs." *Chron. Angl.*, p. 125. "thei of London wold a killid the forseid duk, had thei not be lettid be her bischop." *The Chronicle of England by John Capgrave*, p. 232.

with reversing the duke's arms in the principal streets of the city. The lampoons which were posted about the city, however, so infuriated the duke that he was driven to appeal to the prelates, whom he had but recently attacked, to excommunicate his persecutors.[1] What might have been Wyclyf's reaction to his champion's request?

1. *Chron. Angl.,* p. 129.

3. THE LAMBETH TRIAL

$\mathcal{T}$hree months after the abortive attempt to silence Wyclyf in February, 1377, at St. Paul's, Pope Gregory XI issued five bulls directing that another attempt be made. The pope knew nothing of this first futile effort of the English hierarchy to discipline Wyclyf. He chided Sudbury and Courteney in the name of the English prelates that "no resistance that we know of" has been made to him and that no better proof of their criminal negligence need be cited than that news of the man's heretical activities had been "learned of in Rome, a long distance away, before opposition is offered to them in England." Three bulls were addressed to the archbishop of Canterbury and the bishop of London, one to the king, and one to the chancellor of Oxford. All bear the same date, May 22, 1378.

Since he addressed the three bulls to Courteney as well as Sudbury, one suspects that Gregory wished to make action more probable than would have been the case had he let the matter rest wholly in the hands of the cautious archbishop. For though Wyclyf was preaching and gaining adherents in London he was actually subject not to Courteney's direct jurisdiction but rather to that of the bishop of Lincoln and the chancellor of Oxford. Wyclyf's case, in fact, was of such a nature as to force the archbishop to assume responsibility, for though as pastor of Lutterworth Wyclyf was subject to the bishop of Lincoln, he was voicing questionable opinions in another diocese.

If there was any shortcoming on Courteney's part in regard to Wyclyf, it was at best indirect, and the pope would hardly have considered it so grave as to link his name with Sudbury's in assessing blame. He must have had a better reason for sending the bulls to Courteney. Since the chronicler is particularly caustic in his comments about the archbishop's indifference,[2] it is probable that those who informed the pope of Wyclyf's activities emphasized Sudbury's apathy in the matter.

It is of some interest to note that though Gregory sent bulls to Edward, Sudbury, Courteney, and to Oxford he failed to communicate with Wyclyf's ordinary, the bishop of Lincoln. In fact, one of the perplexing phases of Wyclyf's prosecution is the negative role played by John Buckingham, the bishop of Lincoln. While the bishop's authority over the university had been sharply limited,[3] this had not

2. See above, pp. 27–8.
3. Rashdall, *The Universities of Europe in the Middle Ages*, 3, 124.

affected his position as Wyclyf's superior in the latter's capacity as pastor of Lutterworth. Buckingham would have been the logical person for Gregory to censure for the fact that nothing had been done to silence Wyclyf as well as the logical person to prod into doing something. There is reason to believe that Buckingham lacked the ability to deal with a man of Wyclyf's stature. His nomination to the bishopric back in 1362 had caused the question to be raised of "whether John is of sufficient learning to rule so populous and noble a diocese." [4] Suggestive of his lack of forcefulness is the appeal he made to Courteney during the latter's visitation of his diocese in 1389 that he correct certain irregularities in his own chapter at Lincoln. The archbishop, incidentally, reproved Buckingham on that occasion for failing to carry out in full the instructions he had sent him concerning this visitation.[5] It is also worth noting that it was in the diocese of Lincoln that Lollardy scored its greatest success, in the prevention of which Buckingham must have been remiss.

Yet Courteney commended the bishop of Lincoln in a letter written probably late in 1382 for his vigor in dealing with Wyclyf.[6] Furthermore, an oblique recognition of the bishop's zeal may be found in Wyclyf's complaint of how the "poor priests" were being harassed in the dioceses of London and Lincoln.[7] On the other hand, there is Walsingham's damning statement that the followers of Swinderby, one of the leading Lollards in northern England, had frightened Buckingham into passivity.[8] The fact remains, nonetheless, that Swinderby was eventually driven to submit, possibly as much by Buckingham's as by Courteney's efforts.[9]

Before considering the contents of the bulls, a word should be said about the source of the pope's information. The chronicler simply declares that some 50 of Wyclyf's conclusions were sent to the Curia to be turned over to the pope.[1] Several references to this matter are found in Wyclyf's writings, but as is usually the case when Wyclyf makes one of his infrequent personal notes, he does so in a tantalizingly obscure manner. In his protest to the condemnation of these propositions, he

4. *Cal. of Papal Letters*, 4, 1.
5. "Reg. Court.," fol. 137.
6. See below, p. 138.
7. *Trial.*, p. 379.
8. *Hist. Angl.*, 2, 55.
9. *Knighton*, 2, 189–97. See "Reg. Court.," fol. 338 (Wilkins, 3, 215) for the archbishop's mandate of 1391 forbidding anyone to listen to Swinderby's sermons. The latter had relapsed.
1. *Chron. Angl.*, App., p. 396.

charges "children" with having brought them to the pope's attention.[2] This appellative, unfortunately, is more suggestive of what Wyclyf thought of the intellectual maturity of his informers than of their identity. Another reference to them as "apostates" [3] is no more informative. In the *De Ecclesia* he says that Thomas Brunton, the bishop of Rochester, and "his brethren" were under suspicion,[4] and in a later sermon he specifically blames a "black dog," the "said *tolstanus* or his whelps" for so misrepresenting the fourth of the propositions to the pope that it was condemned.[5] The allusion may have been to Brunton for the bishop was a Benedictine, and one who was referred to in a carefully worded protest as a bishop and his brethren might well have become a black dog and his whelps in the heat of a sermon. The delight with which Brunton revealed to Wyclyf the news that his theses had been condemned makes him appear to have been more than just another interested observer.[6]

Yet if the bishop of Rochester was responsible for acquainting Gregory with Wyclyf's controversial opinions or only for reporting inaccurately his fourth proposition, it is difficult to believe that he was the pope's sole or even most important informant. In his bull to Sudbury and Courteney, Gregory stated that he had secured his information about Wyclyf's teachings from "many credible persons." In the same bull he reproved Sudbury, Courteney, and the "other bishops" for their negligence in permitting Wyclyf to disseminate his views and for their indifference in the matter. This would appear to rule out the bishops,

2. *Hist. Angl.*, 1, 357. See below, p. 68.
3. *Fas. Ziz.*, p. 483.
4. *Eccles.*, p. 354.
5. *Serm.*, 3, 188–9. Workman's argument that the reference is to Uhtred Boldon (see above, p. 22) is not convincing (1, 296). "Boldon" is hardly closer to "Tolstanus" or "Colstanus," the name the manuscripts give to the reporter, than is "Brunton." Furthermore, Wyclyf does not hint, as Workman believes, that the appeal to the pope was made from Oxford by "disciples of Antichrist" and a certain "doctor mixtim theologus." Wyclyf simply states that it was these who attacked his views on clerical poverty, nothing more. In the next paragraph Wyclyf goes on to say how in consequence of the great amount of controversy over that issue some "apostates" informed the pope of his views on the subject. As for Workman's last argument that it must have been Boldon since Gregory sent a bull to Oxford where Boldon was, this point is no stronger than the other two. Gregory wrote to Oxford because Wyclyf was lecturing there. If he did so upon information received from Boldon, some better evidence must be provided.
6. Brunton had spent several years in Rome and owed his appointment to Rochester to Gregory. It would not be unlikely under such circumstances that he should have corresponded with some regularity with Rome. He told Wyclyf that a notary of the Curia had informed him of the condemnation. *Eccles.*, p. 354.

who in any event were sufficiently important to be referred to in more dignified terms than merely "credible persons."

Gregory's information may have come from monks, as Shirley believes.[7] While Wyclyf had propounded theories which were distasteful to the church in general, he had attacked in particular the wealth of the possessioners, while commending the poverty of their rivals, the friars. The monks might have experienced added satisfaction in providing the pope with information which would lead him to reprimand the bishops, with whom they were not always on the friendliest of terms. Still Gregory's words, "credible persons," would fit any number of persons such as pilgrims, papal collectors, or English priests going— or Italian returning—to Rome. Throughout the greater part of her history, the papacy has been able to keep remarkably well informed of developments in the religious-political field not only in England but in all the important countries of the world.

The five bulls are all dated May 22, 1377. In the first of the three letters which he addressed to Sudbury and Courteney,[8] Gregory berated the prelates for their failure to prevent Wyclyf from airing his revolutionary opinions, a remissness which stood in sad contrast to the vigilance with which their predecessors had so effectively shielded England from heresy. In fact, news of Wyclyf's "detestable madness" had actually reached Rome before the English prelates had even undertaken action against him. Several of Wyclyf's views, despite some juggling of terms, the pope declared to be substantially those of Marsiglio of Padua and John of Jandun, which John XXII had condemned. He directed both Sudbury and Courteney or—possibly fearing that the cautiousness of Sudbury might lead him to deter his more aggressive suffragan from acting—either of them to investigate privately the validity of the charges brought against Wyclyf, a schedule of whose propositions he was sending along with the bull. If they found the charges substantiated, they were to seize Wyclyf, extort a confession from him, forward this confession together with whatever he may have written or said on the subject of the propositions to Rome by trusty messenger and in all secrecy, meantime holding Wyclyf in prison to await further instructions. Against any who might seek to prevent their carrying out of these directions, they were to call in the assistance

7. *Fas. Ziz.*, pp. xxvii–viii.

8. This bull is the first of the three recorded in "Reg. Sud.," fols 45ᵛ–6. See Wilkins, 3, 116–17. An examination of its contents indicates that it was the first to be drawn up. The order in which the bulls are found in Walsingham (*Hist. Angl., 1,* 345–53, and *Chron. Angl.*, pp. 173–81) is not correct.

of the civil arm if necessary. The bull closed with a detailed and sweeping nullification of any and all legal straws at which Wyclyf might grasp in an effort to block the process to be undertaken against him. The bull read as follows:

Gregory, bishop, servant of the servants of the Lord, to our venerable brethren, the archbishop of Canterbury and the bishop of London, greetings and apostolic benediction. The kingdom of England, glorious indeed in the power and abundance of her riches, but more glorious in the piety of her faith and brilliant in the fame of holy writ, has been accustomed to produce men gifted with the true knowledge of the divine scriptures, profound in their maturity, illustrious for their devotion, and champions of the orthodox faith, who instructed not only their own but foreign peoples in the truest of documents, and pointed out the path of the commandments of the Lord. And according to the report of the achievement of ancient time in these matters, the directors of said kingdom who were placed in the watchtower of responsibility, exercising with care the proper safeguards, did not permit anything erroneous to appear which might infect their sheep, but if cockle should appear from the sowing of the enemy of man, they forthwith would pluck it out, and there grew constantly clean grain destined for the Lord's barn. But, alas, now it appears that those whose duty it is to be on guard in that kingdom, idle indeed in their negligence, do not make the rounds of the state, while the enemies enter her intent on plundering the most precious treasure of souls; whose secret incursions and open attacks are learned of in Rome, a long distance away, before opposition is offered to them in England.

From many trustworthy persons we have indeed learned to our extreme sorrow that John Wyclif, rector of the church at Lutterworth, of the diocese of Lincoln, a professor of holy writ—would he were not a master of errors!—is said to have rashly burst forth in such detestable madness, that he does not fear to assert in said kingdom, maintain dogmatically and publicly preach some propositions and conclusions, erroneous and false, sounding poorly from the standpoint of faith, which seek to subvert and weaken the condition of the entire church, and of which several, despite the altering of some terms, appear to express the perverse opinions and unlearned doctrine of Marsiglio of Padua and John of Gandun, of accursed memory, whose book was denounced and condemned by our predecessor, Pope John XXII, of happy memory, malignantly infecting by these some of Christ's faithful and causing them to deviate from the catholic faith, without which there is no salvation; concerning which thus sprung up and not eradicated, or at least no resistance that we know of having been made to them, but ignored or tolerated with conniving eyes, you and the other leaders of England, instead of being pillars of the church and attentive defenders of that faith, in so negligently ignoring through some sort of connivance, you should with good cause blush for shame, should feel abashed, and be tormented by your own consciences.

Wherefore, since we are not willing nor ought we through dissimulation pass over so pernicious an evil, which if not cut off or drawn out by the roots can creep into very many to kill, God forbid, their souls with its deadly contagion, we charge and direct your fraternity by apostolic writs, that, upon receipt of this, you or either of you, secretly investigate the preaching of said propositions and conclusions, a copy of which we are sending you included under our seal, and if you find such to be the case, that you have said John seized and incarcerated on our authority and seek to extort a confession from him concerning the same propositions or conclusions, and this confession together with whatever said John may have asserted or written by way of induction or proof of said propositions and conclusions, as well as what you may have done concerning the above, you will transmit to us by trusty messenger under your seals, quietly and unknown to anyone; and you will keep the same John under careful guard in chains until you will receive further instructions from us concerning him.

Those who would object, you will restrain through ecclesiastical censure, disregarding the appeal, and call in for this purpose the assistance of the civil arm if necessary; notwithstanding the constitutions of our predecessor of happy memory, Pope Boniface VIII, in which it is decreed that no one be summoned to a trial outside his own city or diocese, except in certain excepted cases, nor in these beyond one day's journey from the limits of his diocese; or that no judges deputized by the apostolic see presume to summon any beyond a day's journey from the limits of his own diocese, and of a journey of two days in case of a general council; and exemptions and other privileges, constitutions, and apostolic letters of Preachers, Minors, the friars of St. Augustine and of St. Mary of Mount Carmel, and all others of any character whatsoever of the Mendicants, or of other orders and places, or special persons or chapters and their convents, general or special, of whatever character they may be, as well as the contrary statutes and customs of these orders and places by which the effect of the present might in some way be impeded or deferred, even if concerning them and all of their interpretations a verbatim, complete, and specific mention must be made in our letters, or if to the said John or to any others, in general or singly, a privilege might have been extended by the said see, to the effect that they could not personally be seized or that they could not be interdicted, suspended, or excommunicated on the authority of apostolic letters which did not make full and specific as well as verbatim mention of this indult. Dated at Rome at St. Mary Major, 22 May, the seventh year of our pontificate.[9]

The second bull [1] addressed to the two prelates reviewed the contents of the first bull and added instructions as to what was to be done in the event Wyclyf should become suspicious and go into hiding. If he escaped their hands both or either of them were to issue a citation at Oxford and wherever else they might deem advisable that Wyclyf present himself before the pope within three months. They were to supplement the citation with the warning that even were Wyclyf to ignore the summons Gregory was determined to prosecute the case against him until he had received the sentence he might deserve. The bull read as follows:

Gregory, bishop, servant of the servants of the Lord, to our venerable brethren, the archbishop of Canterbury and the bishop of London, greetings and apostolic benediction. From the report of many trustworthy persons we have recently learned to our great sorrow that John Wyclif, rector of the church of Lutterworth, of the diocese of Lincoln, a professor of holy writ—would he were not a master of errors!—has rashly burst forth in such detestable madness, that he does not fear to assert in the kingdom of England, to maintain dogmatically and publicly preach some propositions and conclusions, erroneous and false, and sounding poorly from the standpoint of faith, which seek to subvert and weaken the condition of the entire church, of which several, despite the alter-

9. "Reg. Sud.," fols. 45ᵛ–6; Wilkins, 3, 116–17; Chron. Angl., pp. 178–80; Hist. Angl., 1, 350–2. There are occasional slight, though not significant, differences in the readings of the various sources. My translation is based upon the first listed.

1. This bull follows the preceding in "Reg. Sud.," as also in Wilkins, but not in the Chronicon or the Hist. Angl. See above, p. 38, n. 8.

ing of some terms, appear to echo the perverse opinions and unlearned doctrine of Marsiglio of Padua and John of Gandun, of
accursed memory, whose book was denounced and condemned
by our predecessor, Pope John XXII, of happy memory, malignantly infecting by these some of Christ's faithful and causing them
to deviate from the Catholic faith, without which there is no
salvation.

In the realization that we have not been, neither are we, permitted through dissimulation to ignore so pernicious an evil, which
has been able to creep into very many to kill their souls with its
deadly contagion, we have charged and directed you in another
letter that you or either of you secretly investigate the preaching
of said propositions and conclusions, a copy of which we included
under our seal, and if you find such to be the case, that you have
said John seized and incarcerated on our authority, and that you
keep him in chains under careful guard until you receive further
instructions from us about the matter, as is fully explained in the
above mentioned letter.

Considering, however, that said John may possibly have some
suspicion of this capture and incarceration and, Heaven forbid,
may be able to make his escape or with the aid of a hiding place
defeat our command, to the most grave damage of the faith, we
commission and direct your fraternity through apostolic writs, lest
so damnable propositions and conclusions remain uninvestigated
and their irresponsible advocate unpunished, to the most serious
injury of said faith, that you or either of you, personally or through
another or others, arrange on our authority to peremptorily admonish and cite the said John, if you are not able to seize and
imprison him, by public edict which is to be displayed in the
university of Oxford of the said diocese, and in all other public
places in which it is considered likely that it will come to the notice
of said John, and which you may consider advisable, that within a
space of three months counting forward from the day of this citation, he present himself wherever we might then happen to be and
give answer in person before us concerning these propositions and
conclusions, as well as to say and do concerning the above whatsoever we shall direct to be done and what good reason may suggest,
proclaiming in the order of this citation that whether the same
John presents himself within this interval or whether he does not,
we shall proceed in the above matters and against him up to and
including his deserved sentence as his guilt may require and as it

appears expedient to us according to God and the preservation of said faith.

We desire, however, and by these presents command that the above mentioned citation, thus carried out, shall affect said John in the same manner, as if it were made known and reported to him in person, any constitution to the contrary notwithstanding. You will, indeed, take care to notify us by letter, secured with your seals and in accordance with these instructions, of the day of the citation, and of its form, and whatever you will have done concerning the above, faithfully and as speedily as possible. Dated at Rome at St. Mary Major, 22 May, the seventh year of our pontificate.[2]

The nature of the instructions which Gregory gave the archbishop of Canterbury and the bishop of London in these two bulls made necessary the sending of a third. Gregory must have suspected that in claiming jurisdiction over Wyclyf, ordering his arrest, and citing him to Rome he would reawaken the vigorous antipapal sentiments of the fifties which had produced the statutes of Provisors and Praemunire. Many Englishmen, whatever their attitude toward Wyclyf, would have resented his projecting himself into a controversy which could be handled by the local ecclesiastical authorities. Furthermore, Wyclyf was employed in the royal service. An effort to secure the neutrality of the crown was only judicious under the circumstances. In fact, in his letter to Edward, Gregory confessed that if the prelates were to have any success in carrying out his instructions concerning Wyclyf they would need the crown's assistance.

Incidentally, the view that Gregory's bulls "tended to set up a papal inquisition in England" appears somewhat extravagant.[3] The pope sent no inquisitors to England to try Wyclyf. That the prelates were directed to await further instructions after seizing Wyclyf suggests that Gregory was waiting to see what the royal reaction would be before deciding on the disposition of the case. Had the crown not protested, Gregory in all probability would have commissioned the prelates to proceed with the trial. Sudbury and Courteney had attempted as much on their own initiative in February. That their superior in Rome, unaware of this attempt, was now ordering them to do this need not immediately conjure up visions of the Inquisition. Finally, Gregory in citing Wyclyf to Rome was simply following standard procedure in dealing with per-

2. "Reg. Sud.," fol. 46; Wilkins, 3, 117; *Chron. Angl.*, pp. 176–8; *Hist. Angl.*, 1, 348–50.

3. Manning, 7, 490; Workman, 1, 295–7.

sons whose orthodoxy was under suspicion and whose prosecution by the local authorities might either have been impossible or unsatisfactory.

Gregory directed Sudbury and Courteney in this third bull to assure the king, his sons, Joan the future queen, the nobility, and the royal counselors not only that the doctrines which Wyclyf was promulgating were contrary to faith but that they threatened in their implications the welfare of the state as well. They were to impress upon the king and the others that it was their bounden duty as Christians to cooperate in the suppression of such dangerous doctrines. To assist the prelates in thus instructing the crown and nobility they were to enlist the services of a number of learned scholars who were well versed in the knowledge of Holy Scripture and who were thoroughly orthodox. The bull read as follows:

> Gregory, bishop, servant of the servants of the Lord, to our venerable brethren, the archbishop of Canterbury and the bishop of London, greetings and apostolic benediction. In our other letters patent which we are sending you with this, we have written you in full concerning the highly dangerous errors of certain detestable propositions and conclusions, conducive to the weakening of the entire ecclesiastical order, which listed in the schedule included with this letter, John Wiclif, rector of the church of Lutterworth, of the diocese of Lincoln, socalled professor of theology, is said to inspire both impiously and rashly.
>
> We, therefore, desire and we direct your fraternity that you seek through your own efforts and through those of others who are masters and learned in holy writ and not tainted with these errors, but are sincere and fervent in their faith, to fully inform our most cherished son in Christ, Edward, illustrious king of England, and our dear sons, the noble children of said king, and our beloved daughter in Christ,[4] the noble lady, princess of Aquitaine and Wales, and the other lords of England and the royal counselors, and to make clear to them how great a disgrace will spring thence for the devout kingdom of England; and that not only are those conclusions contrary to faith, but, when carefully scrutinized, threaten the destruction of the entire state; and that you require them most earnestly that as catholic princes and warriors of the said faith, they give aid and support with as much zeal as possible toward the extirpation of such serious errors, out of reverence for

4. Inserted here in the *Chronicon* and the *Hist. Angl.* is the name "Johannam."

God, the apostolic see, and ourselves, as well as for their own merit before God and their honor in this life. Dated at Rome at St. Mary Major, 22 May, the seventh year of our pontificate.[5]

Gregory expressed much the same views in his letter to Edward. He reminded the king that the brilliant record of England in faith and orthodoxy was being tarnished by the vicious doctrines of Wyclyf, whose teachings, unless effectively suppressed, would endanger the very existence of the church. The pope did not point out to Edward the danger inherent in them to the state. That analysis might not be readily apparent and would be better provided by the prelates and scholars he had so commissioned in the preceding bull. But he did acquaint Edward with the nature of the instructions he had sent to the archbishop and bishop, those of seizing, imprisoning, and questioning Wyclyf, although he made no mention of ordering his citation to Rome in the event he managed to escape the vigilance of the prelates. Gregory may not have expected the trouble with Wyclyf to reach the point where a citation would be necessary. Furthermore, the pope may have felt that since the citation would be but a futile gesture in the last analysis, there would be little gained and possibly much lost in telling the king of it. Edward might well tolerate the arraignment of Wyclyf but would bristle at his unauthorized citation to Rome. In any event, if Edward approved of the seizure of Wyclyf, no citation would be necessary. On the other hand, if the king blocked Wyclyf's seizure he would surely forbid his going to Rome in answer to a summons. As it turned out, the latter is what the crown may actually have done.[6]

How futile the citation would be in the event of the crown's lack of sympathy with the prosecution of Wyclyf, Gregory as much as admitted in his letter to Edward. For he concluded his message to the king with an urgent appeal that, inasmuch as the archbishop and bishop could do nothing without his favor, he show himself as concerned about the faith as had his zealous predecessors and assist the prelates in this matter.[7] The bull read as follows:

5. "Reg. Sud.," fol. 46; Wilkins, 3, 118; *Chron. Angl.*, pp. 175–6; *Hist. Angl.*, 1, 347–8.

6. See below, pp. 139–40.

7. See Richardson, "Heresy and the Lay Power under Richard II," *EHR*, 51, 8, for the helplessness of the church against heretics. He declares king and council had undisputed control over the extent to which the Lollards could be prosecuted. "It would be impossible to retain him [that is, the one accused of heresy] in prison, even in the bishop's prison, if the council gave orders to the contrary."

To our beloved son in Christ, Edward,[8] illustrious king of England, greetings, etc. The kingdom of England which the Most High has placed under your authority, glorious without doubt in the power and abundance of its resources, but more famed for the depth of its faith, and brilliant in the renown of holy writ, has ever produced men gifted with the true knowledge of the divine scriptures, profound in their maturity, fervent in their devotion, and defenders of the catholic faith, who instructed in the saving precepts not only their own but other peoples as well, and pointed out the path of the divine commandments.

Recently, however, with great bitterness of heart we have learned from the report of very many trustworthy persons that John of Wiclyffe, rector of the church of Lutterworth, of the diocese of Lincoln, a professor of holy writ—would he were not a master of errors!—has burst forth in such execrable and abominable folly, that he does not fear to maintain dogmatically in said kingdom and publicly to preach, or rather to vomit forth from the poisonous confines of his breast, some propositions and conclusions, full of errors and containing manifest heresy, which threaten to subvert and weaken the condition of the entire church, of which some, despite the altering of several terms, appear to express the perverse opinions and unlearned doctrine of Marsiglio of Padua and John of Gandun, of accursed memory, whose book was denounced and condemned by our predecessor of happy memory, Pope John XXII, infecting some of Christ's faithful through their being sprinkled about, and seducing them from the true paths of said faith into the pit of perdition.

Wherefore, since we do not wish to ignore with conniving eyes so great an evil, nor are we able to without the biting of our conscience, which evil, if not destroyed or torn up by the roots, can creep into very many to kill, God forbid, their souls by deadly contagion, we have commissioned and directed through our letters to our venerable brethren, the archbishop of Canterbury and bishop of London, that they, or either of them, upon receipt of our said letters, should investigate the preaching of said propositions and conclusions, a copy of which we are sending them included under our seal, and if they should find such to be the case, they shall have the said John seized and incarcerated on our authority, and shall seek to secure a confession concerning these propositions or conclusions, and this confession together with whatever the same John

8. Richard's name is substituted for that of Edward in the *Hist. Angl.*

might have said or written by way of induction or proof of these propositions and conclusions, they are not to delay in sending us by trusty emissary. Since, therefore, the said archbishop and bishop are known to require the favor and assistance of Your Highness in the prosecution of this matter, we request and earnestly pray Your Majesty, who together with your predecessors were wont always to be renowned and preeminent zealots of the catholic faith, about which this matter is concerned, that out of reverence for God, our faith, and the apostolic see and our consideration, you deign to extend in this prosecution the protection of your favor and assistance to the said archbishop and bishop, as well as to the others who are attending to this matter; wherefore, in addition to the commendation of human praise, you will receive the reward of divine justice and our fuller goodwill and that of the said see. Dated at Rome at St. Mary Major, 22 May, the seventh year.[9]

The fifth bull was addressed to the chancellor and the university of Oxford. Gregory declared that he could not help but feel greatly distressed that despite the brilliant history of the university as a champion of orthodoxy she should of late have fallen so far from this high estate as to permit unchecked the preaching of error and heresy within her halls. Under threat of having the institution deprived of her privileges, the chancellor and university were peremptorily directed to inhibit the teaching of any theories that might "sound contrary to good works and faith, whatever the curious shuffling of words or terms under which the authors might seek to defend them." They were instructed to seize Wyclyf and hand him over to Sudbury and Courteney. Any others in the community whose orthodoxy was similarly under suspicion were likewise to be turned over to the archbishop and bishop should they prove obstinate. It is interesting to note that Wyclyf was not to be provided an opportunity of recanting as were these latter. Gregory probably realized that there was little likelihood of his doing so, or he may have felt that since Wyclyf's notoriety was so great a more formal method of silencing him would be proper. The bull read as follows:

Gregory, bishop, the servant of the servants of the Lord, to his beloved sons, the chancellor and the university of Oxford, of the diocese of Lincoln, greetings and apostolic benediction. We are obliged to wonder and lament that you, who in view of the favors and privileges which have been granted to your school at Oxford by the apostolic see, and because of the study of the scriptures in

9. *Chron. Angl.*, pp. 180–1; *Hist. Angl.*, *1*, 352–3.

the sea of which, God willing, you row about with fortunate steering, that you who should have been pugilists and champions of the true faith, without which the welfare of souls is impossible, have through some idleness and sloth permitted cockle to spring up among the clean grain on the campus of your said illustrious school, and, what is worse, even to mature; nor, as we have heard recently, do you show any concern about the eradication of this cockle, not without dishonor to your glorious name, peril to your souls, disgrace to the Roman church, and the ruin of said faith. And what distresses us more bitterly is the fact that the growth of this cockle is learned of in Rome before a means of extirpation has been applied in England where it was born.

Since indeed we have learned, to our extreme sorrow, from the report of many trustworthy persons, that John Wyclyff, rector of the church of Lutterworth, of the diocese of Lincoln, professor of holy writ—would that he were not a master of errors!—is said to have burst forth in such detestable folly, that he does not fear in the English realm—which is indeed glorious in the power and abundance of her resources, but more glorious in the glowing piety of her faith, the fame of holy scripture, accustomed to produce men who grew famous through the true knowledge of sacred scriptures, mature in the dignity of their habits, conspicuous for their zeal and defenders of the catholic faith—to assert dogmatically and publicly preach, or rather to spew forth from out the poisonous confines of his breast, some propositions and conclusions, erroneous and false, and heresies savoring of pravity, polluting some of Christ's faithful through his spreading of these and leading them from the right paths of this faith into the pit of perdition, which propositions threaten to subvert and weaken the condition of the entire church and also the secular authority; some of which, despite the altering of occasional terms, appear to express the perverse opinions and unlearned doctrine of Marsiglio of Padua and John of Gandun, of accursed memory, whose book was rejected and condemned by our predecessor, Pope John XXII, of happy memory.

Wherefore, since we are not willing nor ought we through connivance to ignore so deadly a plague, for which, if it is not halted in the beginning and itself plucked out by the roots, a remedy could not be found till at a late hour, when through contagion it might have infected very many, strictly enjoining we order your community through apostolic writs, in virtue of holy obedience and under threat of deprivation of all favors, indulgences, and privileges granted you and your university by the said see, that for the future you do not permit conclusions and propositions which sound contrary to good works and faith, to be affirmed or proposed, whatever the curious shuffling of words or terms under which the authors might seek to defend them; and that you seize the said John on our authority or have him seized, and that you turn him over to our venerable brethren, the archbishop of Canterbury and the bishop of London, or to either of them, under secure guard; and against those too in your university who object and who are under your jurisdiction, if there are any perchance who are tainted with these errors, which God forbid, if they obstinately persist in these, that you proceed firmly and with care toward their capture and transference, and in what other ways you may deem best; in such manner you will redeem the negligence of which you have been guilty in the foregoing matters, and will earn our favor and benevolence and that of the holy see, as well as the reward and blessing of Divine Justice. Dated at Rome at St. Mary Major, 22 May, the seventh year of our pontificate.[1]

The schedule of Wyclyf's propositions which Pope Gregory enclosed with his bulls read as follows:

1. The whole human race without Christ does not have the power of simply ordaining that Peter and all his successors exercise political dominion over the world.
2. God cannot give civil dominion to a man, for himself and his heirs, in perpetuity.
3. Charters which man has devised concerning perpetual civil inheritance are impossible.
4. Anyone who is in that state of grace which finally justifies, not only has the right to, but in fact possesses, all the gifts of God.
5. Man can bestow both temporal and eternal dominion only ministerially to a natural son or to one of choice in Christ's school.
6. If God be, temporal lords may lawfully and with merit take from a delinquent church the blessings of fortune.
7. Whether the church be in such a condition or not, is not for me to discuss, but for the temporal lords to investigate; and if such be the case, for them to act with confidence and seize her temporalities under pain of damnation.
8. We know that it is not possible for the vicar of Christ simply

1. *Chron. Angl.*, pp. 174–5; *Hist. Angl.*, *1*, 346–7; *Fas. Ziz.*, pp. 242–4.

by means of his bulls, or by means of them and his own will and consent and that of his college, to declare anyone fit or unfit.

9. It is not possible for a man to be excommunicated except that he be first and principally excommunicated by himself.

10. No one is excommunicated, suspended, or tormented with other censures to his injury except in the cause of God.

11. Malediction or excommunication does not bind simply, but only in so far as it is used against an enemy of God's law.

12. Power from Christ or His disciples is not exemplified by excommunicating one's subjects, particularly for refusing temporalities, but the contrary.

13. The disciples of Christ have no power to strictly exact temporalities by censures.

14. It is not possible by the absolute power of God that, if the pope or any other pretend to loose or bind in any way, he does thereby loose or bind.

15. We must believe that only then does he loose or bind when he conforms to the law of Christ.

16. This should be universally believed, that any priest, validly ordained, has sufficient power to administer any of the sacraments, and, consequently, to absolve any contrite person from any sin.

17. It is permitted kings to deprive those ecclesiastics of their temporalities who habitually misuse them.

18. Whether the temporal lords, or the holy popes, or the head of the church, who is Christ, have endowed the church with the goods of fortune or favor, and have excommunicated those taking away her temporalities, it is nonetheless lawful, for the condition [2] implied, to deprive her of temporalities in proportion to her offense.

19. An ecclesiastic, indeed even the Roman pontiff, may lawfully be rebuked by those subject to him and by laymen, and even arraigned.[3]

There is some disagreement as to the number of propositions which Pope Gregory condemned. Were there 18 or 19? Sudbury's register, which should provide the correct number, lists 19, a figure which tallies with the schedules in the *Chronicon Angliae* and *Historia Angli-*

2. Sudbury's register reads *additionem* for *conditionem*.

3. "Reg. Sud.," fols. 46–6ᵛ; Wilkins, 3, 123; *Hist. Angl., 1,* 353–5; *Chron. Angl.,* pp. 181–3. Wilkins errs in giving the pagination in Sudbury's register as simply fol. 46.

cana. Additional corroboration of that number is provided by Netter who records Wyclyf's denunciation of Pope Gregory's act in condemning "nineteen theses." [4] On the other hand, while number "nineteen" is specifically mentioned as being "most damnable," [5] Wyclyf's *Protestatio* and *Libellus* list but 18.[6] The error is in the latter figure. All 19 of the theses can be found expressed in the *De Civili Dominio,* eight, in fact, being seemingly lifted verbatim from the text while the remainder are there in substance.[7] Workman declares only 18 were condemned, basing his statement on the *Protestatio.*[8] This would mean the omission of number seven from the list in Sudbury's register. The omission is significant. Of the 19 theses condemned, number seven was most offensive to the papacy. This one thesis carried a number of barbs: the implication that the church was unsound; the right of the civil authorities to judge for themselves whether the church was sound or otherwise; and finally, the duty of these authorities to deprive the church of her temporalities if they found her unsound and to do this not only without concern for such futile ecclesiastical weapons as excommunication but even under pain of eternal damnation. Wyclyf does not list number seven in the *Declarationes* he prepared in defense of his theses, but he does append to his apology for number six a reminder that he had been misquoted on the procedure to be taken in the event the church were found to be delinquent.[9] Yet, since the damning passages are found in

4. *Fas. Ziz.,* p. 484. Wyclyf refers to "nineteen" theses in the course of this tract.
5. *Ibid.*
6. *Chron. Angl.,* pp. 184–9; *Hist. Angl., 1,* 357–63; *Fas. Ziz.,* pp. 245–57. The author of the chronicle printed as the appendix to the *Chron. Angl.* says the pope condemned 13 theses; see p. 396.
7. In the first book of the *Civ. Dom.,* thesis no. 1 is found expressed almost verbatim on p. 251; no. 2 verbatim on p. 252; no. 3 verbatim on p. 252; no. 4 expresses the sense of chaps. vii and ix; no. 5 almost verbatim on p. 253; no. 6 verbatim on p. 267; no. 7 is found expressed on pp. 269, 271–2; no. 8 is based on chap. xxviii; no. 9 verbatim on p. 274; no. 10 verbatim on p. 276; no. 11 almost identical to statement on p. 275; no. 12 verbatim on pp. 277–8; no. 13 verbatim on p. 279; no. 14 essentially the same as on p. 284; no. 15 essentially the same as on p. 284; no. 16 verbatim on pp. 284–5; no. 17 essentially the same as on pp. 265–6; no. 18 largely sums up the force of the majority of the other theses; no. 19 essentially the same principle as on p. 284 and almost verbatim on p. 94 of Bk. II. For a discussion of the question of whether these theses were taken from the *Civ. Dom.,* see above, p. 25.
8. Workman, *1,* 293. But Workman is not consistent; he uses the list of 19 as a basis for his statement that theses 6, 7, 17, and 18 set "forth Wyclif's claim that . . . the endowments of the Church may be secularized . . ." (*ibid.,* p. 298 and n. 2). No. 7 of the schedule of 18 theses concerned excommunication, not secularization.
9. See below, p. 69, on the view that Wyclyf modified his theses.

the *De Civili Dominio* together with the other 18 theses, one may conclude that Wyclyf later found proposition seven embarrassing and difficult to defend and simply proceeded to disown it for the nonce.[1]

Workman, in stating that the propositions "are concerned with the politics and not the theology of the Church," is largely echoing the views of others.[2] The statement is misleading. It creates the impression that the ecclesiastical authorities were concerned only because the propositions threatened the wealth and political authority of the church. Workman himself declares that the first five were based upon Wyclyf's premise that dominion was founded on grace. While the conclusions which Wyclyf drew therefrom did affect the external life of the church, they also carried with them wide theological implications. Proposition number 2, for example, denied God's omnipotence, that He could do with His power as He pleased provided only that the act itself or purpose were not sinful. Proposition number 4 denied that the sacraments imparted special graces and suggested, further, that complete uniformity existed among the just and the blessed. Propositions 6, 7, 17, 18, and 19 would have given the temporal powers the right to pass judgment upon the moral well-being of the church. While these five propositions, if implemented, would have had calamitous consequences for the external order of the church, they also denied the theological principle traditionally accepted—that the church, not the state, was the final judge in spiritual matters. The remaining propositions struck indirectly at the doctrine of the keys, a premise which underlay the entire sacramental and penitential system, to say nothing of the doctrine of a sanctified priesthood. To dismiss the 19 theses, accordingly, as being simply concerned with the external and, presumably, extraneous order of the church is ridiculous.

That the 19 theses of Pope Gregory's schedule did not represent a direct denial of any fundamental doctrine of the church was Wyclyf's doing, not the Curia's. Wyclyf had not as yet gone beyond an attack on what he considered practices which had become corrupted and abused. But he was soon to lay his hand on the theological bases of these practices. From an attack on an unworthy priesthood, he would move against the institution itself. Then, if there were no priest, transubstantiation and the Mass, as well as the sacramental system, would have to go. From a denial of the pope's power to excommunicate, he would come to question the very necessity of having a pope. It may have been partly in the hope of forestalling such a development, one which had

1. See below, p. 69.
2. Workman, *1*, 298.

often proved a natural step with earlier reformers, that Pope Gregory sought to call a halt to Wyclyf's activities.

It is true that Pope Gregory was gravely concerned about the immediate consequences Wyclyf's theories would have upon the external order of the church. They would have been catastrophic. What a windfall for the legion of impecunious, rapacious barons—the right to seize the wealth of priests, bishops, and abbots whom they in their own fastidiously scrupulous fashion might decide were unworthy! Even Wyclyf later realized that he had gone too fast and hastened carefully to limit the powers of the civil authorities in this regard. They might take this wealth only upon the authorization of the church authorities,[3] a far cry, indeed, from proposition number 7. Was this what the chronicler had in mind when he accused Wyclyf of seeking to lure the nobility into supporting him against the church?[4]

The charge that Pope Gregory selected and arranged the propositions in order to produce the maximum effect upon the civil authorities cannot be established. The *De Civili Dominio* provided the source of all the propositions. If Gregory were interested in suppressing heretical views, which he was,[5] he should have noted any questionable proposition in this treatise, whether it affected the church only in her relations with the state or in purely doctrinal respects. This he does. Gregory's schedule begins with those propositions which denied the traditional views on the holding and granting of property and the exercise of authority. These were matters in which the state was as much concerned as the church. That he noted these propositions before taking up those which specifically attacked the church is what should be expected. It is in essentially that sequence that Wyclyf treats the subjects in the *De Civili Dominio*.[6] It appears somewhat absurd, furthermore, to suggest that Pope Gregory left the most damaging proposition to the last, on the assumption presumably that the civil authorities reading or hearing them read would have lost interest and have begun to nod by the time number 19 was reached.[7] Actually proposition number one does not even concern the state, and surely, had Gregory been anxious to impress the temporal lords with the threat which Wyclyf's theories held for their position, he would have reserved the number one place for the most damaging in that respect. Proposition number one heads the list

3. See below, p. 69.
4. See above, p. 17.
5. See above, p. 21, n. 9.
6. See above, p. 51, n. 7.
7. Workman writes: "The last thesis, skillfully put at the end and not at the beginning, would seem to the pope the worst . . ." (*1*, 298.)

simply because Wyclyf discussed it first, while number 19 closes the list probably for a similar reason—it is the last point of the 19 which Wyclyf considered in the *De Civili Dominio*. It is without question merely a coincidence that number 19 was singled out as "most damnable" together with number seven.[8]

That the prelates and their learned assistants, in accordance with Gregory's instructions, were able to impress the crown with the danger to the state inherent in several of Wyclyf's propositions is improbable. While the implementing of Wyclyf's theory that dominion is founded upon grace, not upon authority or inheritance, would have revolutionized politics and society, the crown must have been inclined to ignore the logic in such reasoning in the conviction that Wyclyf's propositions were essentially utopian except insofar as they affected the church. It is significant that, despite the far-reaching implications of his views on grace for both church and state, Wyclyf concerned himself with their practical application only as far as they touched the church. For that reason there were surely some among the royal counselors who were anxious to protect Wyclyf for his nuisance value in bargaining with the pope.

On the other hand, if the prelates failed to convince the crown that Wyclyf's doctrines threatened the existence of the state, there is reason to believe that the government was aroused over the character of his attack on the church, whether as a result of the prelates' arguments or otherwise. For it was about this time that the king in council ordered Wyclyf to be silent on the question of withholding money from Rome even though the crown may have favored this.[9] If the crown felt sufficiently concerned to forbid Wyclyf to speak further on that subject, it is unlikely that it would have been indifferent to his pressing the more fundamental attacks on the church embodied in such propositions as numbers 6 and 19.

It is interesting to speculate on what would have been Edward's reaction to Gregory's bull had it reached him before his death and had he been able to attend to it with a vigor reminiscent of his earlier career. Would he have been more hostile in dealing with Wyclyf than the men, notably Gaunt, who took his place? It is likely that he would have. He was under no obligation to Wyclyf as was the duke who had summoned him to Westminster. Edward also was experienced where Gaunt was not, and the king had learned, like most medieval monarchs, that more could be realized through cooperation with than opposition

8. *Fas. Ziz.*, p. 484.
9. Wyclyf was silenced on other points as well. See below, pp. 59–61.

to the papacy. The duke was to learn the same lesson. To Edward, Wyclyf would have been but another clerk, a possible source of popular unrest, an irritant jeopardizing amicable relations with Rome. One may conclude that Wyclyf could not have chosen a better opportunity to voice his theories than during the period of Edward's dotage and Gaunt's ascendency.

The five bulls were issued May 22, 1377. It was December 18 before Sudbury and Courteney proceeded to carry out the pope's instructions. This delay may be attributed to a number of factors. There is the possibility that the bulls did not leave Rome immediately upon their issuance on May 22 or that their progress to Canterbury was slow even for the Middle Ages. If Gregory had not learned by May 22 of the attempt the prelates had made more than three months earlier to silence Wyclyf,[1] it is quite possible that the troubled times were seriously impeding travel between England and Rome. The chronicler states Gregory's bull reached Oxford just a few days before Christmas.[2]

That the bulls may have required a longer time than usual to reach England is further suggested by the fact that Wyclyf first learned of the condemnation of his theses sometime during the fall session of Parliament. Parliament convened October 13 and rose November 28.[3] While Parliament was sitting, the bishop of Rochester informed Wyclyf "under excitement" that his propositions had been condemned.[4] That the bishop did this under excitement indicates that he had himself just learned of the pope's action. Being a bishop and somewhat close to the Curia,[5] he would very likely have been informed of the judgment almost as soon as Sudbury.

If the delay was not due to physical causes, the political situation in England was such as to counsel prudence on the part of the prelates in their desire to silence Wyclyf. The death of Edward in June precipitated the political crisis which had been brewing since the fatal character of the Black Prince's malady had first been realized. Was John of Gaunt to rule? If the duke's supposed ambitions were thwarted, who would dominate the government—the young Richard, his mother Joan of Kent, or a regency? In a trial in which the defendant was not only

1. See above, p. 35.
2. *Hist. Angl.*, 1, 345; *Chron. Angl.*, p. 173.
3. *Rot. Parl.*, 3, 29.
4. *Eccles.*, p. 354.
5. See above, p. 37, n. 6. Loserth (*loc. cit., 156,* 4 n. 1) maintains that the bishop of Rochester could not have known the contents of the bulls before they reached England. He believes the prelates had them in their hands sometime before their publication on December 18.

an avowed advocate of state supremacy and of the secularization of church property but also one who enjoyed powerful aristocratic support, the English bishops may have decided to delay formal action until the political situation had been clarified.

The atmosphere in Parliament was not encouraging to the bishops. True, Wyclyf's protector, the duke of Lancaster, fared none too well. His old enemy of the Good Parliament, Peter de la Mare, was back in the speaker's chair. Despite Gaunt's bitter denunciation of the vicious slander that he was aiming at the throne, the "continual council," which had been appointed by the great council to direct the government, was remodeled to further reduce his influence.[6] Yet with all the constitutional encroachments that Commons was able to effect at the expense of the crown's prerogatives and the serious attention it devoted to the war with France, Parliament had time during its short session for an attack on the church. A bitter assault was leveled at those French ecclesiastics who were holding English benefices. They were charged with using those endowments to help defeat English arms in France. To terminate that monstrous situation, a statute was enacted which required all foreigners, monks as well as seculars, to leave the kingdom by the following February. For the balance of the war the increments of their holdings were to be applied to war expenses.[7]

The bishops may have found added reason for caution in the honor claimed for Wyclyf by several scholars of having addressed the assembled Lords and Commons on the nature of his anticlerical program and in defense of the condemned propositions. Thus Trevelyan would have him delivering such a long and erudite apology as to leave the honest knights of the shire either nonplused or asleep.[8] The basis for this belief is a document preserved by Netter which bears the arresting caption, "Libellus Magistri Johannis Wycclyff, Quem Porrexit Parliamento Regis Ricardi Contra Statum Ecclesiae."[9] Workman suspects the rubric to be in error chiefly for want of a parliament to which Wyclyf might have been able to present the document. Thus he holds that Wyclyf would not have laid it before the Parliament of the fall of 1377, that is, before the arrival of Pope Gregory's bulls, for in so doing he would only have aroused strife "by assuming a condemnation not yet made public." On the other hand, the next Parliament, the Gloucester Parliament of fall, 1378, would have been too late since "events

6. Lewis, "The 'Continual Council' in the early years of Richard II, 1377–80," *EHR, 41,* 250.

7. *Rot. Parl.,* 2, 322.

8. Trevelyan, p. 81.

9. *Fas. Ziz.,* pp. 245–57.

came too thick and fast for a matter dealt with six months before to continue to be of vital interest." The tract, in addition, contains no reference to the death of Gregory or the election of Urban.[1]

While Workman's reasoning is persuasive, it does not rule out the possibility that upon learning from the bishop of Rochester during the fall session of Parliament in 1377 that his theses had been condemned [2] Wyclyf immediately drew up this *Libellus* and hastily circulated it among the members of Parliament while that body was still in session. Though this might have awakened some controversy, Wyclyf was not one to shun a discussion. Furthermore, he could not afford to have done otherwise than risk stirring up strife. Earlier that year at St. Paul's he had required the assistance of the duke of Lancaster to thwart the efforts of the English prelates to silence him. Now with the pope also arrayed against him, he might well have concluded that there was no time like the present to seek political support for his inevitable clash with the church.

The fact remains, however, that there is absolutely no hint in the *Libellus* itself that it was presented to Parliament. We might expect a more personal approach and some internal evidence to corroborate the rubric. Wyclyf could not count humility among his virtues, and as he often lapses into the first person in his discourses [3] it seems unlikely that so distinct an honor as that of addressing Parliament would have been passed over in silence. There is, finally, no record of such an address in the *Rolls*. It is, as a consequence, dangerous if not impossible to accept the validity of the rubric.

More indicative of the delicacy of the political situation and the caution the prelates would have to employ in their efforts to carry out Gregory's instructions concerning Wyclyf was the query which Netter says was put to Wyclyf by Richard and the great council in the first year of the new king's reign—"whether in view of the critical need for its defense, the kingdom of England might lawfully hold back the treasure of the kingdom lest it be turned over to foreigners, even though the pope were demanding this under penalty of censure and by virtue of obedience." [4] The inquiry had been precipitated by the activities

1. Workman, *1*, 311. Though Workman attacks the accuracy of the rubric—that the *Libellus* was delivered to Parliament—he still uses it as evidence of Wyclyf's influence "with the nation."

2. See above, p. 37.

3. Wyclyf mentioned, for example, that he had personally heard the seven lords discuss the merits of the papal claims to tribute. *Op. Min.*, p. 425. See above, p. 23.

4. *Fas. Ziz.*, p. 258. See also *Pol. Works, 1*, xlii, lvi. For the genuineness of the document, see *ibid.*, pp. lxxv–vi.

of the papal collector, Arnold Garnier, who was gathering such monies as Peter's Pence and first fruits for the papal coffers. Parliament had raised the same issue in the fall of 1377, both inquiry and complaint springing from the great expense of the war which promised to grow still heavier in view of recent exertions of the French.

If Wyclyf's opinion was sought on the lawfulness of withholding money from Rome, no special significance need be attached to that. He was in the crown's service and the logical person to question on the issue. The same inquiry may have been put to other theologians similarly employed. Yet Wyclyf was known to entertain antipapal views, and he had but recently published a tract attacking Garnier. The papal collector had aroused the concern of the crown five years before by his zeal and at that time had been required to take a solemn oath that he would do nothing contrary to the interests of the realm, specifically, that he would "send out of the realm no treasure" to "pope or any cardinal." [5] Now Wyclyf was pointing to the obvious inconsistency in eliciting such an oath from him while at the same time permitting him to continue his collections in accordance with the Bruges agreement.[6]

Like so many of the milestones in Wyclyf's life, this appeal to him by the government has occasioned considerable controversy. Among others, Lewis and Steel, an old and a contemporary scholar, declare that it was Parliament that made the query.[7] They offer no evidence to support their view. There is none. The *Rolls* make no mention of the inquiry, while the rubric which introduces the *Responsio* specifically mentions the king and his great council as requesting Wyclyf's opinion. Since the *Libellus* had specified Parliament, the author of the two documents must have appreciated the difference between the great council and Parliament. Neither could the continual council have sounded out Wyclyf on the problem. While the author of the rubric might be excused for confusing the great council with the continual council, the fact that Bishop Courteney and at least one other prelate were always members of this small group would effectively rule out that contingency.

Since the great council was not entirely replaced by the continual council but continued to meet,[8] that body might have put such a query

5. Rymer, *6*, 709; *Cal. of Close Rolls, 1369–74, 13,* 424.
6. *Pol. Works, 1,* xxx, xlii.
7. Lewis, *The History of the Life and Sufferings of the Reverend and Learned John Wiclif,* p. 55; Steel, p. 45. Steel is confused. He declares Parliament asked Wyclyf's opinion, which request provoked the 19 conclusions. See *ibid.,* n. 1. Loserth (*loc. cit., 156,* 11) also believes Wyclyf addressed Parliament in this connection.
8. Lewis, *loc. cit.,* pp. 246–7.

to Wyclyf. It probably did not. There is not the slightest internal evidence to support the view that the *Responsio* was drawn up in answer to a request by the great council.[9] In fact Wyclyf begins the *Responsio* with the wholly impersonal introduction: "There is some question whether the kingdom of England may lawfully prevent the treasure of the realm from going to foreigners in the event it is required for its own defense . . ." Again, as in the case of the supposed address to Parliament, we should expect a man of Wyclyf's temperament to have expressed himself less modestly had he been formally interrogated on the issue.[1] But the most damaging evidence to cast doubt on the contention that such an inquiry was put to Wyclyf is contained in the abrupt note which follows immediately upon the conclusion of Wyclyf's arguments, namely, "And here silence was imposed upon him concerning the above by the lord king and the royal council."[2] If the great council did ask Wyclyf's opinion, it completely ignored it, first in August, 1377, when Garnier was authorized to take 4,000 pounds out of the country, and again in October, 1378, when he was permitted to proceed with his collections.[3] There is something so unreal about the entire episode—first that the great council asked his opinion only to ignore it so completely, and then that it ordered him to stop discussing such matters—that one must deny the accuracy of the rubric.

In view of the silence enjoined upon Wyclyf for the sentiments he expressed in the *Responsio,* its contents require examination. Wyclyf declared that the crown might lawfully hold up the export to Rome of money which was needed for the defense of the country. He based this view on three arguments: First, God has endowed every natural body with the right and power to protect itself; since England fell into that category, God expected her to exercise this right and authority to keep treasure within the country whenever necessity required its detention. Second, the law of the gospel permitted the pope to accept money only in the form of alms, and almsgiving ceased to be a duty in time of need; in fact, the pope could use the wealth entrusted to him only in the interest of those in need, the poor. Third, the law of

9. *Fas. Ziz.,* pp. 258–71.
1. See above, p. 57.
2. *Fas. Ziz.,* p. 271. Trevelyan (p. 81) paints a realistic scene of a bewildered Commons finally calling halt to the flow of Wyclyf's overwhelming erudition. Actually the *Responsio* appears to be a well-rounded treatise, not one which was abruptly terminated. Workman (*1,* 302) says the "Council asked the advice of Wyclif 'in writing' . . ." His statement is based on the astounding translation of "Infra Scriptum," which here has the force of "noted below," to mean "in writing."
3. See Rymer, *7,* 172, and *Cal. of Pat. Rolls, 1377–81,* p. 276.

conscience required England's rulers to protect the well-being of the realm and respect the pious wishes of their ancestors, which they could not do if they failed to preserve the alms their forbears had given in the condition under which they were bequeathed; their bequests had been made to the English, not the universal, church, and to transfer the income of these to the pope would reduce the spiritual relief the donors would experience in purgatory. Furthermore, such practice would impoverish and depopulate the kingdom, contribute to the growing insolence of the Roman Curia, strengthen the enemies of the realm, and invite the ridicule of the world at the asinine stupidity of Englishmen who were brave enough to attack a foe in worldly combat but too timid to withhold alms from an unworthy spiritual adversary.

And, Wyclyf continued, the fear of papal retaliation should concern no one. Were the pope to lay England under an interdict, God would not recognize such censure since it was not justified. God would not desert those who feared Him more than men. In any event, a Christian is required to give but voluntary alms to the pope, and what alms he gives must not be permitted to enable the pope to live in luxury and to wage aggressive warfare. The danger that the retention of this money in England might lead to arrogance, lewdness, and avarice could be averted by distributing the wealth of the church, restoring endowments to their early condition, and by using the remainder to establish the true peace of the church. England's misfortunes did not have their origin in the failure to give alms to the church; it was just the reverse, for when alms are donated to unworthy ecclesiastics, to a pope who would use them on his relatives, then such almsgivers become accomplices in these crimes. Yet there is some danger in adopting this controversial stand not to permit money to go to Rome. Because of English lack of fortitude and perseverance, divided counsels may lead to civil war. For that reason, before such a revolutionary step is taken, it will be necessary to school the people in resolution and courage.

The contents of the *Responsio* are highly significant. A careful study will reveal how Wyclyf there reaffirmed most of the views which Pope Gregory had condemned in his list of 19 propositions. Several propositions are referred to only indirectly, such as those concerning dominion, but numbers 6 to 18, excepting only number 16, are found expressed in substance. Most vigorously did Wyclyf renew in this *Responsio* his attack on the political pretensions of the church, on the efficacy of papal excommunication, and on ecclesiastical wealth. Therefore, the injunction placed upon him by the government not to discuss these matters further—*fuit impositum sibi silentium super praemissis*—should, in its scope, have all but muzzled Wyclyf, since up to this time these three subjects had drawn the bulk of his attention. To reduce this sweeping prohibition to the simple question of withholding money from Rome, as Wyclyf's champions would do, is to ignore the arguments which Wyclyf proposes in the *Responsio* to justify his position. These arguments are part and parcel of the *praemissis* referred to in the court's order, which from now on were to be closed subjects to Wyclyf.

One can only marvel at the success Wyclyf's biographers have achieved in glossing over this silencing of Wyclyf by the government as a matter of little interest and even less consequence. Some, as noted above, reduce the silencing simply to the question of withholding revenue from Rome, a position which is utterly unrealistic and without foundation. Others, like Workman who devotes two volumes to the man, pass off the event in a sentence.[4] Yet this silencing marks the crucial moment in Wyclyf's career. If there was some question up to this point as to where the government stood with regard to him, that issue was now made crystal clear. The government bluntly ordered Wyclyf to cease attacking the church.

This silencing raises yet another interesting and important consideration. The government had just received an appeal from Pope Gregory that it take cognizance of Wyclyf and his propositions. There is no reason to suppose that the government had knowledge of these propositions before the receipt of Gregory's bull. Consequently, when it ordered Wyclyf to be silent on the matters noted above, since these represented in substance what Gregory had taken exception to, the government was actually cooperating with the pope's request. One might even argue that since the *Responsio* follows immediately upon the *Libellus* in the original Bodleian manuscript as recorded by Netter it is possible that the prohibition to speak *super praemissis* was intended to refer not only to the *Responsio* just concluded but to the *Libellus* as well. The Libellus constituted Wyclyf's apologia for the condemned propositions.[5]

If Sudbury and Courteney wondered what action to take upon receipt of the papal bulls, they were not alone in their hesitation. For when Gregory's bull finally reached Oxford a few days before Christmas[6] that institution's reaction was even more reprehensible, in the words of the chronicler, than the hesitation of the prelates.

4. Workman, *1*, 304.
5. See above, pp. 56–7.
6. *Chron. Angl.*, p. 173; *Hist. Angl.*, *1*, 345.

How seriously the present procurators or rectors of said university had degenerated from the prudence and wisdom of their predecessors can be readily seen from this, that, having learned the reason for the appearance of the said papal messenger, they were for a long time undecided whether they should receive the papal bull with honor, or with dishonor wholly ignore it. Oxford University! How great has been your fall from the summit of wisdom and knowledge, that you who were once accustomed to make known to the entire world inexplicable and doubtful problems, now, blinded by the cloud of ignorance, do not fear to question matters which no lay Christian may doubt. Of the memory of such folly one is ashamed, and I therefore refrain from lingering over this subject, lest I appear to tear out with my teeth the maternal breasts which were wont to give the milk, the drink of knowledge.[7]

Three factors occasioned Oxford's confusion. In the first place, the university felt proud of her eminence in the field of theology and resented the intrusion of any person, even the pope, who would question her ability to maintain orthodoxy within her own precincts. In the second place, a strong party favored the views of Wyclyf, how strong being suggested by the decision of the masters-regent in theology to support him.[8] Finally, if the university were to carry out Gregory's instructions and imprison Wyclyf, they might run afoul of the civil authorities, for English law forbade the detention of any English subject at the behest of the pope. The *Eulogium* describes how the latter quandary was resolved:

The friends of the said Master John Wiccliff therefore took counsel with John himself in the congregation of regents and non-regents, that they should not arrest a subject of the king of England at the order of the pope lest they appear to give the pope lordship and regal power in England. Yet because it appeared necessary in the opinion of the university to do something in view of the pope's command, a certain monk, the vice-chancellor, asked and ordered said Wikcliff that he keep himself in the Black Hall and that he should not leave that place since he wished no one else to im-

---

7. *Chron. Angl.*, pp. 173–4; *Hist. Angl.*, *1*, 345. The *Chronicon* account has the word *parvulis* inserted after "milk." Concerning the dilatoriness of Sudbury and Courteney, Walsingham laments: "Qui quam indevote, quam segniter commissa sibi mandata compleverint, melius est silere quam loqui." *Chron. Angl.*, p. 183; *Hist. Angl.*, *1*, 356.

8. See below, p. 66.

prison him. And because he had pledged his word to the university, it was fitting that he should suffer this for the sake of preserving the privileges of the university.[9]

There has been some misunderstanding concerning this imprisonment of Wyclyf by the vice-chancellor. Workman among others interprets his detention as an ingenious scheme to which Wyclyf was a completely willing partner and by which the university hoped to meet at least the letter of Gregory's instructions. This interpretation rests largely upon a faulty translation of the text of the last sentence in the above quotation. Workman writes: "Wyclyf agreed to do so because he had sworn to the university to preserve its privileges."[1] The chronicler does not say this; he says rather that the vice-chancellor deemed it only proper for Wyclyf to comply with his instructions since the latter had sworn to preserve the privileges of the university.[2] And the vice-chancellor "ordered" Wyclyf to remain in the Black Hall. That Wyclyf's detention actually approximated an imprisonment is borne out by the words of the same chronicler when he declares that the vice-chancellor was himself subsequently imprisoned for having thus detained Wyclyf. The chronicler also states that Wyclyf was later released upon the request of his friends.[3]

Workman, on the other hand, attributes the imprisonment of the vice-chancellor to the university's failure to punish a group of students who had insulted a member of the royal household. The latter had chanced to put up for the night at Oxford, whereupon a number of the bolder blades[4] proceeded to serenade him with improvised verses which did more honor to their poetical versatility than to their respect for the king. For this and for having let fly a shower of arrows against the window of the royal knight's lodging they had remained unpunished. This negligence on the part of the authorities led to a summons to Westminster. To the question of the royal chancellor, Houghton, of why he had done nothing about the outrage, the chancellor of the university, Adam de Tonworth, confessed that he had not dared. Houghton did not accept the cogency of Tonworth's explanation and

9. *Eulog.*, 3, 348.
1. Workman, *1*, 306.
2. The text in the *Eulog.* reads: "Et quia juratus erat Universitati hoc pro conservatione privilegiorum Universitatis decuit ipsum pati."
3. *Eulog.*, 3, 349.
4. To describe these culprits as "bolder blades" might appear somewhat incongruous since, according to the royal writ summoning the chancellor to Oxford, the ringleaders in the affair were three monks. Wilkins, 3, 137.

deposed him, only to be reminded by that self-reliant official [5] that he held his office not only from the crown but from the pope as well. Houghton proved no less resourceful and announced: "we deprive you of the king's part, and now see what you can do with that of the pope . . . The king can remove you and the university from Oxford." Only by resigning his office forthwith did Tonworth save the privileges of the university.[6]

The chronicler interpolates the description of this affair in his account of Wyclyf's imprisonment, but in no other than this physical sense does there appear to have been any relationship between the two episodes. One may not conclude, therefore, as Workman supposes, that the vice-chancellor was imprisoned for his part in neglecting to discipline the students. The *Eulogium,* our only source, states quite clearly that the vice-chancellor was punished for having imprisoned Wyclyf and that Wyclyf was later released upon the request of friends.

The significance of Wyclyf's imprisonment lies in this: first, that the university felt constrained to respect the pope's command despite the danger of arousing the crown's ire; second, that the crown would tolerate not even this mild "imprisonment" at the pope's orders. This last fact underscores the essential weakness of the church in the Middle Ages to cope with heresy and, more to the point of this study, indicates where one must look for a solution of many of the problems attending Wyclyf's prosecution.

On December 18 Archbishop Sudbury proceeded to carry out the pope's instructions. He sent a mandate to the chancellor of Oxford in his and Courteney's names, in which he directed that a thorough though secret examination be made of Wyclyf's propositions by the orthodox doctors of holy scripture in the university. The chancellor was to cite Wyclyf to appear within 30 days before the archbishop and bishop or their representatives in St. Paul's to make answer concerning the propositions. It is worth noting that Sudbury did not direct the chancellor to imprison Wyclyf or to turn him over to him. Such had been Gregory's instructions to the archbishop. The prelates must have realized that without royal authorization such procedure would have been dangerous if not impossible. The mandate read as follows:

> Simon, by divine permission, etc., and William, by the same permission bishop of London, delegated by the apostolic see in that

5. Though Tonworth declared he had been afraid to punish the miscreants, he did not lack the courage to stand up against the royal chancellor or to carry out Gregory's instructions in a very qualified manner. See above, pp. 61–3.

6. *Eulog.,* 3, 348–9.

clause, "that you two, or one of you, specially appointed for the enclosed," to our beloved son and venerable chancellor of the university of Oxford, in the diocese of Lincoln, or his representative, greetings in the Lord and strict obedience to our, more truly indeed to the apostolic, instructions. You will have learned that we have received, with that respect which is fitting, letters from the most holy father in Christ and our Lord, Gregory XI, by divine providence pope, concerning this, that John Wycliff, professor of holy scripture and rector of Lutterworth, of the aforesaid diocese of Lincoln, bursting forth recklessly in detestable madness, did not fear to assert, proclaim, and publicly preach several propositions and conclusions, erroneous and false, and sounding poorly from the standpoint of faith, maliciously infecting with them some of Christ's faithful, and causing them to deviate from the catholic faith without which there is no salvation, as is fully described in said apostolic letters. Wishing, therefore, to carry out the apostolic instructions to the utmost of our ability, as we are obliged, we charge and direct you, firmly enjoining in virtue of the obedience with which you are bound to said see, that upon receipt of this, having called together for this purpose professors who are expert in holy scripture and who think correctly and holily in the catholic faith, informing yourselves secretly concerning the maintaining of said propositions and conclusions, of which a copy is inserted below, omitting completely sophistical words or curious construction of terms, that you notify us, as is proper, of everything which you have learned and think concerning the above, in your private letter and sealed with your seal, clearly, distinctly, and openly in all matters and in every regard. You will, furthermore, cite or cause peremptorily to be cited said John, that on the thirtieth juridical day after the citation has been made to him, he appear personally before us or others delegated by us or our commissioners in this matter, in the church of St. Paul at London, to give answer, hear, and to do further concerning these conclusions and propositions, whatever should be done by apostolic authority in that respect and what right reason may dictate; warning the same that whether he will have presented himself on the assigned date or not, the process will be continued against him, as the apostolic letters themselves direct and require. We charge you, in addition, upon the aforesaid authority, that you execute the apostolic letters, now transmitted to you by us, in every particular and in all respects, diligently and faithfully, in accordance with the force, form, and affect of the same, under the penalties fully indicated in the letters aforesaid; certifying us or our said commissioners or delegates as quickly as it can be done, what you will have done concerning the above, by your letters patent, fully containing the content of this and of your conduct.[7]

The chancellor showed himself scarcely more respectful toward Sudbury's instructions than toward those of the pope. While he did have Wyclyf's propositions examined, this was done neither in secret nor apparently by only the "orthodox" doctors. The masters-regent in theology were directed to scrutinize the questionable theories, and when each had handed in his opinion, the chancellor, in the name of and with the consent of all, announced the verdict—that though the theses sounded poorly to the ears they were orthodox. To which Wyclyf replied that Catholic doctrine should not be condemned simply because it sounded unorthodox.[8] Incidentally, from the language of the chronicler, one might conclude that the judgment was well nigh, if not entirely, unanimous.

Sometime before March 27, 1378, Wyclyf appeared before the bishops at Lambeth. Why he presented himself at Lambeth rather than St. Paul's, as Sudbury's mandate had directed and whether he did so within the specified 30-day period are questions which cannot be answered. A possible explanation for the change of venue may have been the prelates' preference of less conspicuous Lambeth to bustling St. Paul's in their anxiety to avoid publicity. According to the chronicler the populace did break into the meeting,[9] but this may be reading ahead of the event, for if St. Paul's was satisfactory on December 18 when Sudbury's mandate was issued, conditions could hardly have changed so radically within so short an interval as to make meeting there no longer prudent. As for the day on which Wyclyf put in his appearance, in the absence of positive documentary evidence Walsingham's statement that the trial took place before Gregory's death (March 27) is at least of negative value in fixing the *terminus ad quem*.[1] Wyclyf may, accordingly, have presented himself within the grace period of 30 days.

7. "Reg. Sud.," fol. 46ᵛ; Wilkins, 3, 123–4. Wilkins copied the date incorrectly. It is dated "15 calends of January," not 5. Wilkins also erred in noting the folio in the register as 46.

8. *Eulog., 3,* 348. Wyclyf probably had this occasion in mind when he commented in his *Declarationes:* "Absit ab Ecclesia Christi quod damnetur veritas, quia male sonat peccatoribus vel ignoris; quia tunc tota fides Scripturae foret damnabilis." *Hist. Angl., 1,* 363; *Chron. Angl.,* p. 189.

9. See below, p. 68.

1. *Hist. Angl., 1,* 356; *Chron. Angl.,* p. 183.

But these questions may not be disposed of so simply. There is a passage in the *De Veritate Sacrae Scripturae* which has led to the usual confusion which plagues almost every turn in Wyclyf's career. Wyclyf writes that though he had been cited to appear before the archbishop he feared to do so. Some time before, Sudbury had used the text: "A little while and you shall not see me, and again a little while and you shall see me." The archbishop must have added the phrase, "for I go to the Father," since Wyclyf chose to read into the text the fantastic interpretation that Sudbury was about to go to Rome to arrange his death with the pope. Wyclyf goes on to say that many people had been instructed to believe, by whom only God knew, that it would be an act of charity to kill him. This almost sounds like a third summons, for Wyclyf speaks of being cited to appear not at St. Paul's but wherever the archbishop might happen to be in his province. The passage also implies that Wyclyf did not honor this summons out of fear.[2]

Workman, on the other hand, believes that Wyclyf first refused to present himself, then, emboldened by the news that the vice-chancellor of Oxford had been imprisoned, subsequently decided to appear.[3] In proposing this sequence of events, Workman forgets that he dates Wyclyf's appearance at Lambeth "a few weeks previous to Lady Day 1378" (March 25), while the vice-chancellor was still a free man on March 22 when he accompanied the chancellor to Westminster.[4] Furthermore, it is not likely that Sudbury would have had occasion to use the text, "A little while . . ." before Easter, for Christ used those words when warning His disciples of His approaching Ascension. That Wyclyf upon learning of the vice-chancellor's imprisonment, hardly before March 24, immediately notified the prelates that he would be willing to appear before them and that a meeting was hurriedly arranged prior to March 27, the day of Gregory's death, is equally incredible. For another thing the language of the chronicler, "citra mortem Gregorii Pape," [5] implies a longer interval than a day or two.

Yet it is difficult to believe that the archbishop, a timorous soul at best, should have dared to summon Wyclyf yet a third time after the manner in which the crown intervened in the Lambeth trial.[6] The easiest way out of the difficulty is to suggest that Wyclyf erred when

2. *Ver. Script.*, *1*, 374.
3. Workman, *1*, 308.
4. See above, p. 63.
5. *Hist. Angl.*, *1*, 356; *Chron. Angl.*, p. 183.
6. See below, p. 68.

he wrote that he had been cited to appear before the archbishop "wherever the latter might happen to be" and that his words, "he feared to present himself," meant not that he did not go but that he actually did present himself, though in fear of death when he did so.[7] It should be noted in this connection that Wyclyf's fear of death was probably more rhetorical than it was real. Wyclyf was not above adding a little color now and then to heighten the appeal of his sermons.[8]

Of the Lambeth trial, at any rate, there is no question. Nothing quite so dramatic transpired as at the first meeting at St. Paul's,[9] though there was some excitement. On the day of the trial Sir Lewis Clifford, an emissary from the queen mother, appeared before the prelates and "pompously" instructed them not to presume to pass formal sentence upon Wyclyf. The chronicler pictures the prelates, who had been boasting of how they would try Wyclyf whatever the nature of the opposition, as now crestfallen and overawed. Yet they proceeded with the trial, only to have the citizens of London, "not them so much as the dregs of the city impudently force their way into the [archbishop's] chapel in order to speak in behalf of the same [Wyclyf] and to impede that affair, heartened no doubt by the earlier negligence of these prelates."[1]

Though hampered alike by the queen mother's injunction and by the intrusion of the crowd, the prelates questioned Wyclyf on the 19 propositions. In view of all the moral support he was receiving, Wyclyf must have defended his views with confidence, though he qualified the more revolutionary aspects of his theses so as to make them palatable to his inquisitors. Wyclyf implies as much in the introduction to his *Declarationes,* which he apparently presented on this occasion in defense of his propositions. He declares that lest Christians be scandalized by the stories which "children" had carried to Rome he was putting down his views in writing; that he was prepared to make clear the sense in which he had proposed his theses, namely, as they were found in the scripture and in the works of the doctors of the church; that if the theses were shown to be contrary to faith he was most ready to renounce them, "submitting myself humbly to the correction of Holy Mother Church."[2]

7. "licet fuerim citatus ad comparendum nunc coram domino archiepiscopo, in quocunque loco fuerit sue provincie, timui illo ire." *Ver. Script., 1,* 374. Buddensieg assigns the tract to the interval between the second half of 1377 and the late fall of 1378. *Ibid.,* pp. xci–ii.

8. See Workman, *2,* 205.

9. See above, pp. 28–30.

1. *Hist. Angl., 1,* 356; *Chron. Angl.,* p. 183.

2. *Hist. Angl., 1,* 356; *Chron. Angl.,* p. 184.

That Wyclyf modified his stand on several of the theses under questioning by the prelates is clear from a comparison of these *Declarationes* and the *De Civili Dominio* from which they were taken. Thus proposition number 7 of Gregory's list is entirely omitted from the list of the 18 which make up the *Declarationes*. Yet the content of the seventh proposition is found expressed in two passages of the *De Civili Dominio*: "But whether the church is in that state today, it is not for me to inquire, but is the office of the political authorities . . . ," and "that kings and civil authorities are bound to deprive an unworthy church of her wealth under threat of damnation." [3] Still, in concluding his defense of proposition number 6 in the *Declarationes*, Wyclyf explains that it is not his intention, presumably as reported by the above-mentioned "children," to propose that the civil authorities may deprive a delinquent church of her temporalities whenever and by whatever method they might choose or entirely on their own authority but rather only with the authorization of the church and in cases and form dictated by justice. This qualification does not appear in the *De Civili Dominio;* neither does that which he offers in explanation of the sixteenth thesis in Gregory's schedule (the fifteenth of the *Declarationes*). In the *Declarationes*, not the *De Civili Dominio*, Wyclyf points out that, while he believes every priest has the power to administer any sacrament, it is only reasonable that this power should not be exercised by the lower clergy except in case of an emergency.[4]

Finally, Walsingham is witness to the charge that Wyclyf tempered the sense of his theses under pressure of the prelates' questioning. He writes in disgust that Wyclyf was able to deceive his inquisitors, and he insists that the theses, "if they are simply taken in the sense in which he maintained them in the schools and in his public sermons, without doubt breathe the pravity of heresy. For he did not qualify them with any kind of circumlocution when he put them into the ears of the laity, but nakedly and openly, as they are above described, he preached them . . ." [5]

That Wyclyf was able to convince the prelates that his theses were orthodox, as the *Eulogium* declares,[6] may not appear as much an ex-

3. *Civ. Dom.*, 1, 269, 271–2.

4. *Hist. Angl.*, 1, 361; *Chron. Angl.*, p. 188. It should be noted that Wyclyf's interpretation of his theses as expressed in the *Libellus* (see above, p. 56) is similarly more moderate than the original analysis in the *Civ. Dom.* As Loserth writes: "In der Flugschrift sind den Erlaeuterungen der einzelnen Theses hier and da einschraenkende, mildernde Saetze angefuegt . . ." *Loc. cit.*, 156, 13–14.

5. *Hist. Angl.*, 1, 363; *Chron. Angl.*, p. 190.

6. "Et dictus [Wyclyf] probavit coram archiepiscopo Cantuariensi et episcopo Londoniensi conclusiones illas veras esse." *Eulog.*, 3, 348.

aggeration as one might suppose at first glance. When it is remembered that the theologians at Oxford had judged them true, only ill sounding, and that Wyclyf had taken pains to soften the implications of his propositions, the prelates might have had little difficulty, in view of the prohibition of the queen mother, in making a virtue of necessity and dismissing Wyclyf with instructions that "he was to discuss no further such propositions in the schools or in sermons, for fear of scandalizing the laity." [7]

There is one matter touching the Lambeth trial which requires elucidation. That is the interference of Joan, the widow of the Black Prince. She may have intruded herself because of her sympathy for Wyclyf, though the fact that four of the 16 executors of her will were suspected of Lollardy should scarcely be considered ample evidence since among the 16 were included the bishops of London and Winchester.[8] Whether she favored Wyclyf's cause or not is of little moment. The fact is that the emissary from her court, Sir Lewis Clifford, spoke with authority.[9] In whose name he spoke is not clear. It may have been Gaunt's. He was in England at the time, and, whatever the differences between his followers and those of the late Prince of Wales, the duke remained a friend of his widow. If Joan instructed Clifford as the duke desired, her monition would have been respected, for despite the whittling of the duke's power which Parliament had contrived to effect,[1] his voice was still the loudest in England. Where he had publicly befriended Wyclyf just a year before at St. Paul's, he may now have hesitated to do so because of his experience the first time.[2] He was no longer the arrogant, self-confident master of the court that he had been during the closing months of his father's life.

It is unlikely that Sir Lewis Clifford carried a message from the government when he left the court of the queen mother for Lambeth. What came closest to approximating a government at the time was the continual council, and at this moment, early in 1378, three of the nine members who constituted the council were bishops. And one of these was Courteney.[3] Yet if Gaunt was the man behind the scenes he must

7. Hist. Angl., 1, 363; Chron. Angl., p. 190. See also Eulog., 3, 348.

8. Nicholas, Testamenta Vetusta, 1, 14–15. See Workman, 1, 290 n. 2.

9. "pompose vetantis ne praesumerent aliquid contra ipsum Johannem sententialiter diffinire . . ." Hist. Angl., 1, 356; Chron. Angl., p. 183.

1. See Steel, p. 44.

2. "We must suppose that by using the influence of the princess in Wycliffe's favour, instead of interfering personally, the duke avoided provoking the hostile party which had risen to defend Courtenay in 1377." Stubbs, 2, 446 n. 1.

3. See Lewis, loc. cit., p. 247.

have realized that his personal interposition would not suffice to shield Wyclyf indefinitely. Wyclyf had become more than a problem to the church. Now that his teachings were stirring up controversy, the state was growing concerned; he had, in fact, become something of a nuisance. The crown had nothing to gain from his attacks on the church, for it had never seriously contemplated seizing her temporalities and was hardly any more concerned about reform. To permit Wyclyf to continue his revolutionary preaching would have antagonized the pope and hierarchy and occasioned considerable unrest among the people. On the other hand, to have allowed the pope or the English hierarchy to discipline him would have aroused his numerous admirers, to say nothing of enraging Gaunt. It was probably the continual council that threshed the matter through and came up with an eminently satisfactory solution, acceptable at least to the civil authorities and to the English hierarchy. Wyclyf was prohibited to speak further on controversial matters.[4]

This order must be the one recorded by Netter, but rather than having been given by the great council after asking Wyclyf his opinion on withholding money from Rome, it was more probably issued by the continual council following Gregory's appeal. And it was issued in the interest of tranquillity; that is made clear from a similar injunction placed upon one John de Acley at about this same time by members of the king's council. Acley, a monk of Durham, had been delegated by the Benedictines in their provincial chapter to act as their official apologist against Wyclyf. Acley's prior, however, canceled this appointment in view of the council's command to Acley not to take part in any controversy which might lead to schism or disturbance. Pantin suggests that since it was Wyclyf's would-be opponent who was silenced the council's interference indicated a tendency to favor Wyclyf.[5] Pantin is wrong. This would be tantamount to saying that the council was willing that Wyclyf continue to air his controversial opinions, at the same time forbidding an orthodox theologian to differ with him for fear of causing disturbance. There is no evidence, only unwarranted conjecture, that the civil authorities had become so sympathetic to Wyclyf as to have taken such a revolutionary stand. But there is strong evidence of the reverse—that the council had ordered Wyclyf to cease his attacks on the church.[6] Actually it may be no oversimplification to

4. See above, p. 59.
5. Pantin, "A Benedictine Opponent of John Wyclif," *EHR, 43,* 75–6. Pantin includes a transcription of the prior's letter with his article.
6. See above, pp. 60–1.

assert that both Wyclyf and Acley received the same order—to keep silent—from the same group, the continual council, at about the same time—probably 1378 [7]—and for the same reason, national tranquillity. Incidentally, Wyclyf himself admitted that his suggestions might lead to civil war unless the people were first instructed as to their reasonableness.[8]

One may safely conclude, in effect, that Wyclyf was silenced by the government in 1378 as a direct consequence of Pope Gregory's intervention. The pope's bulls precipitated a solution of the problem Wyclyf had created. Gregory made such an issue of his continued teaching, so aroused the already concerned hierarchy, that the civil authorities could no longer ignore the threat to the country's peace which a virulent war of words between Wyclyf and his opponents would pose. Whereupon, in conjunction with the chief ecclesiastical lords, the government proceeded to work out a compromise. Wyclyf was not to be touched—not out of sympathy for him but as a sop to his protector, Gaunt—but he was ordered to halt his attacks on the church.

Another facet of the Lambeth trial deserves mention, the intrusion of the London citizenry. The chronicler's brief though vitriolic comment reveals only why they burst into the chapel, namely, to lend their verbal assistance to Wyclyf and to impede the progress of the trial.[9] Workman declares that the citizens were "probably under the lead of John of Northampton," though he should have used the word "possibly" instead of "probably." [1] That the violence of the crowd brought an abrupt halt to the proceedings, as Trevelyan and Shirley would have us believe,[2] is mere conjecture. It is true that the group forced its way into the chapel, and Walsingham appears to credit the "favor and diligence" of the crowd along with Wyclyf's sophistry for his being let off so easily.[3] Actually the citizens who were able to worm their way into the chapel must have conducted themselves with reason-

7. Pantin believes the injunction was issued sometime between 1377 and 1378. For the date of the order given to Wyclyf, see above, p. 59.

8. See above, p. 60.

9. "non dico cives tantum Londonienses, sed viles ipsius civitatis, se impudenter ingerere praesumpserunt in eandem Capellam, et verba facere pro eodem, et istud negotium impedire . . ." *Hist. Angl., 1,* 356; *Chron. Angl.,* p. 183.

1. Workman, *1,* 308. London sent John Northampton to represent the city at Gloucester in October, 1378. This John was a "staunch supporter of his [John of Gaunt] and a follower of Wycliffe." *Cal. of Letter-Books,* p. 98 n. 1. Thus Northampton might have been among the group that pressed into the archbishop's chapel at Lambeth, though to say he "probably" was is a different matter.

2. Trevelyan, p. 86; *Fas. Ziz.,* p. xxxiii.

3. "favore et diligentia Londoniensium . . ." *Hist. Angl., 1,* 363; *Chron. Angl.,* p. 190.

able decorum, for while they came as Wyclyf's champions they were confronted with Courteney, their bishop. They had taken his part against John of Gaunt the year before.[4] That his popularity with them had remained undiminished was recognized by Gaunt a few months after the Lambeth trial when he threatened to drag the bishop to Westminster in spite of the "ribald knaves" of London.[5]

Before dropping the subject of Gregory's bulls, note might be made of Wyclyf's violent reaction to the pope's action in condemning his theses. Some of his choicest epithets he reserved for Gregory, whom he denounced as a "horrible devil" and an "unremitting heretic."[6] As Loserth writes: "He never forgave this pope for having condemned his theses."[7] Some of Wyclyf's venom arose from his conviction that Gregory had a particular grudge against him. As a matter of fact, Gregory was as much concerned with heresy elsewhere as he was in England, and his efforts to silence Wyclyf were nothing out of the ordinary.[8] Yet it is significant that Wyclyf was convinced his propositions were thoroughly orthodox, and he writes of forwarding an apology for his views to Urban VI by the hands of bishops in the hope of persuading him of the validity of his theses.[9] There is no other confirmation for this astonishing bit of information, and if Wyclyf is not guilty of some distortion it does at least bear witness to the respect and concern he felt for the papal reaction. It also reflects a remarkable degree of optimism on his part.

4. See above, p. 29.

5. See below, p. 76. For Courteney's popularity among the city fathers, see above, p. 31.

6. *Eccles.*, pp. 358, 366.

7. "Die Verfluchung der Thesen hat er diesem Papste nimmer verziehen." *loc. cit., 136,* 112. Loserth also writes: "Die Verurtheilung der 18 Thesen Wiclif's durch Gregor XI. hat auf Wiclif einen so tiefen Eindruck gemacht, dass wir die Folgen davon in allen seinen spaeteren Schriften spueren: in seinen ausserordentlich leidenschaftlichen Ausfaellen gegen diesen Papst, dessen Gestalt in wahrhaft fratzenhafter Weise bei ihm verstellt ist." *Ibid.*, p. 112.

8. Loserth notes numerous letters which Gregory addressed to the church authorities of several countries in his anxiety about heresy. He concludes: "Es ist in seinem Vorgehen gegen Wiclif nichts Ausserordentliches zu sehen." *Ibid.*, p. 113.

9. Wyclyf says he sent the pope his views on the Bible (*Ver. Script., 1,* 274), which he set forth in a tract entitled *Conclusiones Triginta Tres sive de Paupertate Christi* (*ibid.*, pp. 349–50). This tract takes up the theme of the *De Civili Dominio*, which had provided the substance of the 19 condemned propositions. For the tract, see *Op. Min.*, pp. 19–73. The text, incidentally, does not speak of two bishops as serving as Wyclyf's messengers. It reads: "per manus dominorum episcoporum . . ." *Ver. Script., 1,* 274. Workman (*1*, 312) follows Shirley who read *duorum* instead of *dominorum. Fas. Ziz.*, p. xxxiii n. 2. That Wyclyf sent along with these bishops his famous letter of excuse for failing to appear at Rome in answer to a papal summons (see below, p. 141) is simply Workman's gratuitous assumption. Workman, *1*, 312.

4. EVENTS OF 1378–82

The Haulay-Shakyl Incident

An incident took place on August 11, 1378, which momentarily rekindled the court's interest in Wyclyf. This was the breach of sanctuary committed by Sir Alan Buxhill, the keeper of the Tower, when he invaded the precincts of Westminster Abbey in order to seize a Robert Haulay who had escaped from prison. The origin of the case of Robert Haulay and his partner John Shakyl went back 11 years to the battle of Najera in Castile when the two men had had the good fortune, or so at least it had appeared at the time, to capture the count of Denia, a Spanish grandee. Despite the count's rank, the Black Prince had permitted Haulay and Shakyl to hold him for ransom, although the crown apparently retained an interest in him.[1] In 1377 Haulay and his companion were still holding the count's eldest son Alphonso as hostage for a ransom which was then already ten years late in coming. Finally in August of that year the count sent an agent to England with part of the ransom and instructions to arrange for his son's release.[2]

By this time, however, the foreign situation had altered, and the crown decided it could make better use of Alphonso than could Haulay and Shakyl. Whether to expedite an exchange of prisoners or whether to curry the favor of the king of Aragon and the count of Foix in preparation for an attack on Castile,[3] Haulay and Shakyl were ordered to release their hostage to the government. This demand they refused even when Parliament added its command,[4] and for their defiance they were thrown into prison. They remained there until August, 1378, when they managed to make their escape and sought refuge in Westminster. Inasmuch as the possession of Alphonso had by this time become as much a matter of principle as of necessity to the government, the crown gave orders to invade the Abbey.

The group of soldiers which Buxhill took with him, 50 according to Walsingham,[5] almost made it look like an invasion. Shakyl was taken

1. See Workman, *1*, 314 n. 6. See *Eccles.*, pp. 142–3.
2. Rymer, 7, 171.
3. See *Hist. Angl.*, *1*, 376; *Chron. Angl.*, p. 207; *Eulog.*, *3*, 342; *Eccles.*, p. 142.
4. *Rot. Parl.*, *3*, 10.
5. *Hist. Angl.*, *1*, 377; *Chron. Angl.*, p. 208. Workman's "forty" is a mistake. *1*, 316.

through a ruse. The soldiers found Haulay hearing Mass, and after an argument as heated as it was fruitless they attempted to seize him. He broke away from them and was twice chased around the choir before finally being cornered near the altar. There, even though Mass was in progress, one of the soldiers cleft him through the skull while another pierced him through the back. They also slew a clerk of the community who had endeavored to protect Haulay. Then they took the lifeless body of Haulay by the legs and, "horribly dragging it through the most sacred part of the choir and the church, bespattering everything with his blood and brains," they cast it out into the street.[6]

Despite the shocking character of this violation of the right of sanctuary, it was three days before Archbishop Sudbury had summoned up sufficient courage to excommunicate those guilty of the outrage. He issued but a general condemnation at that, for, as he explained, the actual perpetrators of the deed were unknown.[7] Courteney, who must have been straining at the leash, immediately published the condemnation with all possible zeal and solemnity at St. Paul's and repeated the denunciation on Sundays, Wednesdays, and Fridays. The bishop's denunciation was more specific than Sudbury's, for not only did he excommunicate Buxhill by name but he explicitly exempted from the force of his mandate the king, his mother, and the duke of Lancaster. No doubt the bishop experienced an unholy satisfaction in carrying out the archbishop's mandate, for the somewhat pointed exclusion of his enemy, Gaunt, must have had the effect of suggesting to his listeners that the duke might have been involved in the affair.[8]

The Londoners, at any rate, believed the crime had been ordered by the duke or had been carried out with his connivance.[9] The fact that he had been away at the time of the outrage was overlooked, while his returning soon after from his ill-fated expedition to St. Malo, "ingloriously and in military disgrace,"[1] made it popular to impute anything to him. Secure in the knowledge that the burghers had been shocked at the violation of Westminster and that they had no affection

6. *Hist. Angl.*, 1, 377–8; *Chron. Angl.*, pp. 208–9.

7. "Reg. Sud.," fol. 49ᵛ; Wilkins, 3, 132. Even the peaceful entry of a church by bailiffs bearing maces was forbidden. See "Reg. Court.," fol. 193 ("Ex Reg. Morton").

8. Walsingham (*Hist. Angl.*, 1, 379; *Chron. Angl.*, p. 210) states that the archbishop and five of his suffragans published the condemnation and specifically excluded the king, his mother, and Gaunt from its force. This disagrees with the register.

9. *Hist. Angl.*, 1, 379; *Chron. Angl.*, p. 210.

1. *Chron. Angl.*, p. 210.

to waste on Gaunt, Courteney continued his fulminations despite appeals to him by the king that he desist altogether or at least alter the nature of the condemnation. Since Richard was but twelve years old at the time, the appeals must have originated with the duke. When the bishop also contemptuously refused to appear before the council at Windsor to which the king had summoned him, Gaunt proposed that "if the king so directed, he was willing to hasten to London and bring back that obstinate bishop to the council by force in spite of the Londoners whom he called 'ribald.' " [2]

It is probable that Wyclyf became involved in the incident when the duke directed him to assist in the preparation of a case for the government. Supporting this view is Wyclyf's statement that he had prepared a lengthy defense for "my master, the duke," to refute the charge that he had been implicated in the crime. Furthermore, in the course of the defense Wyclyf mentions that the duke had declared in his hearing that he was not opposed to the principle of sanctuary and felt that it should be violated only if the welfare of the realm required it.[3] One wonders whether Gaunt did not make the statement after calling together the clerks, including Wyclyf, and then instructing them on the nature of the assignment—that is, the preparation of an apology for the crown.

The occasion for which Gaunt wanted the assistance of the clerks was the meeting of Parliament at Gloucester in October, 1378. Since the abbot had refused to consent to the reconsecration of Westminster even though the "king sente meny tymes be his writtes . . . forto appere befor him, and forto cece his cursyng, and that he sholde halowe agayn his chirche . . . ," [4] the government must have concluded that the ecclesiastical lords would probably reject any request for badly needed funds until they had received satisfaction for the violation of the Abbey.

Parliament convened at Gloucester hardly two mònths after the murder of Haulay. That it met there rather than London inspired some contemporary wild rumors which seem to have persisted until today. Thus Loserth accepts Walsingham's explanation that the meeting was transferred to Gloucester "for this reason in particular, because they believed that the bishops and the common people of the kingdom, as well as the Londoners, would be less inclined to resist or contradict their votes in so remote a place." And what they planned to do was

2. *Hist. Angl.*, 1, 379; *Chron. Angl.*, p. 210.
3. *Eccles.*, p. 266; *Fas. Ziz.*, p. xxxvi.
4. Davies, *An English Chronicle*, p. 2.

nothing less than to despoil the church of most of her wealth.[5] This analysis must be discounted as one of the vicious rumors which Gaunt's unpopularity caused to spring forth from the prolific minds of the volatile Londoners who hated him. As noted above,[6] there is no act of Gaunt or anything in his character which would substantiate the charge that he ever contemplated disendowment. If a reason must be found for the meeting of Parliament at Gloucester, it might have been the turbulent atmosphere of London.[7]

As Gaunt had suspected, no sooner had Commons succeeded in forcing the government to agree to its scrutinizing the expenditure of the last subsidy than Sudbury rose and in the name of the clergy made a formal protest against the recent pollution of Westminster. In the course of the debate on this point, a number of doctors of theology and civil law, as well as other clerks, came forward with arguments showing that the government had been well within its rights in invading the Abbey. While Wyclyf is not mentioned by name—as are none of the other clerks for that matter—the arguments expressed by the defense remind one of those he voices in the *De Ecclesia* on the same subject. A strong appeal is made to God and to the ethical principles established upon His justice. Privilege of sanctuary is not denied, but it should not cover instances of debt.[8] Wyclyf in the *De Ecclesia* points out in addition that Haulay precipitated the pollution of the Abbey since he was the first to draw his sword.[9]

In view of the uncompromising stand of the prelates, no settlement of the issue was possible at that time. Parliament took up the delicate question again the following year and issued a statute which confirmed sanctuary for felony but withdrew protection from fraudulent debtors.[1] Yet the distinction regarding debtors was more technical than real, and here as in the question of withholding money from Rome,[2] if Wyclyf's opinion was requested by the crown it was largely ignored.

---

5. *Hist. Angl., 1*, 380; *Chron. Angl.*, p. 211. See Loserth, *loc. cit., 156*, 80. Poole (Review of Loserth, *Johannis Wyclif Tractatus de Ecclesia, EHR, 3*, 574) believes that Wyclyf in chaps. xv–xvi of the *De Ecclesia* appears to give credence to this view.

6. See above, p. 14.

7. See Workman, *1*, 318, and Poole, *loc. cit.*, p. 574.

8. *Rot. Parl., 3*, 37. The *Eulogium* declares: "non privilegium sed pravilegium."

9. *Eccles.*, p. 150. See also *Fas. Ziz.*, pp. xxxvi–vii; *Chron. Angl.*, p. 208; *Hist. Angl., 1*, 377.

1. *Statutes of the Realm, 2*, 12; *Chron. Angl.*, p. 223; *Hist. Angl., 1*, 391–2.

2. See above, p. 57.

If Wyclyf's voice can be detected in the arguments offered by the crown at Gloucester in defense of its invasion of Westminster Abbey, that was the last occasion on which the government made use of his services. At no time after the Gloucester Parliament is there any evidence which might suggest the continuance of that relationship between crown and Wyclyf which dated back to just prior to the Bruges conference.[3] That relationship had, in fact, grown embarrassing to both parties and by mutual consent was permitted to lapse. By this time Wyclyf had become convinced that the crown was not even remotely interested in implementing his program of reform, predicated as it was on the secularization of the wealth of the church. Such theories were to be brought within the realm of practical politics only after the course of another century and a half. Wyclyf could have continued to serve the crown, but it would have been simply as another clerk and with the understanding that he eschew the discussion of certain controversial theories. Such a sterile role the indefatigable revolutionary refused to play.

What caused the estrangement between crown and Wyclyf? There were a number of factors. One was the political eclipse of Wyclyf's champion, the duke of Lancaster, who had been excluded from the continual council and who had just returned more unpopular than ever from the disastrous St. Malo expedition. Another factor was the ineffective though not inconsequential efforts the hierarchy had been making to silence Wyclyf. The hierarchy was well represented in the continual council, notably by Courteney, London's popular bishop, and its voice could not be entirely ignored, even though the crown might have been so minded.

That the crown was not so minded was due to two other reasons—one negative, the other positive—which together account for most of Wyclyf's loss of favor at court. The first was the crown's perennial need for funds, a considerable portion of which would have to be voted by convocation. This fact precluded any open encouragement of Wyclyf, if it did not strongly advise a conciliatory policy to placate the hierarchy in its efforts to silence him. The other reason, and the more important, was the election of Urban VI on April 8, 1378. For it is one of the ironies of history that the election of Urban, which Wyclyf warmly acclaimed as the salvation of the church,[4] actually contributed decisively to the elimination of his influence at Westminster.

The election of Urban affected Wyclyf's fortunes in two ways. In the

3. See above, p. 4.
4. *Eccles.*, p. 37; *Op. Min.*, p. 401.

first place the replacement of the French Gregory XI with the Italian Urban destroyed the basis for much of the antipapal sentiment then existing in court circles. The English, along with Wyclyf, were inclined to hail the new pope as "our Urban," [5] particularly after he extended to Richard, in a bull dated May 9, 1378, extensive privileges in the appointment to vacant benefices in his kingdom.[6] With the coming of the schism and the championing by France of Clement's cause, the allegiance of England to Urban became all the stronger. Clement's emissaries were not even permitted to plead their case before Parliament.[7] For Wyclyf the immediate consequence was a sharp drop in prestige. Wyclyf stood above the other clerks in the crown's service chiefly because of his strong antipapal views, which the crown could exploit for their nuisance value when the occasion demanded. Now with the government committed to supporting Urban, Wyclyf's peculiar priority came to an end.

The election of Urban affected Wyclyf's fortunes in a second way, a disastrous one. Urban's election was soon followed by the schism. The schism in turn drove Wyclyf shortly into open conflict with the papacy. He had already grown skeptical of the claims of the papacy, particularly since Gregory had presumed to pass judgment against 19 of his theses. His doubts concerning that institution were confirmed when Urban and Clement began to indulge in their vicious battle of vilification. It is safe to say that, had Urban been of finer stuff and had he carried through the reform which many, including Wyclyf, hoped he would, Wyclyf's subsequent history would have been materially altered. But Urban was no reformer, and so, rebuffed by a crown which needed him no longer and alienated himself by the unprincipled conduct of the new pope, Wyclyf decided to continue his work without the protection of the court and to do so in an even more revolutionary manner. This decision cost him the last of his popularity in government circles.

That Wyclyf terminated his association with the crown after 1378 may provide a clue to the obscurity which beclouds his personal history after that date. Of his controversial theories the chroniclers have much to report, but of his activities there is scarcely a note. We know only that in August, 1380, he took rooms at Oxford, presumably for a

5. See below, p. 148, n. 3.
6. Wilkins, 3, 130–1.
7. The Gloucester Parliament ordered confiscation of benefices which belonged to those cardinals who supported Clement. *Rot. Parl.*, 3, 46–7; *Cal. of Pat. Rolls, 1381–85*, p. 417. For a discussion of the English reaction to the election of Urban, see Ullmann, *The Origins of the Great Schism*, chap. vii.

year.[8] Where he spent the intervening time between the fall of 1378 and the summer of 1380 is a matter of conjecture, although it must have been at Lutterworth. That he took rooms at Oxford in August, 1380, suggests that he had none there during the period immediately preceding; neither is his name connected with the events at Westminster. This does not rule out the possibility that he spent intervals at Oxford. Lutterworth was not far distant, and the bitterness of the controversy raging at Oxford over his views leads one to suspect that it was he, either in person or through trusty disciples, who was keeping the halls in a turmoil.

After 1378 Wyclyf devoted himself almost exclusively to promoting his assault on abuses and practices in the church which he considered unsound. This attack involved aspects of both reform and revolt. Thus the earlier target of his barbs, the wealth and political power of the church, came in for renewed attack. Now he began to press his arguments much deeper, for where in the De Civili Dominio he had discussed the question of disendowment "as a speculative position: now he puts it directly [in the De Ecclesia], in the case of the kingdom of England, and not merely as a possibility but as a present duty." [9] He denounced with more feeling than formerly such abuses as pluralism and absenteeism and excoriated practices, in themselves not abuses but frequently inviting misuse, such as indulgences, the veneration of saints, relics, pilgrimages, excommunication, and mortuaries.

Had Wyclyf contented himself with attacking abuses and nonessential practices, he would have remained relatively unknown. But on the principle that a righteous God could not have entrusted the salvation of mankind to the hands of a corrupt church, he began to question the bases of that institution. He expatiated further on the doctrine of the keys which he had already disputed in the De Civili Dominio in views which Gregory had listed among the 19 propositions and singled out as heretical. He now held that the pope was not indispensable, that he could even be heretical, and that if he were not poor, he was Antichrist. Perpetual vows were unlawful, and even the friars for whom he had earlier had such high regard [1] he now described as members of

8. *Second Report of the Royal Commission on Historical Manuscripts*, p. 142. Wyclyf paid 40s. for two years' rent in 1374–75, while from "August 1380 to some date now effaced" he paid 20s. *Ibid.*, p. 141. On the basis of an annual rental of 20s. it would appear unlikely that Wyclyf was associated with the university after August, 1381. See Magrath, p. 112.

9. Poole, *loc. cit.*, p. 574.

1. See above, p. 26.

"sects." [2] The church of God was composed only of the elect whom God had so designated, and this church was not at all synonymous with the Roman church. More fundamental was his denial of the doctrine of transubstantiation and of the real presence. Like other reformers before and after him, the more he found to question in the church as then established and administered, the more he turned to the scriptures as the foundation stone of Christian faith and morals. [3]

It is important to remember, however, that Wyclyf in his attack on the church never reached the point of open defiance that Luther did. He never actually repudiated the papacy, [4] his position on the doctrine of transubstantiation was sufficiently confused [5] as not to appear unqualifiedly heretical, and despite his belief in predestination he maintained that "each man that shall be condemned shall be damned for his own guilt, and each man that is saved shall be saved by his own merit . . ." [6] Typical of this illogicality and of his refusal to accept the implications of his premises, a fact which may have helped save him from more effective prosecution, was his statement that, while the bishop had no spiritual powers above those of a priest, yet "no one without a revelation should despise the consecration of his bishop." [7] And his actions reflected this inconsistency. The man who was most outspoken in England in denouncing pluralities, nonresidence, and the Caesarean clergy was himself a pluralist, had been cautioned for being away from his cure, and had spent several years in the service of the crown.

Nonetheless, the more radical theses which Wyclyf developed in such works as the *De Veritate Sacrae Scripturae,* the *De Ecclesia, De Apostasia, De Eucharistia,* and the *De Potestate Papae,* all of which fall within the years 1378 to 1380, served to deprive him of much of his upper-class support and to lead ultimately to his exile from Oxford. [8] It was in particular his views on the Eucharist which principally destroyed the esteem in which he was held, for even the untutored gentry

2. *Pol. Works,* 1, 303; *Apos.,* p. 13. See Workman, 2, 103–8.

3. See Loserth, *loc. cit., 156,* 29.

4. See below, p. 148.

5. Of Wyclyf's position on transubstantiation, Workman writes: "his inconsistencies, and his facility for explaining away texts and authorities that are against him, show the shifts to which he was driven. His teaching, in fact, was still developing when death overtook him." 2, 39–40.

6. See *ibid.,* 2, 9–10.

7. *Pol. Works, 1,* 259.

8. See below, p. 135.

which had earlier supported his anticlericalism could appreciate the fact that in his attack on transubstantiation he was embarking on a course where they could no longer follow him. That was the point where Gaunt called a halt.[9]

The Rising of 1381

Then in 1381 two events took place which had fatal consequences for Wyclyf's cause. They were the Peasant Revolt of 1381 and the elevation of the energetic and aggressive Courteney to the see of Canterbury. For any direct responsibility in the rising of June, 1381, historians hold Wyclyf innocent. Of his indirect influence there is some question, while of the disastrous effect the rebellion had upon his fortunes there is none. As for his direct responsibility, one should remember that Wyclyf was himself a member of the squirearchy, that he had earlier benefited not a little from the protection of members of the nobility,[1] and that he was still being shielded by the duke of Lancaster, the largest landholder in England. It may have been for that reason that while he encouraged his listeners to carry out his theory against churchmen—that all dominion was founded upon grace—he never advised them to do the same with regard to the gentry.

Yet it is probable that "Wyclif's ideas, reported second-hand by Poor Priests, or distorted by men indifferent to their subtle distinctions, had not been without their influence."[2] The chronicler's account of the activities of John Ball, one of the leaders of the uprising, would appear to bear this out. Ball, a priest, had a long history of difficulties with his ecclesiastical superiors. He had, in fact, been resting in jail, incarcerated on the charge of heresy, when the first wave of rioters set him free and thus enabled him to join them. For some 20 years he had been preaching up and down England, saying that which pleased his audiences, "disparaging to ecclesiastics as well as to lay lords." He would advise his listeners to withhold tithes from vicars who were richer than they, even to seize tithes from priests whose lives were less worthy than their own. "He taught, in addition, the perverse dogmas of the perfidious John Wiclyf, and the opinions which he held . . ."[3] Were Ball not such an old hand at disseminating views distasteful to the

9. See below, p. 133.
1. See above, p. 28.
2. Workman, 2, 240.
3. *Hist. Angl.*, 2, 32; *Chron. Angl.*, p. 321.

hierarchy [4] one might consider his admonition on the subject of tithes as conclusive proof that he was a disciple of Wyclyf. It is probably rather a case of two minds running in the same channel.

Still the evidence is damaging, particularly since Walsingham charges Ball directly with preaching Wyclyf's doctrines, while Netter presumes to give a confession which Ball made to Courteney. Ball was eventually taken in Coventry and was about to run the gamut of the horrors of medieval executions from drawing through hanging and beheading to quartering when Bishop Courteney intervened and secured a reprieve of two days for the condemned in order to enable him to repent of his sins.

> Who seeing that he was doomed, summoned William, bishop of London, later of Canterbury; also Walter Lee, guard, and John Pro-fete, notary; and there he publicly confessed to them that for two years he had been a disciple of Wycclyff, and that he had learned from him the heresies he was teaching; and that he preached the heresy of the Eucharist which originated with him, as well as others taught by him. He said, furthermore, that there was a company of the sect and doctrine of Wycclyff, which had conspired to form a sort of confederation, and had arranged to travel the breadth of England in order to preach the lessons which the said Wycclyf had taught, in order that all England would accept at one time his perverse doctrine. Then he enumerated to them the said Wycclyff as the principal author, and in second place Nicholas Herford, John Aston, and Laurence Bedeman, master of arts. He then added that had no resistance been offered to the above, the same would have destroyed the entire kingdom within two years.[5]

There is, as Workman points out, something of the sign of a "weapon made to order" about this confession, but it is dangerous to conclude that "No credence need be attached to a confession of which we hear nothing until twenty years later . . ." [6] The same damning indictment can be brought against the bulk of the testimony scholars have used and still use to piece together the history of ancient and medieval times. Granted that the listing of the Oxford stalwarts, Hereford, Aston, and

---

4. Years before he had been cited by Archbishop Islip and had been excommunicated when he failed to answer the summons. Archbishop Sudbury repeated this excommunication on April 26, 1381. "Reg. Sud.," fol. 75ᵛ; Wilkins, 3, 152–3.

5. *Fas. Ziz.*, pp. 273–4.

6. Workman, 2, 237.

Bedeman, adds a note of spuriousness to the confession, the fact that it does not include the names of Repingdon and Purvey, two of Wyclyf's foremost disciples, reduces somewhat the degree of artificiality. Furthermore, it accords so closely with Walsingham's account [7] and, in addition, finds an echo in the purported confession of Jack Straw that it cannot be entirely discounted. Straw, another insurgent leader, stated that it had been the intention of his group to kill, among others, the "possessioners, bishops, monks, canons, and rectors" but to leave the mendicants as adequate in numbers to take care of the spiritual wants of all. [8] Straw and his companions must not have heard that Wyclyf for the past 12 months or so had also been willing to dispense with the friars, although not in quite the scathing terms with which he had damned the others.

Reference should be made in this connection to a letter which the four mendicant orders at Oxford addressed to the duke of Lancaster in February, 1382, against Nicholas Hereford and his "accomplices." The document is revealing. The friars charge Wyclyf with having been the author of the recent uprising, thereby contributing their bit to the growth of that sentiment. More significant is the friars' complaint that Wyclyf had attempted, through the "tongues of a number of pseudo-doctors," to pin the blame for the rebellion upon them. They were accused of having done this in three ways: first, by impoverishing the people, who gave them more than they paid out for all their various taxes; second, by having made the serfs lazy through their own example of lazy mendicancy so that the serfs, "despising their accustomed labors, rebelled against their lords"; third, by having failed, in their role as the confessors of most of the lords and people, to prevent the disturbances. [9] These "pseudo-doctors" must have included Hereford, whom the friars in the same letter describe as their worst enemy, as well as the other Lollard leaders at Oxford. There is no reason to doubt the friars' charge that these men were seeking to place the blame for the uprising on their shoulders. Whether these "pseudo-doctors" were doing so in order to escape the same charge themselves and whether Wyclyf was responsible for their taking this stand are questions more easily raised than answered.

All of this adds up to two conclusions, both advanced with a degree of caution: first, that Wyclyf's doctrines, especially those concerned

7. Of the confession itself Walsingham has only this to say: "plura alia fatebatur et fecit . . ." *Hist. Angl.*, 2, 34; *Chron. Angl.*, p. 322.

8. *Hist. Angl.*, 2, 10; *Chron. Angl.*, p. 309.

9. *Fas. Ziz.*, pp. 292–5.

with dominion, did contribute in a measure to the coming of the revolt; second—and this with less hesitancy—that many contemporaries were quick to hold Wyclyf responsible for the disturbances. The clergy would surely have taken that stand, and they would have convinced others. Gregory had carefully instructed Sudbury and Courteney to emphasize to the king and the nobility the danger to the state inherent in Wyclyf's propositions.[1] There is no doubt that the hierarchy took pains, and with considerable satisfaction, to remind their lay friends of those earlier warnings when the violence broke loose. And in the last analysis, as far as the consequences to Wyclyf's position are concerned, it is not so much whether Wyclyf had anything to do with the coming of the revolt but rather what contemporaries believed that is important.

Similarly, contemporaries had little difficulty in linking the growing discontent of the masses with the increasing number of Wyclyf's adherents, the Lollards. These were being recruited through the untiring efforts of the "poor priests," who roamed about the country preaching not only Wyclyf's views but whatever conclusions unlettered and often radical minds could deduce from them. They must have included saints and rascals, apostles and charlatans, scholars and idiots, priests and laymen. Some, like John Ball, had been itinerant preachers for a decade or more; others had been delegated by Wyclyf, possibly as early as 1377, to disseminate his ideas.[2] They proved a thorn in the side of the hierarchy,[3] and so popular was their appeal that the chronicler—with medieval exaggeration, it is true—could lament: "Scarcely would you see two men on the road but that one of them was a disciple of Wiclif."[4] Doubtless many were inclined to agree with Walsingham that the excesses of 1381 were the inevitable consequences of the negligence of the prelates, of Sudbury in particular, in failing to discipline Wyclyf and his disciples.[5]

The Translation of Courteney to Canterbury

The second event of 1381 that had such grievous consequences for Wyclyf and his program was the elevation of Courteney to the see of Canterbury. It was Courteney who eradicated Lollardy at Oxford and in so doing deprived the movement of that respectability which was essential if it were to be accepted by the middle and upper classes.

1. See above, p. 44.
2. *Hist. Angl., 1,* 324; *Chron. Angl.,* p. 395.
3. "Reg. Court.," *1,* fol. 26; Wilkins, *3,* 158–9.
4. *Knighton, 2,* 191.
5. *Hist. Angl., 2,* 12; *Chron. Angl.,* p. 311.

He did not suppress Lollardy—far from it—but he left it, by common consent, the religion of essentially meaner folk.

That Courteney succeeded the murdered Sudbury as archbishop was not unexpected. As bishop of London he already occupied a position in the province second in importance only to that of the primate himself. Furthermore, in view of the quiescence of Sudbury, Courteney's had been the guiding hand in ecclesiastical policies since his translation from Hereford to London in 1375. To the papacy his promotion was eminently acceptable for Courteney had proved a strong, loyal suffragan.[6] He had courageously denounced the outrage at Westminster in the face of the government's bitter disapproval.[7] He had proved Wyclyf's most persistent prosecutor, and though his efforts to discipline him had thus far been largely unavailing[8] the papacy could expect better results once Courteney was relieved of the restraining hand of his cautious superior, Sudbury.

Early in Courteney's career as bishop of London an incident took place which should have convinced Rome that Courteney would never lack the diligence and courage to carry out the pope's wishes. The affair grew out of Gregory XI's excommunication of the Florentines in March, 1376. Because the Florentines had tortured the papal emissary and buried him alive, among other reasons, the pope had promulgated against them the terrible bull, *In Omnem Fere Terram*.[9] Gregory ordered their goods to be seized, forbade the payment of debts to them, and enjoined all countries under threat of interdict to exclude them from their domains.[1] So as not to render the bull ridiculously impracticable, a saving clause was inserted whereby it would be lawful for them "to remayne in those countryes where they had taiken servitude, and where, as bond men, then [sic] served their maisters."[2] Choosing therefore what was their only alternative, the Florentines in England threw themselves on Edward's mercy, and he accepted them into his service.[3]

Their haven was destined to be of short duration. As it happened Gregory had sent his bull denouncing the Florentines not only to Edward[4] but also to Courteney, who as bishop of London would be the

6. Urban had planned to make Courteney a cardinal in 1378. See above, p. 31.
7. See above, p. 76.
8. They may not have been entirely futile; see above, p. 72.
9. *Chron. Angl.*, p. 110.
1. *Hist. Angl.*, 1, 322–3; *Eulog.*, 3, 335.
2. *Transcript*, p. 249.
3. *Hist. Angl.*, 1, 323; *Chron. Angl.*, pp. 101–2.
4. Rymer, 7, 103–4.

logical person to see to its promulgation.[5] Since the Florentines already
suffered the opprobrium which was the lot of all moneylenders,[6] the
bishop should have realized that the sweeping terms of the bull would
be likely to elicit the all too enthusiastic cooperation of many Londoners,
who would have been happy to do without papal blessing what their
own instincts recommended. Consequently, when Courteney chose to
ignore the Statute of Praemunire and solemnly published the bull at
St. Paul's Cross, the Londoners responded with a vengeance and made
short shrift of Florentine business establishments. The panic-stricken
Florentines appealed to the mayor for protection, and he in turn laid
the matter before the king. Edward immediately ordered their goods
restored to them and threatened with dire punishment anyone who
should dare injure them or interfere with their business.[7]

Courteney had not long to wait for a summons from the chancellor
to explain his part in the episode. To the question of why he had had
the audacity to publish the bull without first consulting the government,
Courteney could find no better explanation than "because the pope so
ordered." Obliged to choose between the loss of his temporalities and
personally retracting the denunciation of the Florentines, Courteney
was able, only with great difficulty, to secure permission to have the
latter done by proxy. The Londoners must have smiled to hear Courteney's agent protest at St. Paul's Cross that "His lord, the bishop, had
not spoken of an interdict" and must have chuckled at the unconscious
humor in his asking how they could have made such a mistake, "you
who hear so many sermons." [8]

To the government, whoever that may have been in 1381,[9] Courteney
was more than acceptable. He had grown so influential politically
that his bid for Canterbury could scarcely be denied. He was the
leader of what Wyclyf denounced as the "Caesarean clergy." He had
been a member of the original continual council of July, 1377, and of
the remodeled one of October.[1] In 1379 he had been appointed to a

---

5. *Chron. Angl.*, pp. 109–10.

6. Even in the expulsion of the Jews in 1290 "there could be no spice of religious bigotry." Capes, *The English Church in the Fourteenth and Fifteenth
Centuries*, p. 22.

7. Rymer, 7, 135; *Hist. Angl.*, 1, 323. See *Eulog.*, 3, 335.

8. *Eulog.*, 3, 335–6. Courteney's friend Brantingham was chancellor, or he
might not have gotten off so easily.

9. "Not until 1383, when he [Richard] asserted his full independence, is it
possible to decide who controlled the Government, though it seems probable that
no individual or party enjoyed undisputed sway." Vickers, *England in the Later
Middle Ages*, p. 262. See Steel, p. 44.

1. See Rymer, 7, 161, and *Rot. Parl.*, 3, 6.

commission to examine the revenues of the crown and the property of the late king.[2] The following year he was a member of a commission delegated to regulate court expenses in the hope that retrenchment there might alleviate the government's fiscal difficulties.[3] On August 10, 1381, he was entrusted with the Great Seal and held the office of chancellor until the following November 30.[4] He was, of course, a member of the powerful Courteney family, and while it may have counted for little, both he and Richard's father had had the same great-grandfather (Edward I).[5] Finally, that Urban supported Courteney's candidacy must have carried some weight in court circles, since relations with Rome were still most cordial.[6]

The duke of Lancaster would have objected vigorously to Courteney's elevation to Canterbury a few years earlier but probably not in 1381. For one thing, he was away in Scotland for much of the summer. He had also grown deeply concerned about having his offspring legitimized, and he would find that easier if the influential Courteney were on his side or his enmity at least mollified. It is even possible that the excesses of the Peasant Revolt had somewhat upset the duke, particularly in view of the heavy property damages he had suffered. He may, accordingly, have been willing to drop his objection to the elevation of that prelate who was the most vigorous opponent of those who many felt had been responsible for the disturbances, that is, the followers of Wyclyf. In any event, Richard gave his approval to the elevation of Courteney on August 5[7] after the monks had unanimously elected him. Urban, presumably in ignorance of their action, provided him with the see on September 8.[8]

2. *Rot. Parl., 3,* 57.
3. *Ibid.,* p. 101.
4. Rymer, 7, 310; *Cal. of Close Rolls, 1381–85,* pp. 84–5, 97.
5. Dugdale, *The Baronage of England,* p. 634.
6. See Steel, p. 64.
7. *Cal. of Pat. Rolls, 1381–85,* p. 33.
8. "Reg. Court.," fol. 1.

5. THE BLACKFRIARS COUNCIL

How ominous Courteney's elevation to Canterbury was for Wyclyf and his followers the new archbishop proved less than two weeks after receipt of the pallium.[9] Almost the first official act of "this sturdy pillar of the church"[1] was to summon a number of his suffragans and many more doctors and bachelors of theology and canon and civil law to meet in the chapter house of the Blackfriars at London on May 17 to pass judgment on various questionable propositions which were then being preached about England. The "Memorandum" read as follows:

> Be it remembered that the report has been circulated among both the nobles and commoners of the kingdom of England how certain conclusions, heretical and erroneous, and repugnant to the determinations of the church have been preached generally, commonly, and publicly in diverse places of our province, which threaten to subvert the status of the whole church and of our province of Canterbury, as well as the tranquillity of the realm. We, William, by divine permission archbishop of Canterbury, primate of all England and legate of the apostolic see, having been informed of these and desirous of executing the duty of our office, have called together certain venerable fellow-brethren, our suffragans, and others, and very many doctors and bachelors of holy writ and of canon and civil law, whom we believed to be the most renowned and expert in the kingdom, considering them also most holy in catholic faith, whose names are contained below. And on the seventeenth day of the month of May, in the year of our Lord 1382, after said conclusions, whose tenor follows below, had been publicly propounded and distinctly and clearly read in our presence and that of our said fellow-brethren gathered together and then personally present in a certain chamber within the precincts of the priory of the Preaching Friars at London, we burdened our said fellow-brethren, doctors, and bachelors, on the faith by which

9. Though Courteney had been formally translated to Canterbury by the pope on September 8, the pallium did not reach England until May 4, 1382 ("Reg. Court.," fol. 9). Until the pallium arrived Courteney steadfastly refused various sorts of pressure to induce him to perform any official acts, even that of uniting Richard and Anne of Bohemia in marriage. See *ibid.*, fol. 3; *Cal. of Close Rolls, 1381–85*, p. 88; *Polychronicon Ranulphi Higden, 9*, 11–12.

1. *Fas. Ziz.*, p. 272.

they were bound to our Lord Jesus Christ, and as they would wish
to answer on the day of judgment in the presence of the all high
judge, that they all and each of them tell us his opinion concerning
the said conclusions. And at length, after deliberation concerning
the above on the twenty-first day of the same month, and with our
said fellow-brethren, doctors and bachelors assembled before us
in the aforesaid chamber, and after said conclusions had been read
for a second time and clearly explained, it was declared with the
common consent of ourselves and of all, that of said conclusions
some were heretical and some erroneous and contrary to the determination of the church, as it will appear more clearly below.
And because we have learned by sufficient information that said
conclusions have been preached, as noted above, in many places
of our diocese aforesaid, and that certain persons have held and
taught some of them and are vehemently and notoriously suspect
of heresy, we have instituted the following processes, both general
and special.[2]

Wyclyf was not invited to attend the session.[3] The council's object
was not to try Wyclyf but rather to judge certain theories of which he
was thought to be the author. Courteney may have wished to avoid
the discouraging denouement that he had experienced at Lambeth
three years earlier;[4] it is even probable that the case of the hierarchy
versus Wyclyf had already been settled out of court.[5] Actually the
problem was not such a personal matter any longer; there were other
"Wyclyfs" to be silenced. Against these, as against Wyclyf himself in
the event his particular disposition had as yet not been arranged, it
would be easier to proceed once a formal condemnation of their
opinions and doctrines had been secured.

The council which met at Blackfriars comprised 8 bishops including
Courteney, 16 masters of theology, 14 doctors of canon and civil law,
and 6 bachelors of theology, besides John Blexham, the warden of
Merton Hall.[6] Of the 16 masters of theology, not including the bishop of

2. "Reg. Court.," fol. 25; Wilkins, 3, 157. See *Fas. Ziz.*, p. 272.

3. Netter makes the statement that Wyclyf was present when the Blackfriars
council condemned his theses (*Fas. Ziz.*, p. 283). There is no confirmation any-
where of this astonishing statement.

4. See above, p. 68.

5. See above, p. 72.

6. "Reg. Court.," fol. 25ᵛ; Wilkins, 3, 158. The *Fas. Ziz.* (pp. 286, 498) enumerates 10 bishops, adding the bishops of London and Lincoln. Though Shirley
writes of the Lambeth registers, "Their accuracy is not as great as might be expected from official copies" (*Fas. Ziz.*, p. lxxxii), I prefer the listings provided by

Nantes, 15 were friars—three Dominicans, four Franciscans, four Augustinians, and four Carmelites. The sixteenth was a monk of Ramsay. The 14 doctors of laws were seculars. Of the 37 members of the council who were not bishops, 21 were friars, one was a monk, and 15 were seculars. It is pertinent to mention this since Wyclyf dismissed the group as a "council of friars," [7] while Workman implies that "this excessive representation of friars" was part of Courteney's careful manipulation to assure a "hung jury." [8]

In rebuttal, it should be noted in the first place that the decision of this council, despite the presence of the 15 seculars, was unanimous in condemning the 24 propositions.[9] In the second place, while Wyclyf, to be sure, had alienated the friars by this time, he had hurled far more abusive invective at the monks, yet but one monk is listed as a member of the group. And in answer to Workman's statement that the secular members of the council were probably prejudiced against Wyclyf in view of the strictures he had leveled at priests who studied law or were employed in the civil service or were guilty of pluralism—on one or the other of which counts all of them were guilty [1]—it should suffice to remind the reader that Wyclyf was himself not free of censure on the last two points. As a matter of fact, Wyclyf would not have been able to meet the qualifications which Workman would lay down for membership on a council to try his own conclusions.

This, of course, does not deny that Courteney selected those whose "orthodoxy" was above question, while anyone with known sympathies for Wyclyf would surely not have been invited. The archbishop is himself witness to this fact.[2] Yet selecting is not quite the same as packing. Those clerics who were willing to go to the lengths that Wyclyf had by 1382—for example, on the doctrine of transubstantiation—were a small minority. Why should Courteney have been required to welcome several of Wyclyf's followers to share in passing judgment upon a matter of such fundamental significance, particularly since they were so few in number and were proposing a view so diametrically opposed

---

Courteney's register to those of Netter for this and for the subsequent meetings of the Blackfriars council. According to the latter, the number of those attending the various meetings of the council increased with every sitting. The opposite is what we should expect, and this is borne out by the figures furnished by the register. See below, p. 115, n. 6.

7. Arnold, *Select English Works*, 3, 503; *Trial.*, p. 374; *Fas. Ziz.*, pp. 283–4.
8. Workman, 2, 262.
9. "Reg. Court.," fols. 25, 26; Wilkins, 3, 157, 159; *Fas. Ziz.*, p. 276.
1. Workman, 2, 263–6.
2. See above, p. 89.

to that traditionally accepted at the time? That would be tantamount to suggesting that in the trial of criminals society have other criminals serve on the jury or leave itself open to the charge of packing.

Workman adds additional weight to his charge that Courteney packed the Blackfriars council by pointing out that the archbishop did not summon all the bishops of the Canterbury province. The inference is that had all the bishops sat in judgment upon Wyclyf's propositions the verdict would have been different.[3] The suggestion that any number of Roman bishops, in the 14th century or any other, would have accepted Wyclyf's views on the sacramental system, the priesthood, and transubstantiation is fanciful to say the least. No sinister motive need be read into the fact that only seven bishops sat with Courteney at Blackfriars. The presence of these particular seven—Rochester, Salisbury, Hereford, Winchester, Exeter, Durham, and Nantes—was probably due to nothing more reprehensible than geography or accident. The bishops of Rochester, Salisbury, Hereford, and Winchester had sees not far distant from London. Brantingham of Exeter may have been in London primarily to attend the meeting of Parliament,[4] as might have been the case with several of the other prelates. Bishop Fordham of Durham had been consecrated at Lambeth but four months previous and may have been "sitting in the synod as archdeacon of Canterbury."[5] It is difficult to account for the appearance of William Bottlesham, the bishop of Nantes, on the council except on the score of his accidental presence in London. In any event, the actual duty of examining and passing upon the propositions was chiefly, if not exclusively, that of the nonprelatical members of the council.[6] Since the bishops happened to be in the neighborhood of London, Courteney probably asked them to sit in with the council in order to lend impressiveness to its decisions.

The bishops, theologians, and canonists gathered at Blackfriars on May 17 as instructed. After the articles under question had been laid before them, Courteney directed the members of the council to scrutinize them carefully and to return in four days prepared to pass judgment upon their orthodoxy. From the language of the register and the *Fasciculi* it would appear that only the 24 propositions which were finally condemned were placed before the council for examination. It is possible, however, if not probable, that other views of Wyclyf which

3. Workman, 2, 253–4.

4. Parliament convened May 7. *Rot. Parl.*, 3, 122.

5. Workman, 2, 258.

6. In the subsequent meetings of the Blackfriars council the bishops are scarcely mentioned, that is, exclusive of the final session at Oxford. See below, p. 126.

were of doubtful orthodoxy were similarly investigated. Since the verdict of the Blackfriars council was unanimous, it may well have been that there were divided opinions on one or the other of Wyclyf's theories, with the consequence that they were not here officially condemned.[7]

The council reconvened four days later on May 21 [8] and took up the debate on the propositions shortly after breakfast. Though this time neither an emissary from the government nor any of Wyclyf's sympathizers intruded in order to interfere with the proceedings, the elements did. About two or three in the afternoon one of England's rare earthquakes, and a violent one,[9] shook the vicinity of London in such fashion that several bishops and other members of the council were for terminating the conference immediately. But the archbishop would have none of this. He warned them that they were not to be found wanting in the cause of the church, that the earthquake should not frighten them, that it was indeed a good omen, for it presaged the cleansing of the realm from heresy. "For as there are held in the bowels of the earth the air and spirit of infection, and which escape by means of some earthquake and so is the earth purified, but not without great violence, so there were previously buried in the hearts of the reprobate many heresies of which the realm has been cleansed after their condemnation, but not without travail and great effort." [1]

The council, thus reassured by the archbishop's analysis of the phenomenon, proceeded to examine the theses and reached unanimity that day on 24 propositions. Ten they declared heretical, 14 erroneous. Those adjudged to be heretical are the following:

1. That the substance of the material bread and wine remains in the sacrament of the altar after consecration.

7. See below, p. 132, for a possibly similar case with regard to Berton's decree.

8. Netter assigns the earthquake to the feast of St. Dunstan, May 19 (*Fas. Ziz.*, p. 272). While that date which specifies a saint's day may appear the more reliable (see Lorimer in Lechler, *John Wiclif and His English Precursors, 2,* 244 n. 46), the fact that the *Fasciculi* supposes the earthquake to have taken place on the same day as that on which the propositions were condemned, May 21 ("Reg. Court.," fol. 25; Wilkins, 3, 157), weakens its testimony to a considerable degree. Walsingham (*Hist. Angl., 2,* 67; *Chron. Angl.,* p. 351) and *William Thorne's Chronicle of St. Augustine's Abbey Canterbury* (p. 616) assign the earthquake to the twenty-first. The register makes no reference to the event.

9. In London chimneys rocked and pinnacles fell. See Workman, 2, 267.

1. *Fas. Ziz.,* pp. 272–3. Wyclyf's interpretation of the earthquake was as apt, though not so ingenious, as Courteney's. He described it rather as God's judgment upon the proceedings of the assembly *Trial.,* pp. 376–7.

2. That the accidents do not remain without the subject in the same sacrament after consecration.

3. That Christ is not in the sacrament of the altar identically, truly, and really, in his proper corporal presence.

4. That if a bishop or priest be in mortal sin, he may not ordain, consecrate, or baptize.

5. That if a man be truly contrite, all exterior confession is superfluous and unprofitable to him.

6. To declare obstinately that it is not established in the gospel that Christ ordained the mass.

7. That God must obey the devil.

8. That if the pope be a reprobate [2] and an evil man, and consequently a member of the devil, he has no power given him over faithful Christians from anyone, except perhaps from the emperor.

9. That after Urban VI, no one is to be received as pope, but every man should live after the manner of the Greeks, under his own laws.

10. To say it is contrary to holy scripture that ecclesiastical ministers may have temporal possessions.

The articles which the council adjudged erroneous are the following:

11. That no prelate may excommunicate anyone unless he already knows that he has been excommunicated by God.

12. That he who excommunicates in such a manner is for that reason himself a heretic or excommunicate.

13. That a prelate excommunicating a cleric who appeals to the king and the royal council, is thereby himself a traitor to God, to king, and country.

14. That those who leave off preaching or hearing the word of God or the gospel preached because of the excommunication of men, are excommunicated and in the day of judgement will be declared traitors of God.

15. To declare that it is lawful for anyone, even a deacon or priest, to preach the word of God without authorization either from the apostolic see or from a Catholic bishop or from any other authority of which there is sufficient proof.

2. The word is abbreviated in the Lambeth register and its identification is doubtful. Wilkins (3, 157) suggests "Perditus vel praescitus, i.e., in Dei praescientia reprobus." *Praescitus* is the reading in Walsingham (*Hist. Angl., 1,* 58; *Chron. Angl.,* p. 343) and Netter (*Fas. Ziz.,* p. 278). Foxe (3, 157) translates the word "reprobate."

16. To assert that no one can be a civil lord, bishop, or prelate while he is in mortal sin.

17. That temporal lords may, according to their discretion, take away the temporal goods from churchmen who are habitually delinquent or that the people may according to their pleasure discipline delinquent lords.

18. That tithes are pure alms and that parishioners may detain them because of the sins of their curates and may bestow them on others at their pleasure.

19. That special prayers applied to a particular person by prelates or religious are no more profitable to him than general prayers, everything else being equal.

20. That any man who enters any private religion is thereby rendered the more incapable and unfit to observe the commandments of God.

21. That holy men who have instituted any private religions, whether of the possessioners or mendicants, sinned in so doing.

22. That the religious living in private religions are not of the Christian religion.

23. That friars are bound to secure their living by the labor of their hands and not by begging.

24. That whoever gives alms to friars or to a preaching friar is excommunicated, as also he who accepts them.[3]

The first reaction to a perusal of the condemned theses is one of astonishment at how far Wyclyf had drifted since Gregory had sent his schedule of 19 theses to England in 1377, just five years before.[4] The ten propositions which the Blackfriars council declared heretical are not found among the earlier 19, although number 8 is largely a reaffirmation of numbers 14 and 15 of the earlier schedule. These ten involve a denial of such fundamental doctrines as transubstantiation, the Mass, the sacrament of penance, the primacy of the bishop of Rome, and the power of a divinely instituted priesthood to perform its

3. "Reg. Court.," fols. 25–25ᵛ; Wilkins, 3, 157–8. Walsingham (*Hist. Angl.*, 2, 58–9; *Chron. Angl.*, pp. 342–4) omits numbers 16 and 24. The *Fasciculi* (pp. 277–82, 493–7) lists the 24 with but slight variation from the reading in the Lambeth register. *Knighton* (2, 158–60) lists 9 heresies and 15 errors, counting number 10 as an error.

4. See above, pp. 49–50. "Whatever share old party feeling may have had in stirring Courteney's theological zeal, no archbishop . . . could safely have neglected to proceed against the author of opinions so profoundly at variance with the ecclesiastical, even more with the theological principles of the day." *Fas. Ziz.*, p. xliii.

proper functions regardless of the administrant's state of grace. This last doctrine had first appeared among the Donatists in the 4th century and had been resurrected more recently by the Albigensians and Waldensians. It is interesting to see that where Wyclyf had contented himself in 1377 with simply denouncing churchmen who misused their wealth he had found by 1382 that the Bible gave them not even the right to hold property; that where in 1377 he would have limited the pope's power of the keys to acts done in conformity with the law of Christ he would dispense in 1382 with the pope himself.

Of particular interest are propositions 16 and 17. They involved much more than an attack on the church. Here we find the implications of Wyclyf's doctrine of dominion now for the first time being extended to the temporal world. Thus, not only bishops in mortal sin but civil lords as well forfeited for the time their authority and power; just as the laity might deprive sinful churchmen of their property, so might the people punish their civil superiors, should these be wicked, in whatever manner they pleased.

But were these Wyclyf's views? Wyclyf says not all, for of the propositions condemned by the Blackfriars council "some are catholic and some are plainly heretical." This statement comes somewhat as a surprise, for one is tempted to make the easy assumption that any dubious doctrine which warranted examination by a learned group of theologians in England in 1382 must have emanated from Wyclyf. More in character is Wyclyf's charge that the friars in the council had persuaded the bishops to join them in maligning Christ, many saints, and even doctors of the church as heretics. Which theses Wyclyf disclaimed he does not say, but since he accused the group with writing their own particular views on the Eucharist, one may conclude that he was willing to accept authorship of those which dealt with that subject.[5]

The ecclesiastical authorities probably attributed all 24 theses to Wyclyf, although there is but one reference to that effect in the official account of the "process" taken against Lollardy in 1382. Archbishop Courteney described the propositions as those "which are said to be conclusions of Wyclyf" in his letter to Braybroke which the latter sent on to the bishop of Lincoln.[6] Since the original archiepiscopal mandate to Braybroke does not include that phrase, one suspects that the words were interpolated. On the other hand, the Council of Constance condemned 45 propositions as those of Wyclyf, and with these

5. See *Fas. Ziz.*, pp. 283–5.

6. *Knighton*, 2, 167. For Courteney's mandate to Braybroke, see below, p. 101.

were enumerated the 24 passed upon by the Blackfriars synod.[7]

An examination of the 24 theses and an attempt to validate them from Wyclyf's writings or statements positively ascribed to him will indicate that the view taken by the Council of Constance was substantially correct. Thus the position taken on the Eucharist in propositions 1, 2, and 3 Wyclyf confirms in the De Eucharistia.[8] Proposition number 4 voices the substance of number 9 of the views attributed to Wyclyf by Netter and here referred to as the "sententiary" list.[9] Substantiation for the view that Wyclyf was willing to subscribe to proposition number 5 can be found in several treatises.[1] While Wyclyf's interpretation of transubstantiation would have deprived the Mass of much of its essence—he even suggested that laymen might consecrate under certain circumstances—it is difficult to establish whether or not he would have accepted the validity of proposition 6.[2]

"That God must obey the devil," proposition number 7 of the Blackfriars list, was one of Wyclyf's proudest conclusions.[3] Proposition number 8 is partially involved in proposition 4, and it follows necessarily from Wyclyf's central thesis that dominion is founded upon grace. Proposition number 9 is substantiated by Wyclyf in the Trialogus.[4] Wyclyf could scarcely have subscribed to the validity of proposition 10 since he himself held temporal possessions. Proposition number 11 corresponds to proposition 9 of Gregory's schedule. Propositions 12, 13, and 14 are conclusions one might logically draw from Wyclyf's position on excommunication. Proposition number 15 was one which Wyclyf both preached and practiced. He had scarcely been authorized by Courteney to air his opinions in the churches of London in 1376[5] and since then had sent out a number of "poor priests" to disseminate his views thoroughout the realm. Proposition 16 corresponds to number 9 of the sententiary list. Proposition 17 reiterates the substance of propositions 6, 7, 17, and 18 of Gregory's list. Proposition 18 corresponds to number 13 of the sententiary list. Proposition 19 is confirmed by Wyclyf

7. See below, p. 153.

8. Euch., pp. 11–29, 51–2, 63 passim.

9. See above, p. 20.

1. See Workman, 2, 42, for references to Wyclyf's works.

2. Trial., pp. 283–5. He attacked the ceremonies of the Mass. See Netter, Doctrinale, 3, 197.

3. See Workman, 2, 268, and Poole, Illustrations of the History of Medieval Thought and Learning, p. 263, for a discussion of this thesis.

4. Trial., p. 446.

5. See above, p. 21. See also Netter, op. cit., 1, 618.

in one of his sermons.[6] Propositions 20 to 24 reflect Wyclyf's violent reaction to his earlier respect for the friars and probably expressed his own views on the subject.[7]

From the above analysis we may conclude that Wyclyf would have refused to acknowledge the validity of but one proposition, that one being number 10. He might also have rejected number 6, at least in the sense in which he interpreted the Mass. It is also probably true that propositions 16 and 17 in their threat to sinful lords and magistrates reflect less Wyclyf's conservative attitude than that of the more radical "poor priests," who were as much concerned with reforming society as he was with the church.

By the evening of May 21 Courteney had the formal statement of the Blackfriars council condemning the 24 theses to bolster his attack on Lollardy. By the evening of the twenty-sixth he had something more formidable, a parliamentary statute which required the chancellor to issue orders to the sheriffs and other officials of the realm to imprison any unauthorized preachers or those who might favor them, whenever a prelate should make such certification to the chancery. The statute read as follows:

> Forasmuch as it is notoriously known that there are divers wicked persons within said realm who go from county to county and from town to town, in certain habits and under pretense of great sanctity, and who without authorization of the holy father, the pope, or the ordinaries of the places, or other sufficient authority, preach daily, not only in the churches and churchyards, but also in markets, fairs, and other public places where there is a large congregation of people, various sermons containing notorious heresies and errors, to the serious corruption of the faith and the destruction of the laws and the estate of holy church, to the great peril of the souls of the people and of the whole realm of England; as is more plainly found and sufficiently proved before the reverend father in God, the archbishop of Canterbury, and the bishops and other prelates, and masters of divinity and doctors of canon and civil law, and a large part of the clergy of the said realm especially assembled for this purpose; and which persons do also preach various slanderous matters in order to sow discord and dissension among the different estates of said realm both temporal as well as spiritual, to the excitement of the people and the serious peril of the entire realm; which preachers, cited or

6. *Serm., 4,* 33; *Select English Works, 3,* 425.
7. See Workman, *2,* 103–4.

summoned before the ordinaries of the places there to give answer concerning that for which they are impeached, they do not obey their summons and decrees, nor respect their monitions or the censures of holy church, but expressly despise them; and, moreover, by their subtle words they attract and entice the people to hear their sermons, and they keep them in their errors by strong hand and great routs: it is ordained in this parliament that commissions of the king be directed to the sheriffs and other ministers of the king, or to other authorized persons, after and in accordance with the certification of the prelates thereof made in the chancery from time to time, to arrest all such preachers and their favorers, maintainers, and abetters, and to hold them arrested and in strong prison until they are willing to justify themselves according to reason and the law of holy church. And the king wills and commands that the chancellor make such commissions at all times that he shall be certified and thereto required by the prelates or any of them, as is described above.[8]

While the statute was aimed specifically at itinerant and unlicensed preachers, there was no obscuring the fact that the order had the spread of Lollardy particularly in mind. A month later, on June 26, the king issued a patent, upon Courteney's request, which corroborated the force of the statute. This patent read as follows:

Richard, by the grace of God king of England and France and lord of Ireland, to all to whom this letter shall come, greeting. Appealing to us, the venerable father William, archbishop of Canterbury, primate of all England, through his petition exhibited to us, we fully understand that very many conclusions, contrary to sound doctrine and notoriously redounding to the destruction of the catholic faith, of holy church, and his province, have been preached, privately and publicly, although damnably, in various places within said province; of which conclusions, indeed, after first holding good and mature deliberation thereon, were sententially and wholesomely declared, upon the common counsel of said archbishop, his suffragans, many doctors in theology, and of other clerks who were skilled in sacred scripture, to be condemned by the church, some as heretical, the others indeed, as erroneous. Concerning which matter it has been requested of us by the archbishop, that we see fit to interpose the arm of our royal power for the correction and just punishment of those who would henceforth preach or maintain

8. *Rot. Parl., 3,* 124–5.

with obstinate mind the aforesaid conclusions. We, inspired by zeal for the catholic faith, of which we are and ever wish in all matters to be the defenders, as is our duty, and unwilling to suffer such heresies or errors to be nourished in any manner whatsoever within the limits of our dominion, do grant and extend special authority and license, by these presents, to the aforesaid archbishop and his suffragans, that they arrest and commit to their own prisons or in others, as they choose, all and every person who shall preach or maintain, privately or publicly, the said conclusions thus condemned, wherever they can be apprehended, and to keep them there until they will have recovered their senses from the pravities of these errors and heresies, or until it will have been provided otherwise concerning those arrested by us or our council. We further charge and direct all and every of our liege men, ministers, and subjects, of whatever estate or condition they may be, upon the fidelity and allegiance by which they are bound to us, that they do not show favor to, counsel, or assist in any way those who maintain or preach said conclusions thus condemned, or their supporters, on pain of forfeiting all that they could forfeit to us in that event; but that they rather obey, comply with humbly and attend said archbishop and his suffragans and ministers in the execution of these presents; so that proper and open publication may be made without fear against said conclusions and their maintainers, as should be wholesomely done for the defense and preservation of the catholic faith.[9]

Workman declares this patent represented a major modification of the force of the statute and that it had been the indignation of the Commons which forced the king to issue this less stringent order.[1] Nothing could be further from the truth. The patent actually established a considerably more effective method for dealing with unauthorized preachers and those accused of heresy. In fact it is probable that Courteney appreciated the impracticability of the statute, at least as far as the itinerant "poor priest" was concerned, and therefore asked the king to issue this supplementary patent. The chief weakness in the statute, from the point of view of the church, was its proviso that the hierarchy work through the office of the chancery. A bishop had first to file a certification with the chancellor; then that official would issue the requisite commission to a sheriff to apprehend the person under

9. "Reg. Court.," fol. 31; Wilkins, 3, 156. See *Cal. of Pat. Rolls, 1381–85*, p. 150.
1. Workman, 2, 270.

suspicion. Thus, even though the chancellor and sheriff were cooperative, which might not always be the case, the process was time consum-
ing. It was also unworkable. For example, a bishop in a far-off diocese
would have to take his appeal to the chancellor at Westminster and
then wait for the chancery office to authorize the sheriff in his county
to make the necessary arrest. The suspect, if he had his wits about him,
could meantime conveniently step over into an adjoining county, thereby
necessitating a repetition of the entire process.

The patent, on the other hand, relieved the hierarchy of the need
for having recourse to the chancellor. They might seize and imprison
any unauthorized preacher or one suspected of heresy and hold him in
their own prisons or any other, presumably those maintained at public
expense, until he had made his submission to the ecclesiastical authorities or until the crown would have decided otherwise. Furthermore,
the sheriffs and other officials were strictly enjoined to assist the hierarchy in ferreting out and punishing such individuals. A refusal to do
so would leave the sheriff open to a charge of connivance with the
suspect, upon proof of which the patent authorized the confiscation of
his property. Incidentally, concerning the hand which Workman believes Commons had in the issuance of the patent, he himself admits
that the influence of that body over religious matters in the 14th century
"was still vague and doubtful." [2] There was nothing vague and doubtful
about the pressure Commons could exert in that century a month after
it had disbanded. In an era of no political parties and no system of
communication worthy of the name, Commons simply did not exist
when it was not in session. And it should not be forgotten that the king
explicitly stated in his patent that he was issuing it at the request of
the archbishop, who would hardly have asked that the force of the recent statute be moderated.

Confident now that there would be no interference from any quarter
such as had paralyzed the plans of the prelates at St. Paul's and Lambeth, Courteney proceeded to go on the offensive against Lollardy.
On May 30 he issued a mandate to Bishop Braybroke of London, the
instructions of which he in turn was to send without delay to all the
suffragans of the province, directing them to publish three times in
every church of their respective dioceses the prohibition against preaching, teaching, or holding the condemned theses or listening to or showing favor toward one so doing, under pain of excommunication. Each
bishop was to serve as his own diocesan inquisitor and personally direct
the work of suppressing the heresies. The mandate read as follows:

2. *Ibid.,* p. 269.

William, by divine permission archbishop of Canterbury, primate of all England, and legate of the apostolic see, to our venerable brother Robert, by the grace of God bishop of London, greetings and fraternal charity in the Lord. The prelates of the church should concern themselves all the more vigilantly about the protection of the Lord's flock committed to their care when they know that wolves inside, but dressed outwardly in sheep's clothing, treacherously go about to attack and scatter the sheep. Truly according to common cry and universal knowledge, which we speak of with sorrow, word has come to us that, even though according to canonical sanctions no one having been prohibited or not sent may usurp, publicly or privately, the office of preaching without authorization from the apostolic see or the bishop of the place, some sons of eternal damnation, nevertheless, brought to mental madness, assume for themselves the right to preach under pretense of great sanctity and are not afraid to affirm, teach dogmatically and generally, commonly, and publicly preach, in both churches and streets, as well as in many other profane places of our said province, certain propositions and conclusions listed below, heretical, erroneous, and false, condemned by the church of God and repugnant to the determinations of holy church, which threaten to subvert and weaken the status of the whole church and of our province of Canterbury, as well as the tranquillity of the realm, infecting therewith many of Christ's faithful and unfortunately causing them to deviate from the catholic faith, without which there is no salvation.

Wherefore, realizing that so pernicious an evil, which could attack very many souls to kill them by its lethal contagion, we might not, as we will not, by dissimulation ignore, lest their blood be required at our hands, but wishing rather to extirpate it as far as it is permitted us from above, with the counsel and consent of very many of our brethren and suffragans, we have called together many doctors of holy theology and professors of canon and civil law, as well as other clerks, whom we believed to be the most renowned and learned in the country, and most holy in catholic faith, that they give their judgement and opinion concerning said conclusions. But because, after said conclusions and assertions had been openly expounded and diligently examined in our presence and that of our fellow-brethren, it was at length found and with our counsel and that of every member of the council declared, that some of those conclusions were heretical, some indeed erroneous, and repugnant to the determinations of the church, as they are below described: we charge and command your fraternity, in virtue of holy obedience firmly enjoining, that you in turn instruct with as much speed as possible all and each of our brethren, co-bishops and suffragans of our church of Canterbury, as we instruct them and each of them and you; that each of them in his cathedral church and all others of his city and diocese and you in your cathedral and in the remaining churches of your diocese, do admonish and inhibit, as we by the tenor of these presents do admonish and strictly warn you, once, twice, thrice, assigning for the first monition one day, for the second another day, and for the third monition, canonical and peremptory, another day, that no man henceforth, of whatever estate or condition, hold, teach, preach, or defend said heresies or errors or any of them, nor that he admit to preach anyone who is prohibited or not sent or of whose right there is some doubt, nor that he hear or listen to anyone preaching these heresies or errors, or any of them, or that he favor him or adhere to him in public or in secret; but that he immediately flee and shun him as a serpent spitting forth venomous poison, under pain of the greater excommunication, which we by these presents pronounce, for now as for then, upon all and each one who is defiant in this matter and who will not obey our monitions, after those three days have elapsed which are assigned for canonical monition, their delay, fault, and offense preceding and that justly requiring; and we peremptorily command that what pertain to them and to you, that it be fulminated by each of our fellow-brethren and suffragans in his city and diocese and by you in yours. We further wish and direct that all and each of our fellow-brethren be admonished by you on our part, by the sprinkling of the blood of Jesus Christ, and we similarly admonish you that, in accordance with the institutes of sacred canons, each of them serve as inquisitor of heretical pravity in his city and diocese, as you do in like fashion in yours, that they and you solicitously and diligently make inquiries concerning such presumptuous persons, and they proceed effectually against them according to the obligations of their office, and you in like fashion, to the praise and honor of the name of the crucified, and for the salvation of the orthodox faith.[3]

3. "Reg. Court.," fols. 25v–26; Wilkins, 3, 158–9. For the letter of the bishop of Lincoln to the officials of his diocese, in which he relayed Courteney's instructions, see *Knighton*, 2, 164–8.

Braybroke lost no time in publishing the archbishop's mandate. On the very day on which it was officially issued, May 30, he headed a long procession which wound its way through the streets of London. The procession had been ordered some time before by the archbishop to be held throughout the province as an act of expiation that God might alleviate the virulence of the plague then raging in England.[4] Both laity and clergy who took part in the procession did so in their bare feet. When the procession had finished its course, a former disputant of Wyclyf, the Carmelite John Cunningham, formally read the archbishop's mandate together with the 24 theses which had been condemned.[5]

Nowhere throughout the province of Canterbury were there any immediate repercussions to the reading of the archbishop's mandate— except at Oxford. And there, before that vigorous little community had again settled down to something like composure, both Courteney and crown had repeatedly to intervene.

On May 28 Courteney sent a mandate, similar to the one he issued two days later to Braybroke, to Peter Stokes, a Carmelite friar at Oxford. The archbishop selected Stokes to be his commissioner in this matter rather than Robert Rigg, the chancellor, as much for the former's zeal in combatting the spread of Lollardy[6] as for the latter's negligence in condoning it.[7] Courteney instructed Stokes to read the list of the 24 theses which the Blackfriars council had condemned and to warn all "that no one, of whatever rank or condition, should hold, teach, preach, or defend in the future in the university of Oxford the aforesaid heresies or errors or any of them, neither in the schools or outside, publicly or in secret, or to listen to anyone preaching any of them, or to show him favour or adhere to him, publicly or in secret, but that he should immediately flee and avoid such as a serpent emitting pestiferous venom, under pain of the greater condemnation . . ."[8] Stokes was directed to read the condemnation of the theses on the feast of Corpus Christi "before the sermon of Philip."[9]

This Philip was Philip Repingdon whom the chancellor of the university, Rigg, had appointed to preach the sermon on the feast of

4. *Reg. Brantyngham*, *1*, 464–5.

5. *Knighton*, *2*, 162–3.

6. "quem novit prae ceteris laborasse contra Lollardos, et sectae Wyclyff restitisse . . ." *Fas. Ziz.*, p. 297.

7. See below, p. 106, for Courteney's letter to Rigg in which he reminds him of his questionable behavior.

8. *Fas. Ziz.*, p. 277. For the mandate, see *ibid.*, pp. 275–82.

9. *Ibid.*, p. 297. Corpus Christi fell on June 5.

Corpus Christi. This was no mean honor, particularly since Repingdon was still not a doctor.[1] What made the selection of Repingdon especially significant, however, was the fact that Philip was one of Wyclyf's stanchest admirers. The "catholics" at Oxford at least considered the appointment of Repingdon highly irregular, and lest he "air on that occasion some errors in defense of Wyclyf" they appealed to Courteney to arrange to have the condemnation of the theses published prior to Repingdon's sermon.[2] Such was the background of Courteney's instructions to Stokes that he make his announcement just preceding the sermon of the day.

It was probably Stokes who had been the spokesman of these "catholics" in their appeal to the archbishop, and in doing so he must have given point to his fears by reminding Courteney how Nicholas Hereford, another well-known Lollard, had just a few days before been privileged to preach the most important sermon of the entire year, that on Ascension Day.[3] Stokes had been battling Hereford the whole year, both in lecture and sermon, and he had even appointed notaries to keep records of what Hereford said. In his Ascension Day sermon Hereford had "preached much that was abominable and detestable . . . exciting the people to insurrection, and excusing and defending Wycclyff." [4]

Two items might be noted before going on with the account: first, that Rigg gave Hereford, one of Wyclyf's disciples, the honor of preaching on Ascension Day over the protest of "other doctors whom he expelled"; [5] second, that Courteney did not see fit to countermand the selection of Repingdon as the preacher for the feast of Corpus Christi even though he had ample time in which to do so. That Courteney did not interfere might be attributed to his fear lest such action antagonize even that element in the university which opposed Wyclyf. How sensitive the university was on the score of outside interference had been revealed several years before when the community had pondered whether to receive or ignore Gregory's bull.[6] The archbishop may also have considered such a risk unnecessary in view of the fact that before Repingdon would begin his sermon his own mandate in condemnation of the preaching of Wyclyf's theses would be read.

1. "etiam antequam fuit doctor; et aliis doctoribus negavit." *Ibid.*, p. 306.
2. *Ibid.*, p. 297.
3. Courteney referred to the occasion as the "most eminent and worthy" of the year. *Ibid.*, p. 298.
4. *Ibid.*, p. 296. The sermon was in English (*ibid.*, p. 306).
5. *Ibid.*
6. See above, p. 62.

But Courteney must have entertained some misgivings in the matter, for two days after sending his mandate to Stokes he addressed a personal missive to Rigg, which read as follows:

> In Christ, son, we wonder not a little and are disturbed, that even though that Master Nicholas Herford is notoriously suspect concerning sermons and the doctrine of heretical and erroneous conclusions, as we recall having brought to your attention at another time, you have since then shown such favor to him, that you have assigned the most excellent and worthy sermon of the year in your university, which, as you know, was appointed to you as chancellor for the time, to this same Nicholas to preach at that time, without any hesitation whatsoever. We, therefore, counsel and admonish you, in the bowels of Jesus Christ, that in the future you do not presume to show favor to such like, lest you appear to be one of their sect and number, and hence make it necessary for us to exercise the duty of our office against you. Inasmuch as against the audacity of these arrogant ones our lord, the king, and the chiefs of the realm have promised, for the furtherance of our process, so to assist us and our suffragans, that, by the grace of God, they will not much longer hold sway, and that you may learn to abhor the society and erroneous opinions of such presumers, you will be careful to give vigorous support to my dear friend, brother Peter Stokes, professor of holy scripture, of the order of Carmelites, in the publication of the letter we have sent him for the defense of catholic faith against these conclusions; and you will have that letter effectually published in the theological schools of said university by the beadle of that faculty in the next lecture to be delivered there, without the slightest alteration, notifying us instantly in reply what you will have done in this matter.[7]

Neither Courteney's positive command nor the reminder that the crown was equally concerned about the growth of Lollardy had any effect upon Rigg. Instead of assisting Stokes in carrying out the archbishop's instructions, the chancellor upbraided him and sought to turn the university against him. He accused him of having acted in a manner detrimental to the liberties and privileges of the institution, "and he declared that nether bishop nor archbishop had any authority over the university, even in a question of heresy." Despite his bluster, however, he felt sufficiently concerned to discuss the matter with the proctors,

7. *Fas. Ziz.*, pp. 298–9.

with the result that he publicly announced that he would cooperate with Stokes.[8]

But Rigg's avowal was hardly borne out by his actions. Netter is our chief authority for what followed:

> he opposed him as much as he could by assembling many armed men against him, around a hundred, with hauberks and swords, either to kill or to oppose Peter [Stokes] should the latter attempt anything. And he even got the mayor on his side by telling him to have a hundred armed men ready against Peter the Carmelite. So with the mayor and his proctors, and his other confederates, he proceeded to the sermon.
>
> And in this sermon Master Philip Repyndon aroused the people to insurrection and to despoiling the churches. And he defended and favored Master John Wycclyff in all things when he preached, among other things, that in sermons temporal lords should be recommended before pope or bishops, and who recommends not in that manner acts contrary to holy scripture. And many other opprobrious things did he say concerning the estates and different persons. And among other things he mentioned how the Lord Duke of Lancaster was very favourably inclined and was ready to protect all the Lollards, whom he even called holy priests.[9]

The high point of Repingdon's sermon was his description of Wyclyf as a "doctor eminently catholic," which compliment he followed up with the assertion that "Wycclyff had never lectured or taught differently concerning the material of the sacrament of the altar than what the whole church of God believes, and that his opinion concerning the sacrament of the altar was most true . . ."[1] After the sermon everyone filed into St. Frideswyde's, Repingdon in the company of 20 men with arms concealed under their gowns. Stokes, in fear lest they intended to attack him, did not venture to leave the church after the services; but Repingdon waited for the chancellor at the door, and to-

8. *Ibid.*, p. 299.

9. *Ibid.*, pp. 299–300. Workman (2, 275–6) forces the following account out of this excerpt in the *Fasciculi*: "This attack on its liberties set Oxford on fire. . . . Wyclyf had united bishops and friars in an alliance against himself; this brought about the equally strange alliance of town and gown in his favour. The whole city was in an uproar. One hundred armed men came to the support of the chancellor—whether students or citizens we are not told." Courteney, on information probably supplied by Stokes, charged Rigg with organizing this demonstration. See below, p. 109.

1. *Fas. Ziz.*, p. 307.

gether they walked away in high good humor. "Great was the joy of the Lollards at such a sermon." [2]

The morning after found Rigg somewhat less confident. Before the full congregation of the university he sought to excuse himself to Stokes for having failed to assist him in publishing Courteney's mandate the preceding day before Repingdon's sermon as he had been directed. He explained that he had had no official sealed document so instructing him. Thus he did not consider sufficiently impelling the letter addressed to him by the archbishop which Stokes had handed him in person the day before the feast of Corpus Christi, together with a copy of his commission. So when Stokes countered this lame apology by producing forthwith the archbishop's mandate under Courteney's private seal, Rigg protested his readiness to facilitate the publication of the mandate, contingent, however, upon the approval of the university. [3]

Stokes was not reassured by Rigg's promise to consult with the university and that very evening sent an account of what had happened to the archbishop. Part of this he put down in writing, but that which he felt would be safer left unwritten he entrusted orally to the messenger to relay to Courteney. He begged Courteney to interpose immediately for he could no nothing further for fear of his life. [4]

The following Tuesday (June 10), however, Stokes did summon up sufficient courage to attempt a rebuttal of Hereford's statement—that temporal lords should be recommended before pope or bishop. His courage soon melted away, though, when he caught sight of the weapons which 12 men had poorly concealed beneath their gowns, and he believed that he would be murdered before he got down from his chair. To his great relief a letter reached him that day from Courteney which ordered him to report immediately in person. [5]

The next morning, accordingly, found Stokes happily shaking the dust of Oxford from his feet. He reached London that night and presented himself to the archbishop at Lambeth early the following morning (June 12). In the course of the discussion of the events of the past week, the archbishop must have informed Stokes that Rigg had already put in an appearance but that he had refused to "hear his excuses" until the following day when the Blackfriars council would reconvene. Rigg may have received a direct summons from Courteney, although there

2. *Ibid.*, p. 300.
3. *Ibid.*, p. 301.
4. *Ibid.*, pp. 300–1.
5. *Ibid.*, p. 302. Stokes must have been a timorous soul, a weakness his opponents exploited. This last episode, at any rate, has all the marks of a practical joke.

is no record of this in the *Fasciculi*. What probably happened was that when Rigg learned that Stokes had been ordered to report back to the archbishop, he concluded that his only salvation lay in hurrying to Lambeth in the hope of getting the archbishop's ear first.[6]

This second meeting of the council convened on June 12. Attending the archbishop were the bishop of Winchester and, besides the original nonprelatical members, 12 additional scholars.[7] Listed among these latter 12 was the name of Robert Rigg, but he appeared less as a jury-man than as a defendant. He and two proctors of the university, Thomas Brightwell and John Lawndreyn,[8] were charged before the council with having favored the heresies and errors of Repingdon, Hereford, and Wyclyf. The specific charges were: that they had failed to silence Hereford when he defended his own views and those of Wyclyf against the religious doctors; that they had not censured Hereford for declar-ing in a sermon before the entire community that no regular could take a degree at the university without apostatizing, even though this statement was in defiance of the customs and statutes of the university; that the chancellor had appointed Hereford and Repingdon to preach the sermons of Ascension Day and Corpus Christi respectively, despite the fact that they were well-known disciples of Wyclyf, and that he had expelled those doctors who had objected to Hereford's appointment; that he not only had refused to assist Stokes in publishing the arch-bishop's mandate condemning the 24 theses, in spite of personal instruc-tions from Courteney, but had prevented Stokes from doing so and had assembled many students and laymen to prevent him from doing so should he have attempted this; that he had approved of Repingdon's sermon; that instead of reprimanding one William James, regent in the arts, who, seeking to justify Wyclyf's views on the Eucharist, had declared that there was no idolatry except in the sacrament of the altar, Rigg had rather commended him and said approvingly, "Now you speak as a philosopher"; and finally, that "the chancellor, proctors, and the greater part of the regents in the arts, were not friendly nor kindly disposed toward the doctors who argued against Nicholas Hereford

6. Rigg reached London "either on that Sunday [June 8] or on Monday, or on Saturday" (*ibid.*, p. 304).

7. There is some question of whether the original members, especially the bishops, were present at this second meeting of the Blackfriars council. Netter (*Fas. Ziz.*, p. 288) says they were. The register mentions specifically the bishop of Winchester, which would appear to rule out the presence of the other prelates. See "Reg. Court.," fols. 26ᵛ, 28; Wilkins, 3, 159, 161.

8. The register (fol. 26ᵛ) supplies Brightwell's name, the *Fasciculi* (p. 288) that of Lawndreyn.

and Philip Repyngdon, but very hostile to them, although they had earlier been friends, and for no other reason than because they had contradicted them. For which reason it appears that they believed the same as did Nicholas and Philip." [9]

After Rigg and his proctors had been thus accused of being "vehemently" under suspicion, the chancellor and his companion Thomas Brightwell, a secular doctor and likewise an admirer of Wyclyf, were interrogated concerning the 24 condemned theses. Rigg capitulated without a struggle and agreed that the theses had been condemned with justice. Brightwell demurred, and only after being diligently examined by the archbishop in person did he also agree to endorse the condemnation. The other proctor similarly hesitated at first but at length declared himself in agreement with Rigg and Brightwell that the theses were heretical and erroneous.[1] To the charge of contempt for having ignored Courteney's letter, Rigg had no better recourse than to throw himself on his knees and beg the archbishop's pardon. This was granted him upon the intercession of Bishop Wykeham.[2]

Courteney then handed Rigg his letters patent, after first having the contents read aloud. These contained the directions he was to carry out in dealing with Lollardy at the university. The mandate read as follows:

> We charge and command you, firmly enjoining, that you publish and cause through others to be published, clearly, plainly, and without curious implication of terms, both in the vulgar as well as in the Latin, to the clergy and people, in the church of St. Mary at Oxford, on those days when it is customary for a sermon to be preached there, and in the schools of said university on lecture days, that those conclusions, heretical and erroneous and repugnant to the determination of the church, have been and are, as noted above, so condemned, which by this letter we so declare to be condemned; furthermore, that you inhibit and canonically admonish and cause to be inhibited and admonished, as we, by the tenor of these presents, do inhibit and admonish, once, twice, and thrice, and peremptorily, that no one for the future hold, teach, preach, or defend, in the schools or outside, the heresies or errors aforesaid, or any of them, even under sophistical cavilling; nor to admit to preach, hear, or hearken to John Wycliff, Nicholas Hereford, Philip Rappyngdon, canon regular, or John Aston or Lawrence

9. *Fas. Ziz.*, pp. 304–8.
1. "Reg. Court.," fol. 26ᵛ; Wilkins, 3, 159.
2. *Fas. Ziz.*, p. 308.

Bedeman, who are vehemently and notoriously suspect of heresy, or any of them so suspect or defamed, or to favor them publicly or in secret, but rather immediately flee and avoid, as a serpent spitting pestiferous poison; and, moreover, we suspend said suspects from every scholastic act until they will have purged their innocence in this matter before us; and that you announce publicly that they have been and are so by us suspended; and that you cause to have faithful and diligent search made concerning their favorers through all the halls of the said university; and when you shall have information concerning their names and persons, that you compel them all and each of them to abjure these their excesses by whatever ecclesiastical censures and other canonical punishments and under pain of the greater excommunication, which against all and each one who will be defiant in this matter and will not obey our monitions, their fault, deceit, or offense requiring in this regard, after the third monition which we consider canonical in this case, we now as well as then, and then as well as now, do pronounce by these presents, reserving the absolution of all and each who will incur, God forbid, this sentence pronounced by us, especially to ourselves. And we exhort you, chancellor, by the sprinkling of the blood of Jesus Christ, that in the future you so employ your greatest efforts that the clergy and people who are subject to you, if there are any deviating from the catholic faith, that they be recovered from this error, to the praise and honor of the name of the crucified and the preservation of the orthodox faith. And what you will have done in regard to the above, and concerning the manner and form of the process you will undertake in this regard, you will certify to us, when you are required on our authority, clearly and distinctly, by your letters patent, having the tenor hereof.[3]

The archbishop next gave Rigg a monitory letter in which he told him that he was under suspicion as one who had proved receptive to the condemned conclusions; that he should no longer discriminate against those in his community who opposed the group which favored Wyclyf; that he should prohibit the teaching of the condemned heresies and errors in the university; finally, that he must suspend Wyclyf, Hereford, Repingdon, Aston, and Bedeman. The monition read as follows:

whereas we have learned on the testimony of trustworthy persons and from experience of the fact, that you, Master Robert Rygge,

3. "Reg. Court.," fols. 26ᵛ–27; Wilkins, 3, 159–60.

chancellor of said university, have been somewhat inclined and even yet incline to the aforesaid conclusions thus condemned, and whom we hold suspect in this regard, that you intend actually to annoy in many ways those clerks so assembled and others who adhere or favor us in this matter, as it is incumbent upon them that they do so adhere and favor, on that very pretext by your crafty devices; you, Master Robert, said chancellor, we admonish once, twice, and thrice, and peremptorily, that you do not annoy, obstruct, or molest, judicially or extra-judicially, publicly or in secret, the said clerks, secular or regular, or those who favor them in these matters in their scholastic acts, or in that case in any other way whatsoever, nor cause or arrange, directly or indirectly, by yourself or another, to have annoyed, obstructed, or molested, or, in as far as you are able, to permit them to be so annoyed; and that for the future you permit no one in said university to hold, teach, preach, or defend the above heresies or errors or any of them in the schools or outside; nor also that you admit to preach John Wycliff, Nicholas Hereford, Philipp Rappyngdon, canon regular, John Ashton, or Lawrence Bedeman, who are vehemently and notoriously under suspicion of heresy, or any other person so suspected or defamed, but those whom we have suspended from every scholastic act until they will have purged their innocence in this regard before us, you will denounce as being so suspended by us, under pain of the greater excommunication . . ."[4]

After handing Rigg these two mandates, Courteney again raised the matter of his failure to assist Stokes in publishing the original mandate. This time, probably by way of afterthought, Rigg defended his failure on the grounds that to have done so would have endangered his life. To this Courteney replied, "Therefore is the university a patron of heresies, since she does not permit catholic truths to be published."[5]

But there remained more gall for Rigg to swallow. Courteney, who must have been a good judge of character, entertained some suspicions

4. "Reg. Court.," fol. 27ᵛ; Wilkins, 3, 160; *Fas. Ziz.*, pp. 309–11. The *Fasciculi* reverses the order in which the archbishop gave Rigg the two letters. Manning (7, 494) is in error when he writes that Wyclyf and the others were to clear themselves before the chancellor rather than the archbishop himself. Since Rigg was a Wyclyf sympathizer, this would have been a simple process. Manning's error can be traced to Shirley's inaccurate transcription of the Latin phrase *coram nobis*. The Lambeth register reads *coram nobis*, and as such did Wilkins transcribe it. Had Shirley noted that the archbishop consistently used the second person singular in referring to Rigg, he would not have confused the *n* in nobis for a *v*.

5. *Fas. Ziz.*, p. 311.

concerning the sincerity of Rigg's submission. He accordingly arranged to have him appear before the privy council on the following day (June 13), to receive a personal warning from the chancellor, Richard le Scrope, to carry out the archbishop's instructions. A much chastened Rigg made his way back to Oxford on June 14, and on the following day, Sunday, he duly published the archbishop's mandate. But he still had some fight in him, for in the course of announcing the contents of the mandate he interpolated sundry unauthorized comments, thereby fanning into a blaze the smoldering antagonism between seculars and regulars in the university.[6] The seculars charged the regulars with attempting to destroy the university. They must have had the better of the battle, for many of the regulars "feared for their lives."[7]

Two of the leading seculars at Oxford, however—Hereford and Repingdon, both disciples of Wyclyf—did not take part in this controversy, for no sooner had they learned from Rigg that they were suspended than they hastened to London to lay their case before the duke of Lancaster. They were confident that he would come to their assistance, as Repingdon, in fact, had publicly declared he would less than two weeks before in his now famous Corpus Christi sermon.[8] Oddly enough, their appeal to the duke came just five months after the friars had taken their own grievances against the Lollards to Gaunt.[9] The facts that the duke had ignored the appeal of the friars and that he had consistently befriended Wyclyf inspired optimism in the breasts of the two men.[1]

The duke's ego, already gratified by these appeals, was further inflated the next morning when a delegation of doctors of theology was announced. They had come to elicit his assistance against heretics, so they declared. Though the *Fasciculi* is not specific, it must have been Repingdon and Hereford whom the doctors had in mind. These two, at any rate, had been accepting the duke's hospitality since the preceding day, during which time they had attempted to convince him that the condemnation of the 24 theses would lead to the "destruction and

6. The passage in the *Fasciculi* (p. 311), "Et venit Oxoniam, et in Dominica sequenti publicavit suum mandatum; et sic tunc excitavit seculares contra religiosos . . . ," lends itself to this interpretation. Such annotating is what we would expect of Rigg, particularly in view of his subsequent treatment of Crump. See below, p. 122.

7. *Fas. Ziz.*, p. 311.

8. See above, p. 107.

9. See above, p. 84.

1. According to *Knighton* (2, 193), the duke had intervened to save the Lollard Swinderby from burning at the stake just shortly before.

weakening of the temporal dominion and of temporal kings." The doctors found him "so informed" when they came to state their case.[2] The fur began to fly as "Nicholas and Philip forced their way in amongst them as veritable Satans." At first the duke "showed the catholic masters a countenance and words tolerably harsh, but after having heard the other side, the lord duke denounced the aforesaid Philip and Nicholas as laymen or devils;[3] and then he heard plainly how detestable was their opinion on the sacrament of the altar, and on that score he called them odious." The duke then proceeded personally to give them a lecture on the Eucharist, forbidding "any doctor to answer them," and he did this so eloquently that "they had nothing to add." When next the condemned theses were read to him "he realized that they [Repingdon and Hereford] had told him falsities, and so he reckoned them liars, and ordered them to accept the regulation of the archbishop."[4]

Repingdon and Hereford thereupon betook themselves somewhat "abashed" to the archbishop. They had been instructed to appear the following morning, Wednesday (June 18), when the Blackfriars council would reconvene. This they did in company with another Oxford Lollard, John Aston. None of the three was prepared to make an unequivocal statement in support of the condemnation of the 24 propo-

2. If Repingdon and Hereford were able to persuade the duke that the condemnation of the theses would be a blow to the state, it could only have been that the duke was unaware of conclusions 16 and 17 and that the two men had left him in the dark.

3. "judicavit dominus dux praedictos Philippum et Nicolaum laicos, vel demoniacos . . ." (*Fas. Ziz.*, p. 318). The duke must have meant that they were no better than unlettered laymen. He was himself one of the laity but far from unlettered in his own opinion.

4. *Ibid.* There is some confusion if not inaccuracy in the *Fasciculi* concerning the chronological sequence of the movements of Repingdon and Hereford. They presumably spent most of Monday (June 16) and Tuesday with the duke, for the delegation of doctors of theology found them there on the seventeenth. Since it is not likely that they just stumbled in on the archbishop while he was presiding at the third session of the Blackfriars group (see below, p. 114) one may assume that they went to the archiepiscopal office the evening of the seventeenth and were told to appear the next morning (Wednesday) at the meeting of the council. This interpretation accords with the account in the *Fasciculi* if the word *sextam* on the second last line of p. 318 is changed to *quartam*. And that is actually what the scribe intended to write. For on the next page, he goes on to refer to *XII. kalendas Junii* as a subsequent date, even though *diem quartam* and *XII. kalendas Julii* were one and the same day. I write *Julii* for *Junii*, for there is no question that the scribe slipped in writing the latter. Had Shirley taken a little more time to unravel the difficulty, he would not have suggested *die* for *Kal.*, for that is no improvement over the original reading (*Ibid.*, p. 289 n. 2). These events took place on June 18 not 14. See "Reg. Court.," fols. 27v–28; Wilkins, 3, 160–1.

sitions. Hereford and Repingdon requested a copy of the theses and a day for deliberation in which to prepare a written answer. This the court granted them with the reminder, however, that their apology was to be free of "sophistical words and disputations." Aston refused the proffered respite but gave his promise at once to maintain silence on the articles in question. This did not satisfy the archbishop, and he forbade Aston ever to preach again within the limits of the province of Canterbury without his permission. When further questioning revealed the fact that Aston had been aware all the time of the prohibition against unauthorized preaching but had simply ignored it, he was ordered to present himself with Repingdon and Hereford on June 20, two days later, to show cause why he should not be condemned.[5]

When the council reconvened at Blackfriars on the twentieth, all three—Repingdon, Hereford, and Aston—were present, together with another suspect, Thomas Hilman, bachelor of divinity.[6] Repingdon and Hereford presented a long written defense in which they explained their positions on each of the 24 conclusions in sequence. Concerning the first proposition, "That the substance of the material bread and wine remains in the sacrament of the altar after consecration," they wrote, "in a sense contrary to the decretal *Firmiter Credimus*, we concede to be a heresy." In a similarly qualified fashion they accepted the condemnation of six other conclusions. They gave unqualified approval to the judgment of the Blackfriars council on ten theses, therein showing that they were not prepared to follow quite the radical course Wyclyf or other Lollards were treading. Of the condemnation of seven other theses their slightly qualified acceptance was not considered of essential importance. In conclusion they made the archbishop the following solemn protest:

> These things, reverend father and lord, are said in humility, with your gracious forbearance and benign correction, as much as at present the measure and meagerness of our faculties will allow, saving always and in all things the honor of God, the verity of

5. "Reg. Court.," fol. 28; Wilkins, 3, 161.

6. "Reg. Court.," fols. 29ᵛ–30; Wilkins, 3, 161–2. There is a major discrepancy in the figures the *Fasciculi* and the register provide for this session of the Blackfriars council. Netter declares that 10 bishops, 30 doctors of theology, 16 doctors of law, 13 bachelors of theology, and 4 or more bachelors of canon and civil law were on hand (*Fas. Ziz.*, p. 319). The register lists but 10 doctors of theology and 6 doctors of civil law. Since this latter list of theologians includes the name of the bishop of Nantes, one might conclude that no other bishops were present. This appears the more probable. The session was not sufficiently significant to warrant the presence of so many prelates.

faith, and a true conscience; beseeching you as humbly as we are able that if it should appear to your discretion and excellency that we should have said something else or in a different manner, your gracious paternity will vouchsafe to inform us, as sons, through holy scripture, the determinations of the church, or the statements of the holy doctors. And verily, with the most ready and obedient hearts, shall we submit to your more wholesome doctrine.[7]

Courteney and his council cross-examined Repingdon and Hereford on the seven theses to which their replies had been considered evasive. These were numbers 1, 2, 3, 6, 11, 19, and 24.[8] Hereford was so convinced of the orthodoxy of thesis number 7, "That God must obey the devil," that he protested his willingness to defend it "under penalty of fire."[9] They were also interrogated concerning thesis 4, even though they had given unqualified approval to its condemnation. The archbishop had a suspicion that their endorsement might have been subject to some mental reservation, so they were asked whether a person in mortal sin could be a bishop or priest. They answered that he could as far as his power was concerned.[1] With this answer the council was content, but they found the position of the two defendants on four of the propositions—numbers 1, 2, 3, and 6—to be "insufficient, heretical, and subtle" and their answers to numbers 19 and 24 as "insufficient, erroneous, and perverse." Courteney then ordered them to make a clear and unequivocal declaration concerning these six propositions. Upon their refusal to modify their answers in any way, they were dismissed with instructions to present themselves again on June 27 wherever the archbishop might then happen to be to receive their sentences.[2]

With John Aston events took a different turn. He had failed to prepare a written apology, an omission which might be attributed to the confidence he felt in his powers of persuasion for he had considerable experience as an itinerant preacher.[3] His demeanor toward his in-

---

7. "Reg. Court.," fol. 29; Wilkins, *3*, 162; *Fas. Ziz.*, p. 162.

8. The Lambeth register enumerates the twentieth conclusion instead of the nineteenth in one place (fol. 29) but corrects itself eight lines below (the third line from the bottom of fol. 29).

9. Hereford's name is given by Netter (*Fas. Ziz.*, p. 328). The register describes the incident but omits the name. The conclusions as listed in the defense of Repingdon and Hereford do not follow in quite the same sequence as those condemned by the first meeting of the Blackfriars council. Number 7 of the original list corresponds to number 6 of Repingdon's and Hereford's series.

1. This is found in the *Fasciculi* (p. 327), not in the register.

2. "Reg. Court.," fol. 29ᵛ; Wilkins, *3*, 163; *Fas. Ziz.*, p. 329.

3. *Knighton, 2*, 176.

quisitors, in contrast to that of Hereford and Repingdon, was one of self-confident impertinence. What made him all the more arrogant was the presence of a group of sympathizers who had broken down the doors of the hall in which the inquisition was being conducted and who sought to impede the proceedings.[4] Despite Courteney's repeated demand that he speak in Latin "because of the lay people that stood about him," Aston insisted on answering the archbishop in English and in a manner likely to arouse the lay audience against his prosecutors. He gave no direct answers to the questions put to him and frequently interpolated the quip that "since he was a layman, it was sufficient for him that he believe only what the church herself believed." To the question of whether the material substance remained after consecration, he answered that that matter transcended his intellect, and in regard to the word "material," "he said by way of deriding the lord archbishop, 'you can put that word "material" in your pocket if you have any.' " Courteney upbraided him for giving "such unwise and foolish answers since he was a clerk and a graduate in the schools" and, possibly as much for his impudence as for his failure to clear himself of the charge of heresy, declared him a heretic and handed him over to the secular authorities.[5]

But jail did not quiet Aston. He prepared an apology for his views on the Eucharist in both English and Latin and had it distributed throughout London. In this *Confessio* he insisted that he accepted without qualification Christ's real presence in the Eucharist, that he believed "in general" what the scriptures and the church defined about the nature of the *materia,* that he had never preached a word about the material bread remaining after consecration since that was a matter of speculation beyond the grasp of his intellect but that he followed the teaching of the Bible in that matter, and finally, that wherever scripture was not clear concerning that *materia* or, in fact, concerning any other matter touching Catholic faith, he believed as Holy Mother Church believed.[6]

Aston's *Confessio* proved such a powerful piece of propaganda that the ecclesiastical authorities felt compelled to publish a rebuttal, also in English and similarly scattered about the city in leaflet form. They pointed out that Aston had refused to accept the statement that the

4. *Hist. Angl.,* 2, 65–6; *Chron. Angl.,* p. 350. In his *Confessio* Aston states he was interrogated on June 19 rather than June 20. (*Fas. Ziz.,* p. 329; *Knighton,* 2, 171).

5. "Reg. Court.," fol. 29ᵛ; Wilkins, 3, 164; *Fas. Ziz.,* pp. 290, 329. The register states he was declared a heretic, not that he was turned over to the civil arm.

6. *Fas. Ziz.,* pp. 329–30. For an English version, see *Knighton,* 2, 171–2.

body of Christ is in the Eucharist identically, truly, and really in its own corporal presence; that he maintained that the substance of the material bread or wine remained after consecration in the Eucharist; finally, that he had refused to subscribe to the condemnation of the 24 theses.[7]

Yet time works many changes, particularly time spent in jail. Several months later Aston drew up a second confession in which he acknowledged his earlier impudence to the archbishop and made a complete retraction of all his errors. He credited his conversion to the abbot of St. Albans, a professor of scripture by the name of Nicholas Radclif, as well as to several of his colleagues.[8] In reply to his request for an opportunity to make a formal recantation, the archbishop directed him to present himself before convocation at Oxford in November.[9] Even then he was not entirely resigned to making a full submission. When Courteney ordered him to accept without further ado the condemnation of the 24 conclusions, he confessed that "he was too simple-minded and ignorant, and for that reason he could not know how to answer clearly and distinctly to said conclusions." Courteney must have been a patient man, for he gave Aston several hours of grace and turned him over to Rigg, now thoroughly orthodox, and to other theologians to be instructed in these matters. Aston's "simple-mindedness" was the last subterfuge his ingenious mind could conjure up, and after dinner he made a complete recantation and was reinstated. The archbishop's formal restitution of Aston may be of interest. It read as follows:

> To all the children of holy mother church to whose attention this letter may come, William, by divine permission archbishop of Canterbury, primate of all England, legate of the apostolic see, eternal greetings in the Lord. Although John Ashton, master of arts and scholar in holy theology, vehemently suspected of heretical pravity, was recently suspended from all scholastic privileges, as justice rightly required, and in view of his manifest contumacy as well as offensiveness committed before us while sitting in judgement, in that to certain conclusions, some heretical, others indeed erroneous, condemned by the institutes of holy canons and by us with the counsel and consent of very many of our suffragans and of other doctors of sacred theology, of canon and civil law, and experts in law, concerning which conclusions he was seriously accused, warned and directed by us to give answer, he was not

7. *Fas. Ziz.*, p. 331.
8. *Ibid.*, pp. 331–3.
9. See below, p. 126.

willing to do so, but contemptuously refused, he was rightfully condemned for his heresy and erring and as a heretic and one erring; yet because the same John, recovering his senses, presented himself to us in person at the council of prelates and clergy of our province of Canterbury, which we very recently held at Oxford, and publicly anathematized and also abjured all heresy, particularly the aforesaid conclusions, and promised, upon his oath, with his hand on sacrosanct articles, that he would never defend or hold those conclusions or any of them as true, but that he would defer in all matters concerned therewith to the judgement of the catholic church and to ours; and that if at any time he should presume to think or preach anything in violation of the above, he would submit himself to the severity of the canons as is fully explained in the form of this abjuration; and because he humbly besought us to absolve him from the sentence of excommunication which he had incurred on that occasion, and to be restored to his former station and repute: we realizing that holy mother church closes her bosom to no one who would return, have absolved him from said sentence in accordance with the form of the law, and have restored him to his scholastic privilege, his former status, and repute, and we have given him this testimonial letter, confirmed by the protection of our seal, to stop up the mouths of those who would speak malicious words.[1]

On June 27 Repingdon and Hereford, together with Thomas Hilman, also suspect,[2] presented themselves to Courteney in the chapel of his manor at Otford, in accordance with the instructions the archbishop had given them on the twentieth.[3] Through deliberate or inadvertent carelessness, none of Courteney's theological and legal assessors was at hand, so the three were instructed to present themselves again the following Tuesday at Christ Church in Canterbury.[4] Whether Repingdon and Hereford wished to show their resentment at this annoyance or whether they had meantime learned of the royal mandate just issued which

1. "Reg. Court.," fol. 32ᵛ; Wilkins, 3, 169.
2. Hilman had left himself open to suspicion of heresy during the discussions of the meeting of June 20 when he had given Aston some encouragement. He had been ordered to return on June 27 to give his opinion of the condemnation of the 24 theses. "Reg. Court.," fols. 29ᵛ–30; Wilkins, 3, 164.
3. See above, p. 115.
4. *Fas. Ziz.*, p. 290. According to the account in the register, they were to present themselves wherever the archbishop might happen to be at that time. "Reg. Court.," fol. 30; Wilkins, 3, 164.

authorized the hierarchy to arrest suspect persons like themselves,[5] they were conspicuous by their absence when the Blackfriars council reconvened at Canterbury early on the morning of July 1. The archbishop adjourned the session until the afternoon, when Hilman finally put in his appearance. After some hesitation Hilman endorsed the condemnation of the 24 theses. Courteney then denounced the other two as contumacious and formally excommunicated them. The sentence read as follows:

> We, William, by divine permission archbishop of Canterbury, primate of all England and legate of the apostolic see, and inquisitor of heretical pravity through the whole of our province of Canterbury, do pronounce Masters Nicholas Hereford and Philip Reppingdon, professors of holy scripture, having by our appointment this day and place to hear our decree in the matter of heretical pravity, having been summoned and for a very long time awaited and in no way putting in their appearance, contumacious, and in punishment of this their contumaciousness, we excommunicate them and both of them, by these presents.[6]

Repingdon and Hereford immediately appealed the sentence to the pope and nailed their appeal to the doors of St. Mary's and St. Paul's in London. This appeal Courteney denounced as "notoriously frivolous and based upon frivolous and false as well as falsely fabricated and maliciously contrived premises, involving at the same time a manifest error in law . . ."[7] On July 13 he issued the following mandate which directed that the sentence of excommunication be solemnly proclaimed at St. Paul's the next Sunday:

> William, by divine permission archbishop of Canterbury, primate of all England and legate of the apostolic see, to our dear son in Christ, whoever will preach the word of God at St. Paul's Cross, London, this coming Sunday, health, grace, and benediction. Inasmuch as to Masters Nicholas Hereford and Philip Reppyngdon, canon regular of the monastery of St. Mary at Leicester, doctors of holy theology, vehemently suspected of heretical pravity, after certain answers not fully but impertinently, heretically, and erroneously made to several conclusions, heretical and erroneous, commonly, generally, and publicly preached and taught in diverse

5. See above, pp. 99–100.
6. "Reg Court.," fol. 30; Wilkins, 3, 164–5. See *Fas. Ziz.*, p. 290.
7. "Reg. Court.," fol. 30ᵛ; Wilkins, 3, 165.

places of our said province, we appointed, judicially appearing before us, a certain convenient day and place to do and receive peremptorily in this matter what the nature of that business should advise; and we excommunicated them because of their contumaciousness in not presenting themselves before us judicially at the said place and day, as justice required: we charge and direct you, firmly enjoining, that you denounce, publicly and solemnly, said Nicholas and Philip, on that same Sunday, when a very large multitude of people will have gathered at said place to hear your sermon, holding up the cross, lighting the candles, and then casting them down upon the ground, that they have been thus excommunicated by us and that they still are.[8]

The archbishop sent Rigg at Oxford a similar order the same day in which he directed him to have the bann published in St. Mary's and in all the schools of the university. He charged him, furthermore, to cite Hereford and Repingdon to present themselves within 15 days of the citation.[9] But Rigg could not locate the two scholars, as he explained in a letter to Courteney dated July 25;[1] Courteney thereupon issued a mandate to Braybroke on July 30 directing him to relay his orders to all the suffragans of the archdiocese that they publish the excommunication of Hereford and Repingdon throughout the province. Braybroke was to instruct the suffragans to cite the two to appear before the archbishop in order that they might "see and hear how we mean to proceed against the same and against each of them in regard to the aforesaid heretical and erroneous conclusions . . ."[2]

The excommunication of Repingdon and Hereford on July 1 was but the harbinger of yet worse misfortune for the adherents of Lollardy at Oxford. The heaviest blow was provided by a royal patent which the crown addressed to the chancellor, Rigg, on July 13. The circumstances were these. Soon after Rigg had published, to his great distress, the condemnation of the 24 theses on June 15,[3] he had attempted to relieve his vexation at the expense of one Henry Crump. Crump was a Cistercian who had challenged Wyclyf some four years before [4] and who had proved in the years since a particularly irritating obstacle to

8. "Reg. Court.," fol. 30ᵛ; Wilkins, 3, 165.
9. "Reg. Court.," fol. 30ᵛ; Wilkins, 3, 165.
1. "Reg. Court.," fol. 32; Wilkins, 3, 168.
2. "Reg. Court.," fol. 32; Wilkins, 3, 167–8; *Fas. Ziz.*, pp. 312–14.
3. See above, p. 113.
4. So Workman believes (*1*, 264). Crump came from Ireland. Netter refers to him as "Monachus albus de Hybernia . . ." (*Fas. Ziz.*, p. 289).

the spread of Lollardy at Oxford. He had been a member of Berton's committee of 12 which had condemned Wyclyf's theories,[5] he had been a member of the Blackfriars council which had passed judgment on the 24 propositions and before which Rigg had been obliged to humiliate himself,[6] and he had of late been referring to those who favored the banned theses as "Lollards."[7]

Rigg summoned Crump to appear before him to answer to the charge that in employing the epithet "Lollard" in his last sermon he had disturbed the peace of the community. Crump had as yet not returned from the sessions at Blackfriars, and consequently he was forthwith suspended for his alleged contumacy in not respecting the summons. When Crump finally did return to Oxford, only to learn of his suspension, he retraced his steps to London and laid his case before the "chancellor of the realm, the lord archbishop, and the council of the king." The upshot was a summons to Rigg and his proctors to appear before the privy council. There, two weeks later, after his own conduct and the situation at Oxford had been carefully reviewed, Rigg was handed two briefs and dismissed.[8]

The first brief, dated July 13, instructed Rigg and the proctors of the university to conduct a thorough investigation of the entire community in search of any who might favor the theses recently condemned at Blackfriars or who associated in any way with Wyclyf, Hereford, Repingdon, or Aston. Such were to be expelled from Oxford within seven days; they might return to the university only after they had purged themselves before the archbishop. The chancellor and proctors were further directed to make diligent search for any book or tract of Wyclyf's or Hereford's authorship and turn the same over to the archbishop without emendation. Finally, on the threat of forfeiting the privileges of the university, they were cautioned to carry out the instructions of the crown and those of the archbishop. The sheriff of Oxfordshire and mayor of Oxford, as well as all other sheriffs, officials, and subjects of the realm, were charged to cooperate with the decree. The patent read as follows:

> The king, to the chancellor and proctors of the university of Oxford, who now are or who for the time being shall be, greetings. Wholesomely inspired and impelled with zeal for the Christian faith, of which we are and always wish to be the defenders, and

5. See below, p. 129.
6. See above, p. 110.
7. *Fas. Ziz.*, p. 312. See also *ibid.*, p. 315.
8. *Ibid.*, p. 312.

wishing with most earnest desire to repress and with condign
punishment to coerce the enemies of said faith, who of late presume
and most viciously dare to sow their depraved and perverse doctrines within our realm of England and to hold and preach condemned conclusions, notoriously injurious to said faith, to the
perversion of our people, as we understand; we have directed you,
with the assistance of all regents in theology of said university,
to cause a general inquiry to be made of all and each graduate,
theologian, and lawyer of the same university, as to whether they
might know any persons within the jurisdiction of that university,
who are probably suspected by them of favoring, believing, or
defending any heresy or error, particularly certain conclusions
publicly condemned by the venerable father, William, archbishop
of Canterbury, on the advice of his clergy, or of any conclusion
which might be similar in sense or in words to any of them; and
if henceforth you will find any who accept, favor, or defend any
of the same heresies or errors, and anything of a similar character,
or who will dare to receive into their homes and houses Masters
John Wycliff, Nicolaus Hereford, Philip Repyngdon, or John Aston,
or any other known to be under probable suspicion concerning any
of the aforesaid heresies or errors, or other view similar in words or
meaning, or to communicate with any of them, or shall presume to
extend to them any protection or favor, that you bann and expel
those favorers, welcomers, associates, and defenders within seven
days after these presents shall be known to you, from the university and town of Oxford, until they will have established their
innocence by manifest purgation in the presence of the archbishop
of Canterbury, then incumbent; and that they may be forced to
purge themselves, you will from time to time within the month,
under your seals, certify those that are such to us and the same
archbishop. We command, furthermore, that you cause diligent
search to be made through the halls of said university and that
inquiry be made without delay as to whether anyone has in his
possession any book or tract put forth or compiled by the aforesaid Masters John Wycliff or Nicholas, and that you have such book
or tract, wherever it might chance to be found, to be laid hold of,
seized, and handed over to the said archbishop within a month,
without correction, corruption, or alteration of any kind as to
its meaning or words; and indeed we command and direct you,
upon the fidelity and allegiance by which you are bound to us, and
under pain of forfeiture of all and each of the liberties and privi-

leges of said university, and of all else which you could forfeit to us, that you diligently arrange to have the above well and faithfully executed, and that you do these things and carry them out in the form aforesaid; and that you obey said archbishop and the lawful and honest commands he will direct to you in this matter, as it is fitting. We give instructions to the sheriff and mayor of Oxford, whoever they may be, and to all and each sheriff, mayor, bailiff, and all our subjects, by these presents, that they lend their assistance, obey, and attend you in the execution of the above.[9]

The second patent, dated July 14, had chiefly to do with Henry Crump. After reviewing the cause of Crump's suspension and stating that the controversy between Crump and Rigg had been threshed out before the privy council, the patent proceeded to declare any action taken in prejudice of Crump to be null and void. Crump was to be restored to full privileges immediately. The chancellor, proctors, masters-regent, in fact the entire community, were warned never to annoy Crump, Stokes, or Stephen Patrington [1] again or any other scholar who might question the views of Wyclyf, Hereford, and Repingdon. The officials of the university were rather to concern themselves with those matters which would promote the peace and tranquillity of the school. The patent read as follows:

The king, to the chancellor and proctors of the university of Oxford, greetings. Inasmuch as a serious complaint has recently been made to us by brother Henry Crompe, monk, regent in sacred theology in said university, how when he was assisting that venerable father, archbishop of Canterbury, and other masters in theology, in the city of London, in the condemnation of diverse erroneous and heretical conclusions, you, upon the suggestion of certain adversaries of his, pretending that the peace of said university had been violated by Henry in his last lecture in the school, had called the same brother Henry to give answer in your presence, and when he did not present himself before you, as he could not, you pronounced him contumacious and guilty of having broken the peace, and thereby did suspend said Henry from his

9. "Reg. Court.," fols. 31–31ᵛ; Wilkins, 3, 166–7; *Fas. Ziz.*, pp. 312–14.

1. For Stephen Patrington, a "remarkable man," see Workman, 2, 247. He had been the author of the letter which the friars had sent to Gaunt against Hereford (see above, p. 84). That the patent lists his name along with those of Crump and Stokes indicates that he was one of the more active of the anti-Wyclyf faction at Oxford.

scholastic acts and lecture; by our writ we did appoint you a day, now past, to appear before our council at Westminster to give answer concerning the above, and to do certain other things, which are expressly contained in said brief; which matter aforesaid and its circumstances having before our said council and in your presence been examined, investigated, and fully understood, it was by the same our council decreed and sententionally determined that the entire process directed and made against said brother Henry, under the circumstances aforesaid, together with everything which might follow from that was null, invalid, vain, and of no effect, and that said Henry be restored and admitted to scholastic acts and customary lecture and former status, as you fully know. Wishing, therefore, that said decree and determination be duly executed and that it receive confirmation, we charge and command you, as strictly as we are able, that you revoke, speedily and entirely, the whole process carried out against that brother Henry in the university aforesaid, as indicated above, and whatever else may have followed therefrom, and that you admit and cause to be restored without delay the same brother Henry to scholastic acts, customary lecture, and former status, according to the form of the above decree and determination. We direct you, in addition, as well as your commissioners or deputies and your successors, and all masters regent and non regent, and other presidents, officers, ministers, and scholars of said university, upon the faith and allegiance by which they are bound to us, that you do not impede, molest, or annoy, or permit in any manner whatsoever, privately or publicly, to be impeded, molested, or annoyed that brother Henry for the causes aforesaid, or brother Peter Stokes, Carmelite, on the occasion of his absence from said university, or brother Stephen Patrington, Carmelite, or any other regular or secular who might favor them, for reason of any word or act concerned in any way with the doctrine of John Wycliff, Nicholas Herford, or Philip Reppyngdon, or the reprobation and condemnation of said heresies and errors, or the correction of their favorers; but that you rather procure and with all diligence nurture and to your utmost preserve those things which will contribute to the peace, unity, and tranquillity of said university, particularly between the regulars and seculars; and that you in no way fail to do these things under pain of forfeiting all and each liberty and privilege of said university and of everything else which you could forfeit to us.[2]

2. "Reg. Court.," fol. 31ᵛ; Wilkins, 3, 167; *Fas. Ziz.*, pp. 314–17.

In the face of such pressure, Hereford and Repingdon had no choice but to recant or flee. For several months they attempted the second alternative, but their convictions were not equal to the inconveniences of a hunted existence. Bedeman was the first of the fugitives to make his peace with the archbishop. He had transferred his activities to the distant diocese of Exeter, where he soon ran afoul of Bishop Brantingham's vigilance and received a summons to appear for questioning on September 14.[3] This summons he must have ignored, for on October 18 Courteney gave him permission to return to Oxford,[4] and he was formally absolved of the charge of heresy by Bishop Wykeham on October 22.[5] A day later, October 23, Repingdon appeared before a council comprising the archbishop and several bishops and doctors of theology at Blackfriars and made his submission.[6]

The seventh and final session of what might be called the Blackfriars council was held in conjunction with the meeting of convocation in November at Oxford. Richard was in great need of a subsidy, and he asked the archbishop to convene the clergy "at St. Paul's or wherever else" it might appear best to him.[7] Courteney preferred Oxford, and it was there that he ordered Braybroke on October 15 to summon the suffragans and other clergy of the province with all possible speed.[8] The archbishop may have chosen Oxford in order to impress the university community with the fact that he had won a smashing victory over organized Lollardy and that he was come, like a victorious general, to dictate final terms in the enemy's former capital.

Convocation formally opened on November 18 with Mass by Courteney and a sermon by Rigg. The clergy had been summoned, so the archbishop explained, for the purpose of "thoroughly rooting out various heresies which have sprung up in the realm, for the correction of crimes and abuses, for the redress of the injuries of the church, as well as for granting some adequate subsidy in order to avert and repel the dangers which notoriously menace the church, the king, and the kingdom of England."[9]

While Courteney spoke of the suppression of heresy as one of the chief purposes for the gathering, he must have considered that battle

3. *Reg. Brantyngham, 1,* 481.
4. "Reg. Court.," fol. 32; Wilkins, 3, 168.
5. *Reg. Wykeham, 2,* 342–3.
6. "Reg. Court.," fol. 32ᵛ; Wilkins, 3, 169.
7. "Reg. Court.," fol. 33ᵛ.
8. *Ibid.,* fols. 33–4.
9. *Ibid.,* fol. 33.

all but won, at least at Oxford. He did, to be sure, appoint a commission made up of the bishops of Salisbury, Hereford, and Rochester, together with Rigg, William Berton, and John Middleton, to ferret out the scholars still remaining who might be maintaining views similar to those condemned at Blackfriars.[1] But from the account in the register, it was not the appointment of this commission but rather the formal recantations of Repingdon and Aston which were to serve as the climax of the session. For only after the meeting had twice been adjourned "in expectation of those absent" did Repingdon and Aston at length put in their appearance and make formal submissions. Repingdon's abjuration follows:

In the name of God, Amen. I, Philip Reppyngdon, canon of the church of St. Mary de Prè, Leicester, of the diocese of Lincoln, confessing the true, catholic, and apostolic faith, do anathematize and abjure all heresy and in particular the heresies and errors underwritten, which were condemned and rejected by the institutes of sacred canons and by you, most reverend father, concerning which I have been hitherto accused; these as well as their authors I condemn and reject, and I confess the same to have been anathematized in a catholic manner. And I swear by these God's holy gospels which I hold in my hands, and I promise, never, neither by the persuasions of any men nor by any other means, to defend or hold as true the conclusions underwritten or any of them; but that I do and shall submit, adhere and shall adhere in the future in all things to the determination of the holy catholic church and to yours in this regard. And, furthermore, all who contravene this faith I declare them, together with their doctrines and followers, to be worthy of everlasting curse. And if I shall at any time presume to hold or preach anything contrary to the above, I shall be willing to suffer the severity of the canons. I, Philip Reppyngdon aforementioned, subscribe to my said confession and profession with my own hand and of my own accord.[2]

The only jarring note to mar the equanimity of the meeting was the accusation which Rigg leveled at Stokes and Crump of having preached heresy. Since Rigg was a member of the committee which Courteney had commissioned to scrutinize the opinions and statements of the members of the community, it may have been in that capacity that he brought the charge. In view of the recent differences between Rigg

1. *Ibid.*, fol. 34.
2. *Ibid.*, fol. 34v; Wilkins, 3, 172.

on the one hand and Stokes and Crump on the other, however, it is possible that the chancellor's accusation was not wholly without malice. In any event, both Stokes and Crump protested vigorously that what questionable theses they might have proposed they had simply suggested in order to stimulate discussion,[3] and with this explanation the archbishop appeared satisfied. But he was quite disturbed at the rancor which seemed to embitter the relations between the university and the regulars, of which he felt Rigg's attack had been but a symptom. After considerable effort, he was able to effect a general reconciliation.[4]

Of the leading Lollards at Oxford in 1382, Hereford appears to have been the only one who was able to escape making a recantation. He dropped out of sight soon after June 27 when he had last presented himself along with Repingdon to the archbishop.[5] Rigg confessed in his report to Courteney on July 15 that he had not been able to locate him at Oxford.[6] Knighton declares he left England to lay his case before the pope since he felt he had thus far been able to avoid prison and even death only through the use of his wits and the protection of the duke of Lancaster. In Rome he fell into the clutches of a council of cardinals who were ready to condemn him to death. The pope, however, intervened lest such action jeopardize friendly relations with England and commuted his sentence to life imprisonment. A subsequent riot in Rome enabled him to escape his prison and return to England.[7] In 1387 he was still at large, for upon Courteney's request the king issued an order for his arrest.[8] He recanted in 1390 and in time became one of the Lollards' most valiant opponents.[9]

3. "causa exercii et doctrine . . ." "Reg. Court.," fol. 35; *Reg. Brantyngham, 1,* 207.

4. "Reg. Court.," fols. 34v–35.

5. See above, p. 119.

6. See above, p. 121.

7. *Knighton, 2,* 173. Knighton (2, 170–1) records a purported confession or, rather, apology of Hereford, similar in content and tone to Aston's (see above, p. 117). Hereford must have prepared this soon after his last appearance before Courteney on June 27.

8. *Cal. of Pat. Rolls, 1385–89,* p. 316. Hereford had failed to appear in answer to Courteney's summons. See *Knighton, 2,* 264.

9. See Workman, 2, 336–9.

6. DID WYCLYF RECANT?

And where was Wyclyf all this time? After reading in the *Fasciculi* and register of the stirring events of the late spring and summer of 1382, one might almost suppose, except for an oblique reference here and there, that the man had been one of the casualties of the Peasant Revolt. And in so supposing, one would not be greatly mistaken so far as Wyclyf's public career was concerned.[1] We scarcely catch a glimpse of him after 1378. He did engage in acrimonious exchanges with a number of opponents at Oxford after that date—with such men as William Remington, formerly a chancellor of the university; John Wells, a Benedictine, over his views on the Eucharist; Henry Crump; and Ralph Strode, a noted Thomist, over his older theses concerning dominion. There were others, some of whom Wyclyf has named, others whom he has simply designated by some such derisive appellatives as "pseudo-friar, idiot."[2] But in all this controversy, one cannot be certain whence Wyclyf provoked his attackers, whether from Oxford or Lutterworth.

An incident took place at Oxford during the fall of 1380 or early 1381 which for the moment and, as it proved, for the last time, cast some light upon Wyclyf. By the summer of 1380 Wyclyf had taken the revolutionary step of questioning the traditional interpretation of transubstantiation.[3] Since his position was finding adherents at Oxford and causing quite a furor as a consequence, the chancellor William Berton, probably a short time before May, 1381,[4] assembled a group of 12 theologians and canonists and directed them to examine the validity of two conclusions Wyclyf was at that time proposing in the university. On the basis of their "unanimous counsel and assent," Berton issued a decree which condemned the two conclusions and prohibited anyone under threat of suspension, excommunication, and imprisonment from setting forth, defending, or listening to a presentation of such theses in the university. Berton's mandate read as follows:

1. See above, p. 82.
2. *Serm.*, 3, 37. For Wyclyf's opponents during this period, see Workman, 2, 120–9.
3. Netter declares he began his attacks "sub anno Domini MCCCLXXXI, in aestate . . ." (*Fas. Ziz.*, p. 104). Matthew, in his article, "The Date of Wyclif's Attack on Transubstantiation," *EHR*, 5, 328–30, suggests a date as early as 1379.
4. For the date, see below, p. 133. Berton had disputed with Wyclyf before he had been elected chancellor. *Fas. Ziz.*, p. 241.

William de Berton, chancellor of the university of Oxford, to all our sons of said university to whom this our mandate may come, greetings and strict obedience to our commands. Not without great displeasure has the news reached us that though all authors of heresies, defenders, or favorers, together with their pernicious dogmas, are through sacred canons damnably enveloped with the sentence of the greater excommunication and as such are rightfully to be shunned by all catholics, nevertheless, some persons, filled with the counsel of the malign spirit, brought to a madness of mind, and seeking to rend the tunic of the Lord, truly the unity of holy church, do in these days, alas, revive certain heresies once solemnly condemned by the church, and do teach dogmatically both in this university as well as outside in public, asserting two among their other pestiferous doctrines: first, in the sacrament of the altar the substance of the material bread and wine, which existed before consecration, really remains after consecration; second, which is more execrable to hear, that in that venerable sacrament the body of Christ and blood are not essentially, nor substantially, nor even corporally, but figuratively or symbolically present, so that Christ is not there truly in his own corporal presence; by which doctrines the catholic faith is endangered, the devotion of the people is jeopardized, and this university, our mother, defamed in no ordinary fashion.

Wherefore, realizing that such assertions in time will produce worse ones, if in this university they are longer so tolerated with conniving eyes, we have called together many doctors of sacred theology and professors of canon law whom we believe to be the most excellent, and, after the above statements had been openly expounded and diligently discussed in their presence, it was at last found and declared to be their judgement, that they were erroneous and repugnant to the determinations of the church, and that those in contradiction of them are catholic truthes and follow manifestly from the statements of the saints and the determinations of the church, namely, that through the sacramental words of the priest duly pronounced, the bread and wine on the altar are transubstantiated or substantially converted into the true body and blood of Christ, so that after consecration the material bread and wine do not remain in that venerable sacrament as before, according to their substances or natures, but only their appearances; under which appearances the true body and blood of Christ really remain, not only figuratively or symbolically, but essentially, substantially, and corporally, so that Christ is truly there in his own corporal presence. This must be believed, this taught, this courageously defended against those who would deny.

We, therefore, in the Lord admonish and on our authority warn, once, twice, and thrice, and strictly inhibit, assigning for the first monition one day, for the second another day, and for the third monition, canonical and peremptory, yet another day, that no one for the future, of whatever degree, estate, or condition he may be, publicly hold, teach, or defend the two aforesaid erroneous statements, or either of them, in the schools or outside in this university, under punishment of imprisonment and suspension from every scholastic act, and also under punishment of the greater excommunication, which we lay upon all and each rebel in this matter and those who do not obey our monitions, after those three days assigned for canonical monition have elapsed, their delay, fault, and offense committed and justly so requiring, the absolutions of all of which and the power to absolve, except in the moment of death, we specifically reserve to ourselves and to our successors. Furthermore, in order that men may be drawn back from such illicit doctrines and that their erroneous opinions be laid to rest, if not because of fear of threatened sentence, at least for want of an audience, we warn by the same authority as before, once, twice, thrice, and we strictly inhibit that no one for the future hear or hearken in any manner to anyone publicly teaching, holding, or defending the two aforesaid erroneous statements or either of them, in the schools or outside of the schools in this university, but that he immediately flee and shun one so teaching as a serpent spitting forth venomous poison, under pain of the greater excommunication which is to be fulminated, not unjustly, against all and each opposing, and under the other penalties noted above.

The names, moreover, of the doctors who especially gave their attention to this decree and who consented to it unanimously, are these: (The names follow.)

Therefore, having called together the aforesaid doctors, as is related, and after full deliberation in their house over the above, we decreed this mandate to go forth upon the unanimous counsel and assent of us all. In testimony of every and all, we have had the seal of our office affixed to this.[5]

---

5. "Reg. Sud.," fol. 76ᵛ; Wilkins, 3, 171; *Fas. Ziz.*, pp. 110–13. The phrase "in their house" in the last paragraph of this mandate is found only in Netter.

A word is in order about this council of 12 before going on with the events which followed upon the publication of the decree. As might be expected, Workman finds this also a "packed council of friars and monks, four only of the twelve being seculars." [6] It is interesting to note the name of Robert Rigg among the latter. Two of the 12 were monks, six friars, the latter being selected "because they could be trusted to give the right verdict," so Workman assures us. As a matter of fact, seculars to the contrary notwithstanding, the decision of the council on the two conclusions was unanimous, which meant that Rigg, the secular, who later became somewhat receptive to Wyclyf's views, cast his vote with the other seculars against the theses. Workman declares, on the other hand, that the verdict was seven votes to five on the strength of a reference in Wyclyf's *De Blasphemia*.[7] But Berton twice states in his mandate that the verdict was a unanimous one. It is dangerous to suppose that Berton could have been guilty of such a brazen distortion as to speak of unanimity had the vote been actually so divided. The members of the council, at least those who accepted the validity of the two conclusions, would have been quick to proclaim the chancellor's deception. The discrepancy between Berton's and Wyclyf's analysis of the vote on the question as to whether Christ was substantially present in the Eucharist must be explained in this way: the first reaction of the group was a divided one, but after discussion or the exertion of pressure the 12 finally rendered a unanimous decision. Incidentally, the council probably examined other theses ascribed to Wyclyf, for Berton's mandate asserts that two of "other pestiferous doctrines" were singled out for consideration and condemnation. If other theses were discussed, the chancellor may have withheld specific mention of these in view of a lack of unanimity on the part of the council.

Netter writes that Berton's decree was published in the schools of the Augustinians while Wyclyf was in the very act of maintaining the contrary. This must have been the first inkling Wyclyf had of what was afoot, for the chronicler describes how the publication of the mandate came as a shock to Wyclyf. Momentarily taken aback, he recovered himself and declared that "neither chancellor nor any of his accomplices could confute his judgement." [8] To the horror of the

6. Workman, 2, 142.

7. *Ibid.*, p. 144. Wyclyf speaks of this council in the *Blas.*, p. 89.

8. "Reg. Sud.," fol. 76ᵛ; Wilkins, 3, 171; *Fas. Ziz.*, p. 113. Workman's translation of the phrase (2, 145) is not entirely accurate. The original reads: "dixit quod nec cancellarius, nec aliquis de suis complicibus poterat suam sententiam infringere . . ."

chronicler, Wyclyf proceeded to appeal the condemnation of his conclusions "not to the pope or to the bishop or to his ecclesiastical ordinary, but as a heretic he appealed to the secular authority in defense of his error and heresy, he appealed to King Richard . . ." [9] The king must have turned the matter over to his uncle, for the "noble and eminent duke, valiant soldier, and wise counselor . . . faithful son of holy church" [1] came over to Oxford in person and ordered Wyclyf to abide by the decision of the council and to speak no further on that subject.

To this order Wyclyf turned a deaf ear, according to Netter, and instead defended his views in a lengthy *Confessio* dated May 10, 1381. [2] But Gaunt's visit must have produced more fruit than this dubious "confession." From a reference in the *Trialogus* one may safely conclude that Wyclyf discussed the doctrine of transubstantiation with the duke and upon the latter's insistence compromised his stand to the extent of promising "not to use those terms 'substance of material bread and wine' outside the school." [3] As usual when Wyclyf makes one of his rare personal references, he does so in a manner which casts as many shadows as light. He fails to indicate when and to whom he made this promise. It must have been while he was still at Oxford, or the limitation, *extra scholam,* would have had little meaning. If he made the promise at Oxford, this can be narrowed down to sometime between early 1381 when his views on transubstantiation first drew official fire, that of Berton's council, [4] and August of that year, after which time there is no record of his renting rooms at the university. [5] By a process of elimination, Gaunt appears to have been the logical person to whom Wyclyf made the promise. It was not to Berton, for as chancellor Berton would have no immediate responsibility outside the environs of Oxford. Wyclyf could not have made the pledge to Courteney, for the archbishop was not formally installed until September 8, 1381, and in any event, the new metropolitan was not the sort to be satisfied with half measures. [6] As direct evidence that it must have been the duke who received Wy-

9. "Reg. Sud.," fol. 76ᵛ; Wilkins, 3, 171; *Fas. Ziz.*, p. 114. Workman writes: "An appeal would lie to the Congregation of Regent Masters and from their decision to the Great Congregation of the whole university." (*2*, 145.)

1. This is from the pen of Netter, not Walsingham, although even the latter was preparing to change his tune; see Galbraith, *loc. cit.*, p. 19.

2. *Fas. Ziz.*, pp. 115–32. This "confession" should rather be termed a "defense." Wyclyf does not qualify his position.

3. *Trial.*, p. 375.

4. This was probably early in 1381; see above, p. 129.

5. See above, p. 80.

6. Courteney refused to exercise the powers of archbishop prior to the arrival of the pallium in May, 1382; see above, p. 89, n. 9.

clyf's promise there is the fact that Gaunt journeyed to Oxford to caution Wyclyf on the subject of transubstantiation. We also know that the duke had a high opinion of his knowledge of that doctrine.[7]

At first glance some incompatibility may appear to exist between Berton's decree and Wyclyf's promise not to discuss transubstantiation outside the schools. The problem can be resolved in this way. Berton's decree concerned the promulgation not the discussion of certain theories touching upon the doctrine of transubstantiation. While Berton might have preferred to make the entire subject of transubstantiation a closed field, such a restriction would have been beyond his authority and would have been resented even by those who disagreed with Wyclyf as an un-necessary if not vicious limitation upon their intellectual freedom. The type of "mental exercise" in which Stokes and Crump insisted they had been indulging [8] could hardly be anathematized. In effect then, the duke must have forbidden Wyclyf to do two things: first, to promulgate his theories at Oxford; second, to discuss them outside the school.[9]

And in this visit of the duke's to Oxford we probably have the clue to the mystery of why Wyclyf, alone of the leading Lollards at Oxford, managed to escape Courteney's clutches in the summer of 1382. For Wyclyf was no longer at Oxford when the archbishop convened the Blackfriars council preparatory to his attack on Lollardy in the uni-versity. As noted above, there is no record of his renting rooms at Queen's after the summer of 1381.[1] Furthermore, when the friars ap-pealed to Gaunt in February, 1382, against those who were slandering them, they singled out "Hereford . . . and his accomplices," not Wy-clyf, as the cause of their unpopularity.[2] Stokes, the most active oppo-nent of Lollardy at the university in 1382, had been attacking Reping-don, not Wyclyf, "throughout the whole of that year." [3] Finally, when Rigg suspended the leading Lollards at Oxford as Courteney and the crown had directed,[4] efforts were immediately made by Hereford, Re-pingdon, Aston, and Bedeman to have the sentence rescinded. There is

7. See above, p. 114.
8. See above, p. 128.
9. Speaking of Wyclyf's promise, Matthew (*The English Works of Wyclif*, p. xxx) writes: "This sounds as if he had been called to account, and had been dis-missed on undertaking some formal condition as to future controversy. But the form is not suitable to a man who was prohibited from all scholastic acts, and the passage may allude to the silence enjoined at an earlier period by the Duke of Lancaster."
1. See above, p. 80.
2. *Fas. Ziz.*, p. 294.
3. *Ibid.*
4. See above, p. 113.

no record of a similar effort on Wyclyf's part. He must already have turned his back irrevocably on Oxford and was no longer interested in recovering his scholastic privileges. Since Courteney must have been aware of Wyclyf's absence from Oxford, the fact that he included Wyclyf's name with the others to be suspended [5] can be explained as rising from his desire to bar him from returning to academic life.

What must have happened then was that Wyclyf, after binding himself not to promulgate his views at Oxford or to discuss them outside the university, found this an intolerable commitment. Either out of respect for this promise or from fear of the duke's displeasure, he decided to leave the university and to continue his work in the freer atmosphere of Lutterworth.[6] It was only after Wyclyf had gone that his admirers, Hereford and Repingdon, who had not been cautioned by the duke, proceeded to turn Oxford into a hotbed of Lollardy.

That the duke of Lancaster figured prominently in Wyclyf's escape from formal prosecution at this time appears certain. Though Gaunt refused to take Wyclyf's part against Berton, the very fact that he made a special trip to Oxford in order to advise Wyclyf personally is in itself conclusive proof that his failure to support Wyclyf in no way amounted to a repudiation. In all probability they continued to be friends, and Wyclyf, as late as 1384, referred gratefully to the duke as the protector of the "poor priests" and as the innocent victim of the malicious plots of the friars.[7] Furthermore, Repingdon and Hereford evidently considered the duke a friend even after he had "silenced" Wyclyf, for they both appealed to him in similar fashion against the archbishop.[8] And while Gaunt never gave any indication of approving the doctrinal innovations of Wyclyf, it is a tribute to the loyalty of this maligned duke that he continued to shield Wyclyf from the hierarchy even after this former agent of the crown had become a source of embarrassment if not injury to him.[9]

---

5. See above, p. 112.

6. Rigg became chancellor on June 1, 1381 (Salter, p. 331). Wyclyf may have left before his election. If he left subsequent to that date, his leaving may have been prompted by his recollection of Rigg's having voted with the other members of Berton's council against his propositions (see above, p. 132). If Rigg reassured him on that score, Wyclyf was still bound by his promise to the duke.

7. *Pol. Works, 1,* 227. Workman says Wyclyf made this reference to Gaunt in June, 1384 (*2,* 306). Repingdon likewise commended the duke for his friendliness toward the "poor priests" in his sermon on Corpus Christi. See above, p. 107.

8. See above, p. 113. Swinderby, the leading Lollard in northern England, appealed to Gaunt in similar fashion in 1382. *Fas. Ziz.,* p. 340.

9. See above, p. 133.

It may have been that Gaunt's defense of Wyclyf at this late date had no higher motivation than the negative one of his enmity for Courteney, his political opponent of earlier years. The crown had decided in 1378 to place restrictions upon Wyclyf,[1] and the duke must have realized, if he had not been so informed by the king,[2] that this clerk would not be permitted to continue his attacks upon the church with impunity, particularly now that they included an assault on transubstantiation. Rather than suffer his personal enemy, the archbishop, to discipline Wyclyf, the duke undertook the silencing himself. Whether Gaunt informed Courteney that Wyclyf had promised to confine his activities to that of theorizing at Oxford on certain debatable doctrines or whether the archbishop learned of this through other channels, it would not have been politic for him in either case to consider the matter still open.

It is true that Courteney did not entirely overlook Wyclyf in his efforts during the summer of 1382 to suppress Lollardy at Oxford. The mandate he issued June 12 to Rigg, the chancellor of the university, had instructed that official to suspend Wyclyf together with the other leading Lollards from all academic privileges.[3] The king, upon the request of Courteney, had bolstered this order with his own letters patent on July 13 in which he directed Rigg to expel from the university anyone found guilty of favoring Wyclyf's theories. The chancellor was also to see that all of Wyclyf's books and tracts were turned over to the archbishop.[4] But Wyclyf himself was never cited.

The attempt is made by several scholars to establish that Wyclyf appeared before the provincial synod which convened at Oxford in November, 1382, and before which Repingdon and Aston made formal submissions.[5] Wood and Knighton provide the basis for the story, with the account of the former resting substantially on that of the chronicler. But Knighton's evidence may be dismissed as worthless. The Lambeth register makes no mention of Wyclyf, although it reports the recantations of Repingdon and Aston. Knighton lists seven bishops, among them

1. See above, pp. 59, 61.

2. In view of the king's opposition to Lollardy, it is possible that upon receiving Wyclyf's appeal against Berton's decree he cautioned Gaunt that Wyclyf's revolutionary preaching could no longer be countenanced. It is not difficult to draw that interpretation from Netter's statement: "[Wyclyf] appellavit ad regem Ricardum . . . Et post appellationem advenit . . . Dux Lancastriae prohibens . . . quod de cetero non loqueretur de ista materia." *Fas. Ziz.*, p. 114.

3. See above, p. 111.

4. See above, p. 122.

5. See Lechler, *1*, 696; Vaughan, *John de Wycliffe, D.D., a Monograph*, App., pp. 571–6.

the bishop of Worcester, as being present at Oxford, while the register enumerates ten prelates but no bishop of Worcester.[6] More damning is Knighton's statement that Wyclyf made a full recantation, inserting what he terms a "confession" but which, despite its obscure language, is simply a reaffirmation of Wyclyf's revolutionary position on the Eucharist.[7] Knighton concludes his remarkable story by telling how the prelates, after presumably accepting this strange confession, proceeded to condemn the 24 propositions.

Lechler's suggestion that the Lambeth register omits all reference to Wyclyf's appearance and trial at Oxford in November, 1382, because the issue was one over which "there was not the slightest reason to be proud"[8] is an untenable conjecture. While it is possible that a proud Courteney would not have permitted the fact that Wyclyf refused to recant to be officially recorded, it is unlikely that an instance of such open defiance would not at least have been proclaimed by the less concerned chroniclers. In addition, a positive refusal to recant would have greatly strengthened the hands of the ecclesiastical authorities against Wyclyf and could scarcely have led to anything less than his eventual submission or sentence.

It is improbable that Wyclyf owed his escape from prosecution to the sympathetic attitude of the government, specifically of the Commons. What influence he may have enjoyed in official circles in 1377–78[9] had been dissipated by the Peasant Revolt with which his name had been linked at the time.[1] There was no question about the position of the king. The crown had secured the acceptance of the statute issued in May, 1382, which required the sheriffs of the realm to imprison anyone who, upon the certification of a bishop, was guilty of heresy.[2] A royal patent dated a month later corroborated this order. On July 13 the king sent a brief to the chancellor at Oxford instructing him to confiscate Wyclyf's books and to expel his adherents from the university.[3]

It is true that Commons had not given its approval to the statute issued in May and that in the fall session of Parliament they demanded "that that statute be therefore annulled, for in no way was it ever their intention to be justified or to bind themselves or their successors

6. See Wood, 1, 500; Knighton, 2, 160; "Reg Court.," fols. 34–34ᵛ.

7. According to Arnold (3, 499), this "confession" is but a summary of the longer *Confessio* which Wyclyf drew up in May, 1381. See above, p. 133.

8. Lechler, 1, 698.

9. See above, pp. 56–8.

1. See above, p. 82.

2. See above, pp. 98–9.

3. *Cal. of Pat. Rolls, 1381–85*, p. 153; see above, pp. 122–3.

to the prelates any more than their ancestors were in times past." [4]

While the champions of Wyclyf draw the ready conclusion from this protest that the Commons was favorably inclined toward Wyclyf, such was not necessarily the case. The language of the protest indicates nothing more than that Commons did not wish to extend to the hierarchy the privilege of giving orders to the officials of the realm. It would have been no more ready to permit the hierarchy, as a policy, to direct the apprehension of murderers or traitors. That attitude sprang not from their supposed sympathy for Wyclyf but from anticlericalism. It is significant that Commons did not continue to press for the repeal of the statute, for despite the crown's acceptance of their protest the law was not withdrawn. The Commons must have been satisfied with the *Yl plest au Roi* as recognition of the point it probably wished to make by its protest, namely, that no statute might be promulgated without its consent. Even assuming that Commons sought the repeal of the statute because of its sympathy for Wyclyf's cause, it is an anachronism to propose that such opposition would have been sufficient to overawe the wishes of the king and council in the 14th century.[5] In any event, the Parliament which saw Commons requesting the repeal of this statute convened in October, 1382, when, if Courteney had planned to arraign Wyclyf, he would already have done so.[6] One must conclude, in view of the complete absence of any corroborative evidence other than this debatable protest, that the tendency of certain scholars to attribute pro-Wyclyf sentiment to Commons in the fall of 1382 rests upon the utterly unhistorical premise that since Commons was anti-Catholic in the 17th century it must have been similarly so in the 14th.

If Courteney felt constrained to recognize Gaunt's admonition to Wyclyf as closing the case, there is reason to believe that he was not entirely satisfied with this disposition of the problem. In a letter addressed to the bishop of Lincoln, the archbishop commended that prelate for the zeal with which he was fighting the Lollards, in particular for his efforts "in the felicitous execution of the matter concerning the Antichrist . . ." [7] Since there is no reason to suppose that the bishop of

4. *Rot. Parl.*, 3, 141.

5. See above, p. 101.

6. Parliament met in October. *Rot. Parl.*, 3, 132. Hereford, Repingdon, and Aston, the chief Lollards at Oxford in 1382, had already appeared before the archbishop on June 18. See above, p. 114.

7. "Reg. Court.," fols. 32–32ᵛ; Wilkins, 3, 168–9. The letter is not dated. Wilkins (3, 168) assigns it to the year 1382 because it appears in the register among documents dated from the fall of that year. However, the somewhat cramped style of the handwriting together with the letter's position on the bottom of two

Lincoln had·anything to do with Wyclyf's leaving Oxford,[8] these words suggest that restrictions in addition to those dictated by the duke at Oxford had been placed upon Wyclyf by Bishop Buckingham subsequent to his retirement to Lutterworth. Courteney's reference to Wyclyf as "Antichrist" may be significant, for he would probably not have employed such a term had he been a partner to Gaunt's handling of the affair.

If Courteney was obliged to accept the arrangement the crown and Gaunt may have decided upon in the case of Wyclyf, the pope was under no such constraint. There is little doubt that the attempt made by Pope Gregory in 1377 to have Wyclyf appear before the Curia in Rome was renewed late in Wyclyf's life by Urban VI. Wyclyf is himself witness to this summons. In a treatise entitled *De Citationibus Frivolis,* in which he lists illness and a royal countermand as legitimate grounds for refusing to comply with a papal summons, he seeks to justify his own failure to obey such a citation on both bases: that of illness in the words, "and so speaks one who is disabled and crippled and cited to this curia"; and that of a royal countermand in the words, "because a royal prohibition prevents him from going, for the king of kings requires and wills effectually that he do not go." [9] The facts that Wyclyf was "disabled and crippled" during the last two years of his life [1] and that his words concerning his having been cited are expressed in the present tense in a tract written at the end of 1383 or the beginning of 1384 would appear to disprove the contention that the citation to which Wyclyf referred was that of Gregory back in 1377 and not a more recent one.

That this treatise, the *De Citationibus Frivolis,* was written not prior to 1383 is an issue of such crucial significance to this study of Wyclyf's prosecution that its analysis merits elucidation in the text rather than in a footnote. Two Wyclyf scholars disagree as to the dating of the treatise.

separate folios strongly suggest that the letter was interpolated sometime after the accompanying documents had been recorded.

8. Though Oxford lay within the diocese of Lincoln, it had virtually thrown off the episcopal yoke by 1368. See Rashdall, 3, 124.

9. *Pol. Works, 2,* 556. It is not clear whether Wyclyf had God in mind rather than King Richard in the phrase, "because a royal prohibition prevents him from going." Surely the second part of the phrase, "for the king of kings requires and wills effectually that he do not go," must refer to God despite the failure of scholars to so interpret it. For a similar reference, see below, p. 146.

1. John Horn, a priest who lived with Wyclyf during his last years at Lutterworth, related to Thomas Gascoigne, under oath, how Wyclyf had been paralyzed during the two years preceding his death. There is no suggestion of any earlier incapacitation. See Lewis, p. 336.

Buddensieg declares the work was written "at the end of 1383 or the beginning of 1384 . . . that the citation may . . . be regarded 'as an historical fact,'" and that "it is unmistakably proved by the words: et dicit quidam debilis et claudus etc."[2] Loserth, on the other hand, assigns the tract to 1378, chiefly because he had taken the same position with regard to the disputed dating of Wyclyf's letter to Pope Urban.[3] Loserth argues that the treatise could not have been written as late as 1383, for the king could not then have forbidden Wyclyf to answer a citation to Rome since he was no longer in the royal service. Loserth, in effect, would have us believe that Richard's authority did not extend to his subjects but was limited to his agents! Furthermore, he sees no reason to suppose that Wyclyf was not "disabled and crippled" until two years of his death. Loserth fails to appreciate the fact that the burden of proof is on him. Since he offers no evidence which might suggest this possibility, we must assume, on the basis of the picture we have of Wyclyf prior to his retirement to Lutterworth [4]—that of a man actively engaging in polemics at Oxford [5]—that he was not crippled before that date. It is true that Wyclyf's health may not have been robust and that he could actually have been ill in 1378, but the illness to which he refers in the *De Citationibus Frivolis* was of neither a minor nor a temporary character. Wyclyf writes that the "king of kings"—in other words, God—had willed "effectually" that he did not go to Rome. The word "effectually" leads one to infer something quite serious, such as paralysis, which would have left Wyclyf "disabled and crippled."

Loserth's last argument in support of an early date for the appearance of the *De Citationibus Frivolis* is extremely labored. He notes that there are similarities in expression between that tract and the *De Servitute Civili et Dominio Seculari* which also has something to say about papal citations. The language of this latter tract he in turn compares with that of Gregory's bull of 1377, and here likewise he has no difficulty finding certain resemblances (only in terminology, not in particulars), whereupon he draws the wholly unwarranted conclusion that the bull precipitated the publication of the two tracts.[6] Incidentally, the reference in the *De Citationibus Frivolis* to the controversy over transubstantiation Loserth labels an interpolation,[7] the reference to

2. *Pol. Works*, 2, 542, and n. 2.
3. See below, pp. 143–5.
4. He probably left Oxford in 1381; see above, p. 80.
5. See above, pp. 129, 132.
6. *Op. Min.*, pp. xxvii–viii.
7. For the date of Wyclyf's attack on the Eucharist, see above, p. 129.

Hereford's imprisonment, which rules out a date prior to 1382, he ignores.[8]

If the *De Citationibus Frivolis* did not appear before 1383, that fact would prove that Pope Urban cited Wyclyf late in the latter's life. Such a summons Wyclyf appears to confirm in a letter which he addressed to Pope Urban in 1384. The contents of this letter are of considerable interest. Wyclyf declares that he is glad to make known to all persons his particular belief, especially to the Roman pontiff, because he supposes that if the pope finds his views orthodox he will confirm them, if not he will correct them. Wyclyf goes on to say that since the pope is Christ's highest vicar on earth he is bound in a special manner to abide by the law of the gospel, to wit, that as Christ and His apostles eschewed worldly wealth and dominion he should do the same; and Wyclyf declares that this is his conviction, in defense of which he is willing to die. Finally, he expresses a willingness to go to Rome, but finds this impossible as God had determined differently, and one ought to obey God rather than man. The letter reads as follows:

> I am happy to reveal fully to anyone and especially to the Roman pontiff the faith I hold, for I suppose that if it is orthodox, he will graciously confirm this faith and if it be erroneous he will correct it. But I submit that the gospel of Christ is the body of the law of God, that Christ, indeed, who directly gave this gospel, I believe to be true God and true man, and in this the law of the gospel excels all other [9] parts of scripture. Again I submit that the Roman pontiff, inasmuch as he is Christ's highest vicar on earth, is among pilgrims most bound to this law of the gospel. For the majority of Christ's disciples are not judged according to worldly greatness, but according to the imitation of Christ in their moral life. Again, from out this heart of the Lord's law I plainly conclude that Christ was the poorest of men during the time of his pilgrimage and that he eschewed all worldly dominion. This is clear from the faith of the gospel, Matthew VIII and 2 Corinthians VIII.[1] From all this I deduce that never should any of the faithful imitate the pope himself nor any of the saints except insofar as he may have imitated the Lord Jesus Christ. For Peter, Paul, and the sons of Zebedee, by seeking worldly dignity, brought that sort of imitation into dis-

8. *Pol. Works, 2,* 554. See Buddensieg's note, *ibid.,* p. 542.

9. Shirley failed to transcribe the word *alias* from the original manuscript (Bodleian MS, e Mus. 86).

1. The original lacks the verse designations which Shirley has added: "Mat. VIII. 20, et 2 Cor. VIII." *Fas. Ziz.,* p. 341.

repute, so that they are not to be imitated in those errors. From this I infer, as a counsel, that the pope should leave temporal dominion to the secular arm, and to this he should effectually exhort his clergy. For in such wise did Christ have signified through his apostles.

If in the above I have erred, I am willing humbly to be corrected, even through death if necessary. And if I were able to travel at will in person, I should like humbly to visit the Roman pontiff. But God has obliged me to the contrary, and he has always taught me to obey God rather than men. But since God has given our pope true and evangelical instincts, we should pray that those instincts are not extinguished through deceitful counsel, nor that the pope or cardinals be moved to do anything contrary to the law of the Lord. Therefore, let us ask God, the lord of everything created, that he so inspire our pope, Urban VI, as he began, so that he and his clergy may imitate the Lord Jesus Christ in their moral lives, so that they may effectually teach the people to faithfully imitate them in this. And let us pray spiritually [2] that our pope be preserved from malicious counsel, for we also know that a man's enemies are of his household, and God does not suffer us to be tempted above that which we are able, much less does he require of any creature that he do that which he can not, for such is the manifest condition of Antichrist.[3]

Considerable controversy rages around both the authenticity of the letter as well as its dating. Lechler rejects its genuineness on the score that it lacks the form of a personal communication: it opens with no salutation, the pope is referred to in the third person, while the writer lapses from the first person singular in the early part of the letter to the first person plural toward the close. He also finds the somewhat impudent tone of the missive incompatible with the avowed purpose for which the letter was sent, that is, to apologize to Urban for the writer's inability to answer his citation to Rome. He points out, finally, that a study of the handwriting of the original document leads him to suspect that the rubric was added some 30 years after the letter itself had been recorded, not an uncommon history for the captions of several of Wyclyf's shorter works.[4]

But Lechler's criticism of the missive rests upon a misconception of

2. The abbreviation in the manuscript might be read as *spiritualiter* or *specialiter*.
3. *Fas. Ziz.*, pp. 341–2 (Bodleian MS, e Mus. 86).
4. Lechler, *1*, 713–15, 715 n. 1.

the purpose for which the letter was written. It should not be considered an ordinary letter in the usual sense but rather a "missive or tract, destined to pass through as many hands as might be, and thus eventually get into the Pope's hands too." [5] A tract composed with that end in view could be expected to be written both in the third person and in language less respectful than that Wyclyf would have employed in a personal letter to the pope. And as far as Lechler's last objection is concerned, that the rubric was added some years later, that conclusion might be drawn from one or the other of the eight original manuscripts in which this particular letter is found,[6] but it is not borne out by the form and handwriting of the Bodleian manuscript. Here the rubric lies between two documents—one telling of Swinderby's appeal to the duke of Lancaster, the other the letter to Pope Urban. The caption lies in the body of the text not on the margin, neither is it cramped in any way in order to fit it into the intervening space. Furthermore, the handwriting of the rubric and of the letter appears to be the same. There is no reason whatsoever to suppose that it was interpolated some years after the letter itself had been recorded.

Loserth, while accepting the letter's authenticity,[7] insists it must be assigned to a year earlier than 1379 for a reason, oddly enough, which is the direct opposite to the one upon which Lechler bases some of his objections. He says that it is too friendly in tone to the pope. According to Loserth, Wyclyf could not, in 1379 or after, have proposed that "since God has endowed the pope with true evangelical instincts . . . we should pray that he is not tempted to do anything contrary to the law of God," since in that year he had assumed a hostile attitude toward the papacy in his *De Potestate Pape*.[8] In the first place, Loserth predicates his argument on the premise that Wyclyf was thoroughly consistent and

5. *Op. Min.*, p. ii. Loserth declares the letter resembles one of similar character which Wyclyf addressed to the bishop of Norwich.

6. *Ibid.*, p. iii.

7. "An der Echtheit des Schriftstueckes, das, was Lechler uebersehen hat, uebrigens auch in den *Protestationes* schon als *Epistola* verzeichnet wird, moechte ich nicht zweifeln. Ein jeder Satz is Wiclifisch." Loserth, "Das vermeintliche Schreiben Wiclif's an Urban VI. und einige verlorene Flugschriften Wiclif's aus seinen letzten Lebenstagen," *HZ*, 75, 479.

8. To quote Loserth: "the following sentence could not possibly have been written in 1379, much less in 1384: Cum autem Deus dederit pape nostro instinctus iustos evangelicos, rogare debemus quod instinctus illi non per subdolum consilium extinguantur, nec quod papa aut cardinales aliquid agere contra legem Domini moveantur. Igitur rogemus Deum . . . quod sic excitet papam nostrum Urbanum VI, sicut inceperat . . ." *Op. Min.*, pp. ii–iii.

logical in what he said and wrote, which he was not.[9] In the second place, one wonders whether Loserth would not have assigned the letter to a year even earlier than 1378 were it not that Pope Urban's name is specifically mentioned in the letter, since Wyclyf had taken a hostile stand toward the papacy some time before 1379. An examination of the propositions which Pope Gregory had condemned in 1377 will reveal that as early as 1376 or before Wyclyf would have stripped the pope of some of his authority.[1]

This is the root of Loserth's conviction that the letter could not have been written in 1384: by that time Wyclyf had passed irrevocable judgment upon the papacy as a usurped, unnecessary, and vicious authority. For how could one and the same person, in the same year, refer to the pope now as a "devil's head," [2] now as "Christ's highest vicar here on earth?" Yet the eminent Wyclyf scholar Buddensieg denies Loserth's contention and declares that "Wiclif in no passage goes so far as to downright and without modification to identify the Pope with the Antichrist or the Devil . . . ," but that he says that "the Pope is Antichrist only so far as he does, or leaves undone, this or that." [3] That is the position Wyclyf takes in the *Opus Evangelicum,* a work left unfinished at his death. He admits that the Christian must obey the pope but only when the order conforms to the law of God.[4]

There are other difficulties, if not inconsistencies, which weaken the position Loserth has taken concerning this letter. How, for example, can one reconcile the enthusiastic statements with which Wyclyf hailed the election of Urban in 1378 with the veiled sarcasm of the letter if it is assigned to that year? Wyclyf thanked God for giving the church a "catholic head, an evangelical man," one who by his past life gave promise of living "in conformity with the law of Christ" and of carrying out long-delayed reforms.[5] In a sermon probably written in 1379 Wyclyf commended Pope Urban for his correct views on the Eucharist and denounced those of the Clementines as false.[6] This last reference, incidentally, is a critical one as far as Loserth's chronology is concerned. Clement was elected in September, 1378. That news probably reached England no earlier than December in view of the slowness with which

9. See above, p. 81.
1. See above, pp. 49–50.
2. Loserth, *HZ, 75,* 478.
3. *Pol. Works, 1,* xxi.
4. *Op. Evang., 4,* 189.
5. See *Eccles.,* pp. 37, 358. See also *Op. Min.,* p. 401.
6. *Serm., 2,* 70; *4,* 499–500.

dispatches traveled at the time,[7] and surely additional months would have had to elapse before Wyclyf could receive such additional information as would have enabled him to distinguish between the views of Urban and those of the Clementines on the question of transubstantiation. Such information would not have been at hand prior to 1379. Consequently, that fact alone clearly destroys Loserth's case that the letter was written in 1378 or earlier, for as late as 1379 Wyclyf was saying commendable things about the pope.

Loserth would deny the letter a date as late as 1384 because of its failure to make any reference to the Eucharist. He argues that in 1384 Wyclyf was not concerned with the apostolic poverty of the church or with her temporal power but rather with the doctrine of the Eucharist. Since Wyclyf makes mention of the first two points in his letter but ignores the third, Loserth concludes that the letter could not have been written late in Wyclyf's life. But there are similarly no references to the Eucharist in the *Cruciata* or the *De Christo et Suo Adversario Antichristo,* treatises which date from 1383 or later.[8] There is no such reference in the *De Contrarietate Duorum Dominorum* where we would most expect to find one. From the allusion to the persecution of the "poor priests," Buddensieg assigns this tract to the eighties, and he finds it "curious" that though Wyclyf lists the heresies of the mendicants he makes no mention of their position on transubstantiation "which . . . is his main reproach against them . . ."[9]

In this question of the dating of Wyclyf's letter to Pope Urban it has been advisable to consider at length the position of Loserth because later writers have usually appealed to him as their authority in this matter.[1] Yet Loserth's view is not shared by other noteworthy Wyclyf scholars. Shirley, Vaughan, Arnold, and Lewis accept without hesitation both the genuineness of the letter and the trustworthiness of the rubric, that is, that the letter was written in 1384, the year of Wyclyf's death.[2]

There are strong positive grounds for accepting that date. In the first place, there is the rubric which introduces the letter. This reads: "Copy of a certain letter of Master John Wycclyff, sent to Pope Urban VI, to excuse his not coming in answer to his summons. The year of

7. See above, p. 55.
8. See *Pol. Works,* 2, 582, and *Tractatus de Christo et Suo Adversario Antichristo,* p. 19.
9. *Pol. Works,* 2, 696.
1. See Workman, 2, 315 n. 2; Ullmann, p. 132 n. 2.
2. *Fas. Ziz.,* pp. xliv–v; Vaughan, 2, 121–3; Arnold, 3, 504; Lewis, p. 122.

our Lord 1384." [3] It is true that I have had occasion to attack the rubrics of two other documents printed by Netter; [4] the force of the rubric of this letter, however, in contrast to that of the other two documents is substantiated by the contents of the text which follows. Thus Wyclyf does write as though he is addressing Pope Urban, and he makes a reference to his poor health and his inability to come to Rome. No similarly convincing internal evidence which would establish the validity of their rubrics is provided by the other two documents. The letter, furthermore, appears in chronological order in Netter, that is, after documents dated before 1384. And as I have noted above, the rubric which introduces Wyclyf's letter is not placed on the margin but is part of the running page of the document and is in the same hand as that of the letter itself. [5]

A second piece of persuasive evidence that the letter was written late in Wyclyf's life is found in Wyclyf's reference to his poor health. He explains that he is unable to make the trip to Rome because God had decided differently and one must obey God rather than man. This can only be interpreted to mean that he was in no condition physically to travel such a distance. As pointed out above, there is no basis for believing that Wyclyf was paralyzed before he left Oxford in 1381. [6] The reader is reminded of the same excuse which he offered to a papal citation in the *De Citationibus Frivolis,* a treatise which cannot be assigned a date earlier than 1382. [7]

A third argument that the letter was written sometime after 1378 is suggested by the language of the letter itself. This is Wyclyf's use of the pluperfect tense when speaking of the behavior of Pope Urban. The pertinent phrase reads: "Therefore, let us ask God . . . that he so inspire our pope, Urban VI, as he began . . ." What Wyclyf has in mind is this, that we should ask God to so inspire Urban that he conduct himself again in the manner in which he had begun. Wyclyf was not the only one whose high expectations at the election of Urban were later dashed by the pope's subsequent activities. If Wyclyf had no such criticism in mind, we should expect him to have used the perfect rather than the pluperfect tense, thus, that Urban continue as he has begun

3. "Copia cuisdam littere Magistri Johannis Wycclyff misse pape Urbano Sexto ad excusacionem de non veniendo sibi ad citacionem suam. Anno Domini millesimo trecentesimo lxxxiiii." (Bodleian MS, e Mus. 86.) See *Fas. Ziz.,* p. 341.

4. See above, pp. 57–9.

5. See above, p. 143.

6. See above, p. 140.

7. See above, pp. 139–41.

(*incepit*) rather than as he had begun (*inceperat*).[8] Such a tense and sentiment would echo the words Wyclyf expressed in the *De Ecclesia* in 1378 concerning the election of Urban, namely, "blessed be the Lord . . . who has provided [*providit*] a catholic head . . ."[9] In fact, we find Wyclyf voicing the same thought, though significantly, using not the pluperfect *inceperat* of the letter but the perfect *incepit* in his *Responsiones ad Decem Questiones Magistri Ricardi Strode,* which probably appeared late in 1378. He writes: "Blessed therefore be the Lord who . . . has placed us under the wings of Urban, but only so long as he will observe the virtues of the vicar of Christ as he has begun [*incepit*]."[1] Only two dates have been assigned the letter—1378 and 1384 —and if Wyclyf used the pluperfect to convey the meaning just suggested, the only choice left is to respect the language of the rubric and accept the later date.

It is clear from Wyclyf's own words that he penned this letter after Urban had dispelled his earlier hopes of conducting a thoroughgoing reform of the church. He admits that God had given Urban "true and evangelical instincts," but he says we must pray that these be not vitiated by wicked counselors. Further on he again raises the danger of evil counsel and for the second time asks that we pray that the pope be preserved from falling under vicious influences. One may reasonably conclude that such concern about evil counselors could only have sprung from Wyclyf's knowledge that Urban was not living up to expectations as a reformer and from his analysis that Urban's wrongdoings could be attributed to the criminal advice he had accepted from members "of his own household." As I noted above, Wyclyf could not have learned of such a turn in Urban's conduct prior to 1379.

The reason for the great concern about this letter[2] is that it clarifies the attitude Wyclyf had assumed toward the church by 1384 and in so doing throws considerable light upon the study of his prosecution. Particularly significant is Wyclyf's reference to the pope as Christ's

8. "Igitur rogemus Deum Dominum cuiuslibet creature quod sic excitet papam nostrum Urbanum sextum sicut inceperat, ut imitetur cum clero suo . . ." (Bodleian MS, e Mus. 86). See *Fas. Ziz.,* p. 342.

9. *Eccles.,* p. 37.

1. "Benedictus itaque dominus qui . . . posuit nos sub alis Urbani, dum tamen servaverit mores Christi vicarii ut incepit." *Op. Min.,* p. 401.

2. While Wyclyf's attitude toward the papacy can be found treated at length in several of his works, the language nowhere is so pointed and unequivocal as in this letter. It is because this letter is of such vital significance in any consideration of Wyclyf's position with regard to Rome that Loserth was prompted to attack the date 1384 so often and with so much feeling.

highest vicar on earth. That Wyclyf publicly subscribed to the traditional belief in the West that the pope enjoyed that eminent position in the ecclesiastical hierarchy conclusively dispels any notion that he broke with Rome or with the official body of the church.[3] Other than that he became more critical of the papacy as he grew older, Wyclyf maintained a fairly consistent position toward the pope throughout his career, namely, that the pope is to be obeyed only insofar as he himself obeys the laws of God. This sentiment he expressed on many different occasions, such as in his early treatises on dominion, in the *De Ecclesia,* the *De Potestate Pape,* and in the *Opus Evangelicum,* which was left unfinished at his death.[4] As he protested in the *De Veritate Sacrae Scripturae* against the charge that he was seeking to evade the papal jurisdiction,[5] he might have written in similar fashion at almost any time during his life.

It is true that one has difficulty reconciling such a statement as "I am happy to reveal fully to anyone and especially to the Roman pontiff the faith I hold, for I suppose that . . . if it be erroneous he will correct it" with the unmeasured invective Wyclyf so frequently leveled at the papacy. But isn't that equally true whether the expression is assigned the year 1378 or 1384? Even before Urban became pope, Wyclyf was convinced that the pope could teach heresy,[6] yet he could later send a defense of his views on ecclesiastical poverty to Rome in the hope of convincing the pope of their orthodoxy.[7] Why should he have been concerned about the views of the pope, if the pope was not above teaching heresy? Or would anyone be so credulous as to suppose that Wyclyf would have altered his own views at any time after 1375—whether in 1378 or 1384—if the pope had directed him to do so? What Wyclyf wrote in this letter of 1384 reminds one of the declaration Repingdon and Hereford made to Archbishop Courteney in concluding their exposition of their views on the 24 theses.[8]

One must ever bear in mind that Wyclyf never considered himself a revolutionary or a heretic. He was first and last a reformer, and one who would effect his reforms within the organization of the church.

3. In his letter to the pope Wyclyf speaks of him as "our Urban." Loserth finds no significance in this phrase (*loc. cit., 156,* 85), but Workman does (2, 75).

4. See *Eccles.,* pp. 34, 38–9; *De Potestate Pape,* pp. 247, 360; *Op. Evang., 4,* 189. See Workman, 2, 73.

5. *Op. Min.,* p. 19. Manning (7, 504) writes: "The papacy is not identified with the Anti-Christ, but a Pope who works the work of Anti-Christ, may bear his name."

6. *Civ. Dom., 1,* 414; *2,* 114; *4,* 398, 404.

7. See above, p. 73, n. 9.

8. See above, pp. 115–16.

While he may not long have continued as optimistic as when he forwarded his treatise on *The Thirty Three Conclusions on the Poverty of Christ* to the Curia, he never became a Luther or a Calvin. Though he found much to his distaste in the practices of the church and in the lives of churchmen, he never withdrew from the institution. He presumably found nothing contradictory between maintaining on the one hand views almost as revolutionary as those of the Protestants of the 16th century while continuing on the other to serve his community at Lutterworth in the traditional role of a Catholic priest. And though his interpretation of what constituted the Eucharist was hardly that of Pope Urban, according to the only evidence we have he suffered his last stroke while hearing Mass.[9]

Such an analysis of the position of Wyclyf with regard to the church enables us to understand how it came about that he was permitted to live out his life neither in prison nor in exile but in the performance of his pastoral duties at Lutterworth. Had he broken formally and irrevocably with the pope, not even Gaunt could have, or for that matter would have, shielded him from further prosecution. Circumstances which may have united with the fact of his retirement, the favor of the duke, and his own failing health to protect him from molestation on the part of the hierarchy were the advanced age of his bishop and the absenteeism of his archdeacon.[1]

Above all else in accounting for Wyclyf's escape from formal sentence was the protection which Gaunt could afford him through his influence with the crown. Gaunt was the most powerful man in England next to Richard himself, and his relations with his nephew were still amicable. It should have required but little insistence from Gaunt to secure for his clerk the protection of the crown. And of the finality of this protection there can be no doubt. Gregory confessed how helpless he would be should the king refuse to cooperate with him against Wyclyf.[2] The punishment of the vice-chancellor of Oxford for having dared to "imprison" Wyclyf upon the pope's instructions [3] made it clear that the crown, not the church, would handle Wyclyf's case. Thus Wyclyf's statement in the *De Citationibus Frivolis* that he was stayed from answering a papal summons by a royal countermand is what we might expect. That the king blocked Wyclyf's summons because of the latter's poor health, as Wyclyf writes "Because a royal prohibition prevents him

9. Leland, *Antiquarii de Rebus Britannicis Collectanea, 3*, 409; Lewis, p. 336.
1. See Workman, 2, 294.
2. See above, p. 45.
3. See above, p. 64.

from going, for the king of kings requires and wills effectually that he do not go," [4] probably impressed the pope no more than it does us. In view of Gaunt's unwavering interest in Wyclyf, if Richard did justify his countermand on the basis of Wyclyf's health he must have done so in order to place the most palatable explanation possible on an action which he would have taken in any event.

On the other hand, it is impossible to attribute the crown's decision to protect Wyclyf to its sympathy for his views. It had none. The council had placed severe restrictions upon his activities as early as 1378.[5] Three years later the duke of Lancaster hurried to Oxford to lay additional curbs upon his freedom of speech.[6] Wyclyf's leaving Oxford might have been due, in large measure, to pressure from the crown. At any rate, we can be reasonably certain of this, that after his retirement to Lutterworth Wyclyf did no more preaching, there or elsewhere, of a polemical nature. To have done so would surely have aroused the royal ire. It would as certainly have drawn the attention of the chroniclers, who are significantly silent. From this silence as well as from the uncertainty of his death, "we deduce that Wyclif had fallen into obscurity with the public." [7]

This silence of the chroniclers presents yet another puzzling aspect of the problem of Wyclyf's position after 1381. Knighton alone advances any information, and his words are only of doubtful value.[8] Netter has a great deal to relate concerning Courteney's efforts to eradicate Lollardy at Oxford in 1382 but nothing about Wyclyf after 1381 except the letter to Pope Urban. Yet this reticence on the part of the chroniclers is not difficult to explain. If, as I have sought to show, Wyclyf made his submission to Gaunt, it would be only natural that little of the affair should have been permitted to become known. It would not have been in Gaunt's interest to have the world learn that his protégé had become such a religious revolutionary that he personally had been obliged to quiet him. Wyclyf would certainly have said little or nothing about his promise to qualify his public utterances. Finally, it would scarcely have enhanced Courteney's prestige to have the public hear how he, the archbishop of Canterbury, had to be content not only with an informal and incomplete submission on the part of Wyclyf but with one which had been made to his former political rival. Such an analysis

4. See above, p. 139.
5. See above, pp. 59–61.
6. See above, p. 133.
7. Workman, 2, 316 n. 3.
8. See above, p. 136.

of the circumstances accompanying Wyclyf's submission not only accounts for the silence of the chroniclers, who would under those conditions have been left largely in the dark about the facts, but likewise
goes far to explain why so much of the problem of Wyclyf's submission
remains in the realm of speculation.

Wyclyf dead, however, proved easier to deal with than Wyclyf alive.
He died December 31, 1384, and for some ten years he and his writings
were largely ignored. Then in July, 1395, the king ordered the chancellor of Oxford to have all the doctors of theology examine the
Trialogus for possible heresy and error and to report back to him without delay.[9] The following year a provincial council which Archbishop
Arundel had assembled at London condemned 18 articles in this
treatise.[1] Early in 1397, on the occasion of the archbishop's first convocation, a group of Oxford scholars complained to the assembly that
members of their community were maintaining the 18 condemned
articles. They asked convocation for an official statement as to the
orthodoxy of the articles in question. The archbishop appointed a
commission to investigate the theses, and their condemnation was
upheld.[2] Arundel next delegated William Woodford, Wyclyf's erst-
while adversary, to prepare a refutation of the 18 articles.[3]

But Lollardy at Oxford would not down. In October of 1406 there was
issued in the name of the "chancellor of the university of Oxford and
the unanimous assembly of the masters" a document which extolled
the virtues of Wyclyf and which asserted among other disquieting
claims that Wyclyf had never been judged guilty of heretical pravity
nor had his body been ordered exhumed or burned.[4] The document is
manifestly a forgery on a number of counts, the most obvious being
the incumbency of the late Archbishop Courteney's nephew Richard
in the office of chancellor at the time.[5] If the tract originated at this
time,[6] however, it has two points of interest; it indicates the aggressive-

9. Rymer, 7, 806.

1. Gratius, *Fasciculus Rerum Expetendarum ac Fugiendarum*, fol. cxxxiii.

2. "Register Arundel," fols. 47–47^v; Wilkins, 3, 229. See Lewis, pp. 372–81, for
the articles.

3. Gratius, *op. cit.*, fols. xcvi–cxxxiii. Tanner, *Bibliotheca Britannico-Hibernica*,
p. 784. For Woodford, see above, p. 2.

4. Wilkins, 3, 302. See Workman, 2, 347 n. 4, for other copies of this testimonial.

5. For Richard, see Salter, pp. 106–7, 332. For a discussion of the forgery, see
Workman, 2, 347–51, whose better sense will not permit him to hold the document
genuine, as much as his prejudices so incline.

6. Salter (p. 91 n. 1) denies Lyte's statement (*History of the University of Oxford*, p. 279) that the manuscript is that of "an early transcript." He declares, on
the contrary, that "the hand need be no earlier than 1590 . . ."

ness of the Lollard group at Oxford, and it may also have contributed to Arundel's decision to secure papal condemnation of Wyclyf and authorization to destroy his body as the only way of disproving the notion that Wyclyf had not been a heretic.

In the November convocation of 1407 [7] Arundel issued a number of constitutions which prohibited the reading of any theological tract, whether of Wyclyf's authorship or otherwise, already published in his day or since or still to be published, unless it was first approved by the university of Oxford or of Cambridge or unanimously passed upon by at least 12 persons selected from their communities by both universities or either of them at the discretion of the archbishop and then finally expressly approved by the archbishop. The constitutions stated, furthermore, that no translation of Wyclyf's on the scriptures could be read, publicly or privately, until the translation had been sanctioned by the bishop of the diocese or by a provincial council. [8]

It seems as though Oxford did not interpret this directive as obliging it to proceed immediately with the organization of a committee, [9] for close upon the meeting of convocation in January, 1409, and presumably on the strength of his discussions with his suffragans, Arundel sent the university a second mandate. This instructed the community to organize a committee of 12 which was assigned the specific task of "diligently" scrutinizing the works of Wyclyf for possible heresies and errors. [1] Two years later [2] this committee forwarded its report that after "long deliberation" on "many books and pamphlets and other tracts and many *opuscula*" its members had uncovered and agreed upon

7. I follow Salter's dating which differs from that of Wilkins. The latter's account of these events "is full of mistakes." See Workman, 2, 359 n. 4.

8. Wilkins, 3, 317; Salter, p. 115.

9. Salter (p. 99) believes Arundel intended that the university organize such a committee. Actually his directive does not say so.

1. Wilkins, 3, 322; Salter, p. 121. Salter (p. 99) states that the convocation of January, 1409, repeated the constitutions of November, 1407, "for the very reason that so little had been done." As pointed out above (p. 151, n. 9), Arundel had not actually ordered a committee to be organized. In a letter to Oxford dated December, 1409, the archbishop mentioned that it had been decided in the January convocation of that year to have a committee of 12 organized which would examine Wyclyf's writings. He infers that he sent them a directive to this effect some time before. For this reason, it appears that the letter of explanation which Oxford sent to Arundel apologizing for its delay in organizing this committee might better be assigned to August, 1409, than to the year previous, as Salter dates it (p. 117).

2. No date is provided by the Faustina manuscript. Wilkins assigns the report to 1412, Salter to March 17, 1411. Salter's dating appears preferable for it was in May, 1411, that Arundel wrote to Oxford to notify the university of the condemnation of Wyclyf's 267 theses. Gascoigne, *Loci e Libro Veritatum*, p. 116.

a listing of 267 heresies and errors. They were omitting from the list almost as many similarly unorthodox conclusions, since these were akin to the 267. They were likewise omitting "many other conclusions" which sounded poorly but which "might be sustained sophistically in a sterile battle of words . . ." They did not deem it necessary to burden their report with the reasons why they found the 267 views false, since their unorthodoxy was obvious. Inasmuch as the committee considered its own authority insufficient to enable it to pass formal judgment upon the theses, it was deferring to the "more mature" judgment of the archbishop and his suffragans, although it expressed the hope that the list would be forwarded to Rome.[3]

This Arundel did in March, 1411,[4] after he had formally condemned the 267 theses with the consent of a provincial synod. In the archbishop's letter to the pope, he was careful to reassure John that he had done this "saving in all things and always the authority of the holy see." He asked the pope to pass final judgment upon the theses and, if he found them heretical, to authorize him to have Wyclyf's body exhumed and cast onto a dung heap or burned.[5]

This was in 1411. Early in 1412, possibly in response to Arundel's request, Pope John convened a council at Rome which condemned several of Wyclyf's works including his *Dialogus* and *Trialogus*, whereupon John issued a decree which prohibited the reading or keeping of any of Wyclyf's books and ordered them burned.[6] The Council of Constance took up the matter and on April 17, 1415, appointed a committee of four to examine the writings of both Wyclyf and Hus. Its report, later supplemented by a more searching investigation of Wyclyf's writings, led to the condemnation first of 45 theses, which included the 24 condemned by the Blackfriars council, then of 260 articles as either "heretical, seditious, erroneous, audacious, scandalous, or infamous," and of almost all of them as "contrary to good morals and catholic truth." Pursuant upon this judgment Wyclyf was declared a heretic, his writings were to be burned and his "bones to be dug up and cast out of consecrated ground, provided they could be distinguished from those of Christians buried near-by." [7]

3. Wilkins, 3, 339–49; Salter, pp. 128–30.

4. Salter assigns Arundel's letter to March, 1411; Wilkins to 1412.

5. Wilkins, 3, 350–1; Salter, pp. 133–5.

6. See Finke, *Acta Concilii Constanciensis, 1,* 124, 162–3; *Cal. of Papal Letters,* 6, 343–4.

7. Mansi, *Sacrorum Conciliorum . . . Collectio,* 27, 632–4; Hardt, *Corpus Actorum et Decretorum Magni Constantiensis Concilii, 4,* 153–6. See Netter, *op. cit.,* 2, 25–6, and Gratius, *op. cit.,* fols. cl–cli.

This order was issued May 4, 1415. Possibly because Wyclyf's old disciple, Philip Repingdon, was bishop of Lincoln at the time, nothing was done to carry out the sentence. There is, however, no record of any papal directive to that effect, which might account for Repingdon's failure to act. In any event Pope Martin V issued an order in December, 1427, to Fleming, Repingdon's successor.[8] In the spring of 1428, 44 years after Wyclyf's death, his bones were dug up and, on the authority of Fleming, burned.[9]

8. *Cal. of Papal Letters*, 7, 23.

9. Netter, *op. cit.*, 3, 830; Lyndwood, *Provinciale seu Constitutiones Angliae*, p. 284; *An English Chronicle*, p. 6; *Eulog.*, 3, 367.

SUMMARY

 $\mathfrak{T}$ hus Wyclyf's contest with the church finally ran its course. It was a long one, beginning with his arraignment in 1377 at St. Paul's and ending with the burning of his remains in 1428, a span of over 50 years. That he was finally declared a heretic and his bones disinterred is no surprise. What is a source of wonder is how he managed to live his life through without incurring formal sentence and punishment as a heretic. The first attempt to silence him was directed by the English hierarchy; this failed when the duke of Lancaster and other noblemen appeared at St. Paul's to take Wyclyf's part. The duke's motive in protecting Wyclyf on this occasion sprang from no more ulterior consideration than his desire to shield the clerk he had just five months before summoned from the halls of Oxford. If we could know why the duke sought the services of Wyclyf in the first place, we might be able to suggest other motives to explain the favor Gaunt so consistently showed the man. That the duke remained a faithful friend until Wyclyf's retirement, if not death, forces one to conclude that his interest in Wyclyf was personal. It may have been more. Gaunt's enemies accused him of contemplating the expropriation of the church's wealth, in which project Wyclyf would have been of great assistance. But the charge cannot be established. Neither can the accusation be supported that the duke wanted Wyclyf's help in his plan to drive the hierarchy out of politics. Gaunt's support of Wyclyf was probably unselfish. It would otherwise not have endured.

In 1378 Wyclyf appeared at Lambeth to explain his position on 19 heretical propositions which he had been accused of preaching. The list had been prepared in Rome, and Pope Gregory enclosed it with his bulls to Archbishop Sudbury and Bishop Courteney in which he directed them to proceed against Wyclyf. This attempt to silence Wyclyf proved somewhat more successful than the first. Even though the queen mother intervened, probably at the request of the duke, and forbade the prelates to pass formal judgment upon Wyclyf, there is strong evidence to support the view that Wyclyf modified his position on several theses, at least in their implications, and that he received an admonition from the prelates to cease discussing the controversial issues he had raised. This admonition the government bolstered with its own prohibition that same year, a course which a concern for national tranquillity must have dictated, for in similar fashion the crown silenced John de Acley who was about to take up the task of refuting Wyclyf which had been assigned him by the Benedictines. There were additional factors which inspired the government's decision about Wyclyf; the schism threw Rome and England together, while the ever-continuing need for funds to prosecute the war with France forced the crown to placate the ecclesiastical lords.

The government made this decision to silence Wyclyf in 1378, the year Wyclyf's influence reached its peak, so his admirers maintain. They base this view on two documents which Netter supplies, one which purports to be an address Wyclyf delivered to Parliament in defense of his theses, the other a reply to a query by the great council as to the lawfulness of withholding money from Rome. But Netter's evidence is suspect. It consists of the rubrics which introduce the two documents, but in neither case does the content of the tract which follows drop any hint which would tend to corroborate the force of its caption. It is extremely improbable that Wyclyf ever enjoyed anything approaching the political stature which would have warranted his addressing either Parliament or the great council.

Already under orders to curb his activities, Wyclyf found that time, instead of easing these restrictions, tended to crystallize them. Part of this was his own doing. In laying his hand to such a fundamental doctrine as transubstantiation he lost the greater part of his following and the more influential. He was no longer simply a reformer; he had become a revolutionary. Then came the Peasant Revolt of 1381, which cost him further support, and finally the elevation of the energetic Courteney to Canterbury. Courteney forced Wyclyf into the background and Lollardy on the defensive. As the leading ecclesiastical member of the continuous council, he probably represented the English church in working out a compromise with the government over the disposition of the problem Wyclyf had created. Wyclyf was to be cautioned to be silent, possibly asked to leave Oxford, but he was not to be molested beyond that point.

Thus it was that when Courteney proceeded in 1382 to destroy Oxford as the citadel of Lollardy Wyclyf was already in retirement. His disciples at the university proved unequal to the pressure exerted by the archbishop, and Wyclyf's last years were darkened by the realization that several of his most stalwart associates had made their peace with the ecclesiastical authorities.

But Wyclyf never did. That he was not obliged to do so, as had Repingdon, for instance, was due chiefly to the "settlement" arranged among the lay and ecclesiastical lords in 1378. That this settlement held up was due in part to the fact that Wyclyf cooperated with it to a considerable degree. He promised to cease discussing transubstantiation outside the schools, and he left Oxford. It also held up because Gaunt chose to continue his interest in Wyclyf. Had he withdrawn his support, there is no reason to believe that Wyclyf could have escaped formal arraignment before Archbishop Courteney with subsequent recantation or punishment.

The pope was not partner to the arrangement whereby Wyclyf was not to be prosecuted, and it is reasonably certain that late in his life Wyclyf received a summons to Rome from Pope Urban. Wyclyf appears to admit as much, and in the *De Citationibus Frivolis* he seeks to justify his failure to comply with a papal summons on the grounds of poor health and a royal countermand. Wyclyf makes a more direct reference to a papal summons in a letter addressed to Urban which is dated 1384, the year of his death. Here he speaks again of his crippled condition as a cause for not going to Rome. The language of this letter reveals yet another reason why he escaped formal prosecution. He refers to the pope as Christ's highest vicar on earth. This is significant; it proves that Wyclyf never broke with Rome, either officially or in his own mind.

Still, the decisive factor which made possible Wyclyf's escape from effective prosecution was not his health or the advanced age of his bishop or the occasional muddled character of his thinking; neither was it the support of the Commons or the people, a support he did not enjoy. It was the favor of the duke of Lancaster.

BIBLIOGRAPHY

This list does not presume to be exhaustive. It does, however, include the important sources which are pertinent to the subject.

Calendar of the Close Rolls Preserved in the Public Record Office, 1369–74, 1381–85. Rolls Series.

Calendar of Entries in the Papal Registers Relating to Great Britain and Ireland, Papal Letters, 4, 7. Rolls Series.

Calendar of Entries in the Papal Registers Relating to Great Britain and Ireland, Petitions to the Pope, 1. Rolls Series.

Calendar of Letter-Books . . . of the City of London, Letter-Book H, ca. 1375–99. Ed. R. R. Sharpe. London, 1907.

Calendar of the Patent Rolls Preserved in the Public Record Office, 1370–89. 5 vols. Rolls Series.

Finke, Henry. Acta Concilii Constanciensis. Muenster, 1896.

Gascoigne, Thomas. Loci e Libro Veritatum, Passages Selected from Gascoigne's Theological Dictionary. Ed. J. E. T. Rogers. Oxford, 1881.

Gratius, Ortuin. Fasciculus Rerum Expetendarum ac Fugiendarum, 1. London, R. Chiswell, 1690.

Hardt, Hermann von der. Corpus Actorum et Decretorum Magni Constantiensis Concilii, 4. Frankfort and Leipzig, 1699.

Issues of the Exchequer. Extracted and translated by Frederick Devon. London, 1837.

Lyndwood, William. Provinciale seu Constitutiones Angliae. Oxford, 1679.

Mansi, John D. Sacrorum Conciliorum Nova et Amplissima Collectio, 27. Venice, 1784.

Munimenta Academica, or Documents Illustrative of Academical Life and Studies at Oxford, 1. Ed. H. Anstey. Rolls Series. London, 1868.

Nicolas, Nicholas H. Testamenta Vetusta, 1. London, 1826.

Rotuli Parliamentorum; ut et Petitiones, et Placita in Parliamento Tempore Edwardi R. III, 2; et in Parliamento Tempore Richardi R. II, 3. Ed. J. Strachey. 1767.

Rymer, Thomas. Foedera, Conventiones, Literae, et Cujuscunque Generis Acta Publica, 6, 7. London, 1709.

Snappe's Formulary And Other Records. Ed. Herbert E. Salter (Oxford Historical Society). Oxford, 1924.

Statutes of the Realm, Record Commission, 2. London, 1816.

Wilkins, David. Concilia Magnae Britanniae et Hiberniae, 3. London, 1737.

EDITIONS OF WYCLYF'S WORKS

PUBLISHED BY THE WYCLIF SOCIETY

De Apostasia. Ed. M. Dziewicki. London, 1889.

De Blasphemia. Ed. M. Dziewicki. London, 1893.

De Civili Dominio, 1. Ed. R. Poole (1885), 2, 3; ed. J. Loserth (1900, 1903).

De Ecclesia. Ed. J. Loserth. 1886.

De Eucharistia. Ed. J. Loserth. 1892.

De Potestate Pape. Ed. J. Loserth. 1907.
De Veritate Sacrae Scripturae, *1.* Ed. R. Buddensieg. 1905.
Opera Minora. Ed. J. Loserth. 1913.
Opus Evangelicum, *4.* Ed. J. Loserth. 1896.
Polemical Works in Latin, *1, 2.* Ed. R. Buddensieg. 1883.
Sermones, *2, 3, 4.* Ed. J. Loserth. 1888–90.
The English Works of John Wyclif. Ed. F. D. Matthew. London, 1880.
Joannis Wiclif Trialogus. Ed. G. Lechler. Oxford, 1869.
Select English Works of John Wyclif, *1, 3.* Ed. T. Arnold. Oxford, 1869, 1871.
Tractatus de Christo et Suo Adversario Antichristo. Ed. R. Buddensieg. Dresden, 1880.

EPISCOPAL REGISTERS

MANUSCRIPTS:

"Register of Thomas Arundel, Archbishop of Canterbury, 1396–1414."
"Register of John Buckingham, Bishop of Lincoln, 1362–98."
"Register of William Courteney, Archbishop of Canterbury, 1381–96." (A part of Courteney's acts is assembled with those of Bouchier, Morton, and Dean. Wilkins refers to such folios as "Ex Reg. Morton.")
"Register of Simon Sudbury, Archbishop of Canterbury, 1375–81."

PRINTED:

Register of Thomas de Brantyngham, Bishop of Exeter, 1370–94. Ed. F. C. Hingeston-Randolf, *1, 2.* London, 1901, 1906.
Registrum Willelmi de Courtenay, Episcopi Herefordensis, 1370–75. Ed. W. W. Capes. Canterbury and York Society Publications. London, 1914.
Register of John de Grandisson, Bishop of Exeter, 1327–69. Ed. F. C. Hingeston-Randolf, *3.* Exeter, 1899.
Wykeham's Register. Ed. T. F. Kirby. Hampshire Record Society Publications, *2.* London, 1899.

CHRONICLES

Adami Murimuthensis Chronica Sui Temporis. Ed. T. Hog. English Historical Society Publications, *1.* London, 1846.
The Chronicle of England by John Capgrave. Ed. F. C. Hingeston. Rolls Series. London, 1858.
Chronicon Angliae, 1328–88, T. Walsingham. Ed. E. M. Thompson. Rolls Series. London, 1874.
Chronicon Henrici Knighton, *2.* Ed. J. R. Lumby. Rolls Series. London, 1895.
An English Chronicle of the Reigns of Richard II, Henry IV, Henry V, and Henry VI. Ed. J. S. Davies. Camden Society, *64.* 1856.
Eulogium Historiarum sive Temporis (Continuatio), *3.* Ed. F. S. Haydon. Rolls Series. London, 1863.
Fasciculi Zizaniorum Magistri Johannis Wyclif. Ed. W. W. Shirley. Rolls Series. London, 1858.
Historia Anglicana, T. Walsingham, *1, 2.* Ed. H. T. Riley. Rolls Series. London, 1863, 1864.
Polychronicon Ranulphi Higden Monachi Cistrensis, *9.* Ed. J. R. Lumby. Con-

taining a continuation of the Polychronicon by John Malverne. Rolls Series. London, 1886.

William Thorne's Chronicle of Saint Augustine's Abbey Canterbury. Ed. A. H. Davis. Oxford, 1934.

Transcript of a Chronicle in the Harleian Library of MSS, No. 6217 entitled "An Historical Relation of Certain Passages about the End of King Edward the Third and His Death." Archaealogia, 22, 204–84. London, 1828.

ARTICLES

Cronin, H. S. "John Wycliffe, the Reformer, and Canterbury Hall, Oxford," Transactions of the Royal Historical Society, Third Series, 8 (London, 1914), 55–76.

––––––. "Wycliffe's Canonry at Lincoln," English Historical Review, 35 (1920), 564–9.

Dahmus, J. D. "Further Evidence for the Spelling 'Wyclyf,'" Speculum, 16 (1941), 224–5.

Galbraith, V. H. "Thomas Walsingham and the Saint Albans Chronicle, 1272–1422," English Historical Review, 47 (1932), 12–29.

Lewis, N. B. "The 'Continual Council' in the Early Years of Richard II, 1377–80," English Historical Review, 41 (1926), 246–51.

Lloyd, M. E. H. "John Wyclif and the Prebend of Lincoln," English Historical Review, 41 (1946), 388–94.

Loserth, J. "Das vermeintliche Schreiben Wiclif's an Urban VI. und einige verlorene Flugschriften Wiclif's aus seinen letzten Lebenstagen," Historische Zeitschrift, 75 (New Series, 39) (1895), 476–80.

––––––. "Studien zur Kirchenpolitik Englands im 14. Jahrhundert," Sitzungsberichte der philosophisch-historischen Classe der Kaiserlichen Akademie der Wissenschaften (Vienna). Teil I: "Bis zum Ausbruch des grossen Schismas," 136 (1897), 1–135; Teil II: "Die Genesis von Wiclifs Summa Theologiae und seine Lehre vom wahren und falschen Papsttum," 156 (1908), 1–118.

––––––. "The Beginnings of Wyclif's Activity in Ecclesiastical Politics," English Historical Review, 11 (1896), 319–28.

Matthew, F. D. "The Date of Wyclif's Attack on Transubstantiation," English Historical Review, 5 (1890), 328–30.

Pantin, W. A. "A Benedictine Opponent of John Wyclif," English Historical Review, 43 (1928), 74–7.

Poole, R. L. Review of J. Loserth ed., Johannis Wyclif Tractatus de Ecclesia, English Historical Review, 3 (1888), 571–5.

Richardson, H. G. "Heresy and the Lay Power under Richard II," English Historical Review, 51 (1936), 1–28.

Salter, H. E. "John Wyclif, Canon of Lincoln," English Historical Review, 30 (1920), 98.

Thomson, S. H. "Wyclif or Wyclyf?" English Historical Review, 53 (1938), 675–8.

Twemlow, J. A. "Wycliffe's Preferments And University Degrees," English Historical Review, 15 (1900), 529–30.

Wedgwood, J. C. "John of Gaunt and the Packing of Parliament," English Historical Review, 45 (1930), 623–5.

SECONDARY ACCOUNTS

Armitage-Smith, Sydney. John of Gaunt. New York, 1905.

Capes, W. W. The English Church in the Fourteenth and Fifteenth Centuries. London, 1903.

Clarke, Maude V. Fourteenth Century Studies. Oxford, 1937.

Dugdale, William. The Baronage of England, 1. London, 1675.

Foxe, John. The Acts and Monuments, 2, 3. Ed. J. Pratt. 4th ed. London, 1837.

Lechler, Gotthard V. Johann von Wiclif und die Vorgeschichte der Reformation, 1, 2. Leipzig, 1873.

———. John Wiclif and His English Precursors, 1, 2. Tr. Peter Lorimer. London, 1878.

Leland, John. Antiquarii de Rebus Britannicis Collectanea, 3. Ed. T. Hearn. London, 1770.

Lewis, John. The History of the Life and Sufferings of the Reverend and Learned John Wiclif. Oxford, 1820.

Little, A. G. The Grey Friars in Oxford. Oxford, 1892.

Lowth, Robert. The Life of William of Wykeham. London, 1758.

Lyte, H. C. M. History of the University of Oxford. London, 1886.

Magrath, J. R. The Queen's College, 1. Oxford, 1921.

Manning, B. L. "Wyclif," Cambridge Medieval History, 7. Cambridge, 1932.

Netter, Thomas. Doctrinale Antiquitatum Fidei Catholicae Ecclesiae, 1, 2, 3. Ed. F. B. Blanciotti. Venice, 1757–59.

Poole, R. L. Illustrations of the History of Medieval Thought and Learning. New York, 1920.

Rashdall, Hastings. The Universities of Europe in the Middle Ages, 3. Eds. Powicke and Emden. Oxford, 1936.

Second Report of the Royal Commission on Historical Manuscripts, pp. 141–2. London, 1874.

Steel, Anthony. Richard II. Cambridge, 1941.

Stubbs, William. The Constitutional History of England, 2. Oxford, 1875.

Tanner, Thomas. Bibliotheca Britannico-Hibernica. London, 1748.

Trevelyan, G. M. England in the Age of Wycliffe. London, 1900.

Ullmann, Walter. The Origins of the Great Schism. London, 1948.

Vaughan, Robert. The Life and Opinions of John de Wycliffe, 1, 2. London, 1831.

———. John de Wycliffe, D. D., a Monograph. London, 1853.

Vickers, Kenneth. England in the Later Middle Ages. London, 1913.

Wilkins, H. J. Was John Wycliffe a Negligent Pluralist? London, 1915.

———. Westbury College from a. 1194 to 1544 A.D. Bristol, 1917.

Wood, Anthony. The History and Antiquities of the University of Oxford, 1. Ed. John Gutch. Oxford, 1786.

Workman, H. B. John Wyclif, a Study of the English Medieval Church, 1, 2. Oxford, 1926.

INDEX

Acley, John de, silenced, 71–2
Arundel, Thomas, appoints commission to examine Wyclyf's theses, 151; delegates Woodford to prepare refutation, 151; orders Oxford to scrutinize Wyclyf's works, 152; prohibits reading of Wyclyf's works, 152; condemns 267 theses, 152; sends these theses to pope, 153
Aston, John, incriminated by Ball, 83; barred from preaching at Oxford, 110–12; at Blackfriars, 114–15; declared heretic and imprisoned, 117; his *Confessio*, 117; submits, 118, 127; restored by Courteney, 118–19

Ball, John, itinerant preacher, 82, 85; incriminates Wyclyf, 83
Bedeman, Laurence, incriminated by Ball, 83; barred from preaching at Oxford, 110–12; submits, 126
Berton, William, assembles council to examine Wyclyf's theses, 129; council not packed, 132
Binham, William, attacked by Wyclyf, 22
Black Prince, Courteney's patron, 12; death, 13; permits Haulay and Shakyl to keep prisoner, 74
Blackfriars council, convened by Courteney, 88; members, 90–1; not packed, 91–2; earthquake frightens, 93; condemns twenty-four propositions, 93–5; propositions compared with those Gregory condemned, 95–6; Wyclyf's position on propositions, 96–8; second meeting, 109; last session, 126–8
Boldon, Uhtred, 37 n. 5
Brantingham, Thomas, dismissed as treasurer, 9; influential member of court circle, 10; member of Blackfriars council, 92
Braybroke, Robert, ordered to publish Blackfriars condemnation, 101; leads procession, 104

Brightwell, Thomas, present at Blackfriars, 109; accepts condemnation of propositions, 110
Brunton, Thomas, Wyclyf attacked him, 37; close to papacy, 37 n. 6; informs Wyclyf of condemnation of theses, 55, 57
Bryan, Sir Guy de, addresses London mob, 32–3
Buckingham, John, grants Wyclyf license for nonresidence, 1; received no bull from pope concerning Wyclyf, 35–6; negligence, 36; commended by Courteney, 36, 138–9
Buxhill, Sir Alan, invades Westminster Abbey, 74; excommunicated, 75

Clifford, Sir Lewis, orders bishops not to sentence Wyclyf, 68, 70
Courteney, William, early career, 10–12; threatens not to contribute tenth, 11; urges Wykeham's recall, 13; dispute with friars, 27; prods Sudbury to summon Wyclyf, 27; at St. Paul's, 28–9; quarrels with Percy and Gaunt, 28–31; popularity, 31; saves Savoy from mob, 33; member of continual council, 70, 87; condemns pollution of Westminster Abbey, 75; Ball confesses to, 83; Florentines, 86–7; political and ecclesiastical eminence, 86–8; elevation to Canterbury, 88; convenes Blackfriars council, 89–90; charge of packing council, 90–2; reassures council on earthquake, 93; secures statute and patent against Lollardy, 98–100; orders publication of condemnation of propositions, 101–3; orders condemnation of propositions at Oxford, 104; appealed to by "catholics" at Oxford against Repingdon, 105; reluctance to interfere at Oxford, 105; letter to Rigg, 106; crossexamines Rigg, 109–10; orders Rigg to bar Wyclyf and others from preaching at Oxford, 110; cau-

his position on twenty-four condemned propositions, 96–8; Hereford defends him in Ascension Day sermon, 105; Repingdon praises him in sermon, 107; barred from preaching at Oxford, 110–12; royal brief against his supporters at Oxford, books to be turned over to Courteney, 122–4; opponents after 1378, 129; views condemned by Berton's council, 129–32; his reaction to condemnation, 132–3; appeals to king against condemnation, 132–3; promises to cease discussing transubstantiation, 133–4; not at Oxford in 1382, 134–5; not overlooked in 1382, 136; Gaunt still a friend, 135; restrictions placed upon him, 136; made full recantation according to Knighton, 136–7; government and Commons unsympathetic, 137–8; cited by Urban on evidence provided by the *De Citationibus Frivolis*, 139–41; dating of this tract, 139–41; letter of excuse to Urban, 141–2; authenticity of letter, 142–3; date of letter, 143–8; importance of letter, 147–8; not paralyzed before retirement, 129, 132,

140; attitude toward papacy, 141–4, 147–9; never considered self outside church, 148–9; decisiveness of Gaunt's protection, 72, 135, 149–50; crown not sympathetic, 149–50; silence of chroniclers, 150–1; crown orders *Trialogus* searched for heresy, 151; Arundel appoints commission to examine theses, 151; forged document supporting, 151; Arundel prohibits reading of his works, 152; Arundel instructs Oxford to search his writings for errors, 152; Oxford committee lists 267 heresies and errors, 152–3; Pope John prohibits reading of his books and orders body exhumed, 153; Council of Constance condemns works and orders bones burned, 153; exhumed, 154; political stature exaggerated, 156; why escaped prosecution, 72, 156–7

Wykeham, William, dismissed as chancellor, 9; influential member of court, 10; supports Courteney, 12; banished from court, 13; recalled, 13; excluded from general pardon, 13 n. 1; member of Blackfriars council, 92; persuades Courteney to pardon Rigg, 110

Date Due